Capitalism with Derivatives

Capitalism with Derivatives

A Political Economy of Financial Derivatives, Capital and Class

Dick Bryan and Michael Rafferty

First published in 2006 by
PALGRAVE MACMILLAN
Houndmills, Basingstoke, Hampshire RG21 6XS and
175 Fifth Avenue, New York, N.Y. 10010
Companies and representatives throughout the world.

PALGRAVE MACMILLAN is the global academic imprint of the Palgrave Macmillan division of St. Martin's Press, LLC and of Palgrave Macmillan Ltd. Macmillan® is a registered trademark in the United States, United Kingdom and other countries. Palgrave is a registered trademark in the European Union and other countries.

ISBN-13: 978-1-4039-3645-5 hardback
ISBN-10: 1-4039-3645-5   hardback

This book is printed on paper suitable for recycling and made from fully managed and sustained forest sources.

A catalogue record for this book is available from the British Library.

Library of Congress Cataloging-in-Publication Data

Bryan, Dick.
    Capitalism with derivatives: a political economy of financial derivatives, capital and class / by Dick Bryan and Michael Rafferty.
        p. cm.
    Includes bibliographical references and index.
    ISBN 1-4039-3645-5
        1. Derivative securities. 2. Risk management. I. Rafferty, Michael, 1961–.
    II. Title.

HG6024.A3B79 2005
332.63'2—dc22   2005051550

10 9 8 7 6 5 4 3 2 1
15 14 13 12 11 10 09 08 07 06

Transferred to Digital Printing 2006

Contents

Acknowledgements

In the development of this book, there have been several important contributions. We have benefitted from research assistance undertaken by Roni Demirbag and Mark West, and work on graphs and tables by Lisa Savage and Husam Al Makawi.

Many people have heard presentations based on chapters and made useful comments. A number of people have read draft chapters: Simon Mohun, Sue Himmelweit, Nick Coates, Sam Gindin, Leo Panitch, Scott MacWilliam and Verity Carney. Their comments, suggestions and contributions have been invaluable. We also take this opportunity to acknowledge the assistance provided by funding from the Australian Research Council and the Swedish Baltic Sea Foundation.

There are some other people to whom we owe a large debt. The first is Neil Ackland, whose determination over a decade ago to write a PhD on a political economy of financial swaps set us on a path of thought and discovery.

We also owe an enormous debt to Scott MacWilliam, Geoff Kay and the late Mike Cowen who, over many years, taught us how to do political economy. We both see ourselves as direct products (and, to coin a phrase, 'derivative') of their profound influence. While they may not necessarily agree with all the arguments presented here, they have always been encouraging of their development.

Amanda Hamilton and Katie Button, at Palgrave Macmillan, provided excellent encouragement and editorial support for the project, while Vidhya Jayaprakash at Newgen Imaging helped to turn a rough manuscript into a readable book. Carolyn Schmidt produced the index.

Finally, to our respective families, we express deep appreciation for their tolerance of (sometimes) long periods of pre-occupation and absence.

1
Introduction

If we were to select a handful of adjectives to describe the current economic world (or most previous periods, for that matter) 'volatile' would be prevalent. Volatility is both a threat and an agent of change, and how volatility is addressed is itself part of that change.

This book is about how financial volatility is currently being addressed by corporations and states, for we show that how this is occurring is having profound implications for labour. What we observe is the rise to prominence of capital's own system of regulation: the market, and specifically the market for financial derivatives. But we cannot simply take the current period in isolation, for processes of volatility and systems of regulation are themselves products of history. So this book is also about situating the current issues of financial derivatives and financial volatility in historical context. It is a broad issue.

One way of approaching this has been to think of volatility in terms of risk and the management of risk. As this book proceeds, the discourse of risk will be seen to offer a limited perspective, but it can suffice to set our analysis in motion.

Risk is everywhere. Sometimes it is welcome, for if there is no risk there are no profits. Sometimes it is feared: risk and disaster often go together.

What if you could explicitly decide exactly what sorts of risk and what amount of risk you wanted to take on, and you could, for a small charge, eliminate the others? The world of business would be very different, but so too would be the wider social world that centres on business.

In limited forms, that possibility has been around for a long time. We would all understand it readily as some sort of insurance contract, but we tend to think of insurance as applying to a limited range of facets of life. In one respect, derivatives can be seen as the massive extension of insurance to a wide and increasing range of 'exposures'. The main things

1

derivatives provide insurance against are interest rate and exchange rate changes, but there are also derivatives that insure against anything from the weather (the Chicago Mercantile Exchange trades weather futures) to the celebrated future price of pork bellies, to the threat of terrorism (the Pentagon, for a short time in 2003, was offering a terrorism futures market as a way to elicit information on likely terrorism threats (Wolfers and Zitzewitz 2003)).

But derivatives are a different sort of insurance.[1] While an insurance contract for your health or your car is thought of as a pool that everyone pays into and only the unlucky ones – those who get sick or crash their car – get to claim, derivatives are somewhat different. There is no pool, just a set of contracts where someone else, with a different perspective on risk, is prepared to buy your risk.

Is the person who buys your risk simply gambling? Perhaps. But they may also have a different vulnerability to risk from you. Your company may fear the dollar falling; another may fear the dollar going up. There may be scope for a contract here: to lock in some agreed dollar value for a future date, a futures contract could be written. But there are other possibilities, too. Perhaps that locked-in future price would be too rigid and you would rather keep options open. Instead of settling for an agreed price, irrespective of what turned out to be happening in the market, there could be an agreement to locking in an *option*, but not a binding obligation, to exchange at an agreed value in the future in case the future value of the dollar strayed too far from its current level. An options contract could be written to do this. There are more, and more complex, functions that derivatives perform, but the insight that we can frame risk, and consider transferring it in elaborate ways, will suffice at this point.

A critical question emerges. How do you price risk? How much should you charge someone to give them a guarantee or an option about future price? It is a question of profound significance. For economics, this is the equivalent of the discovery of DNA. If you could precisely estimate the price of risk, two ubiquitous problems could be solved.

First, risk could, to all intents and purposes, be reduced to a conscious choice. Risk would cease to be so risky. In particular, if it were possible to get the 'right' price for one of those options contracts, business would be able to use options to offset the impacts of future market volatility.

---

[1] Initially also, the joint stock company was often explained as a way of insuring that investors in a company were not exposed to potentially unlimited losses in the event of corporate bankruptcy. Of course, no one today would limit their analysis of the joint stock company simply to a form of insurance.

Successful business could then focus on being creative, not rely on being lucky. Perhaps the threats of all market volatility could be eradicated.

Secondly, and just as significantly, if all risk could be priced accurately, there could be a dollar value basis to compare all risk, everywhere, and over time. Next year's cotton crop could be measured against tomorrow's US dollar/Yen exchange rate. The NASDAQ index in three months could be measured against the price of gold in a year. Future pork belly prices could be measured against terrorist threats! All these different forms of capital valuation could be compared for their risk – and hence their risk-adjusted expected rate of return. The implications would be extraordinary, especially if people could, by trading in derivatives, move their risk exposure easily from one asset to the other. In this world where risk exposures can be moved around in a blur of transactions, we would see the basis of a blended, universal and intensively competitive valuation of 'capital'.

Orthodox economists would be delirious about the efficiency that would follow. Others might see a massive intensification of competition, as money floods between asset types, searching the best rate of return. 'Who suffers when competition becomes so intense?' may well be the concern. Whatever the attitude, the scenarios all depend on being able to crack the formula to price risk.

In 1973, Fischer Black and Myron Scholes published the so-called Black–Scholes formula for pricing options (Black and Scholes 1973). Many had previously attempted to develop a pricing formula, but Black and Scholes got it right. This was the key to those big economic questions that followed from risk.

With the development of hand-held computers, their formula was soon in use on trading floors of financial markets around the globe. In 1997 the Nobel Prize for Economics was awarded to Myron Scholes and Robert Merton (a colleague of Black and Scholes) for this theory.[2] In presenting the award, the Nobel Foundation (Näslund 1997) said of the work of Black, Scholes and Merton:

> Your methodology has paved the way for economic valuations in many areas. It has also generated new financial instruments and facilitated more effective risk management in society.

The formula also offered the possibility of making money: Scholes and Merton themselves went into business in an attempt to exploit this

---

[2] Fischer Black died before the awarding of the Nobel Prize. The Prize can only be awarded to living scholars.

potential. They (and associates from large financial institutions) formed a private investment partnership called Long-Term Capital Management (LTCM).

With their formula now public, making money was not simply a matter of advising on option prices, for traders with their hand-held computers could now calculate that, but of finding options or other assets that were mispriced. There would rarely be many that were grossly mispriced, so the object was to search the world's financial markets to find even tiny mispricings. If they borrowed large amounts of money and then invested on these mispricings, they could generate substantial and riskless revenue. These are the activities of what are now called 'hedge funds'.

In 1994 LTCM started with an equity capital of $1.3 billion.[3] Within four years, LTCM had successfully traded a range of options, especially in peripheral markets, and made very high returns. It had accumulated an equity of $4.8 billion. This capital was being used to support a derivatives book that was estimated to be in excess of $1 trillion.

In 1997 and 1998, LTCM formed a view on the Asian financial crisis, and how recovery after the crisis would impact on US Treasury bonds. They believed that these bonds were mispriced, and they traded in bond derivatives to reflect this view. But the Asian financial crisis did not abate as quickly as they had predicted and LTCM lost nearly half its equity. Then, in August 1998, completely without warning, the Russian government defaulted on some foreign loans and devalued the rouble. LTCM was left heavily exposed, and by September rumour was spreading in the markets that some large traders like LTCM were unable to support their existing positions. LTCM was forced to go to the Federal Reserve and report that it was almost broke, with losses somewhere around $3.5 billion, and exposure to losses many times this.

If that experience was not a stark enough statement of the complex and unpredictable world of derivatives, what happened next was just as astounding. LTCM had traded not in the formal, regulated exchanges, where mispricing of options was less apparent, but in products and markets outside the capacities of state regulation. But as LTCM faced bankruptcy, the US central bank, the Federal Reserve, feared that the collapse of this secluded hedge fund would set off a wave of bankruptcies across financial markets. Despite the lack of state regulation, and the precedent that might be set (perhaps signalling to other hedge fund operators that they would similarly be looked after if they were also

---

[3] The basic facts about LTCM come from Edwards (1999) and Lowenstein (2001).

deemed too big to fail) the Fed pressured the major banks and financial houses, most of whom were financial backers of LTCM, to fund a bailout. And they did.

That one short corporate history encapsulates much of what is fascinating about financial derivatives, such as options. First, derivatives offer a highly sophisticated process for protecting people and corporations against unwanted risk – but they can themselves turn into massive risks. Second, those who theorise the mathematics of risk management often fail to appreciate the wider social processes of which derivatives are part and which are themselves transformed by derivatives. Third, derivatives show the tensions in the relations between states and capital. They perform functions integral to accumulation, but outside of the formal state system of regulation.

These are three dimensions of derivatives we explore in this book. But if we were to address simply the realms of speculation – be it about corporate crises (such as LTCM, Enron or Worldcom) or about national crises (such as Mexico, Russia or East Asia) – our analysis would fail to capture the deep significance of the evolution of derivatives. Derivatives are not significant just because of their attachment to some spectacular failures, but because they are transforming the system of calculation under capitalism.

Our purpose in this book is in part to explain the social role of derivatives: a role that both permits their use in risk management and, in turn, follows from that pervasive use. Overall, therefore, the emphasis is squarely in the sphere of class relations and, especially, competition between capitals. Our central proposition is that derivatives are intensifying the process of competition between capitals, with direct pressure on labour (as workers and consumers). For any corporation, at any time and any place, derivatives present a real-time measure of asset values. They signal what assets to buy and sell, and at what price. Just as importantly, they reveal to all corporations that there are no longer easy profits to be made by being ahead of the market – the most secure way to increase profits is to get workers to produce more, and for lower cost. Derivatives, we argue, are revealing an intensification of capitalism, with all the contradictions that this entails.

So central also to our project is an engagement in debates about the transformations of capitalism that are associated with financial derivatives. As the chapters unfold, it will be apparent that we identify a deep seated problem with money and finance in each of neoclassical Keynesian, radical and Marxist economics, and, in each case, it shows up starkly in relation to financial derivatives. This book is an attempt to begin to redress that problem. In so doing it will be necessary to challenge many existing precepts.

What is at issue?

Most people have no idea what financial derivatives are. For those who do, it seems you either love them for the elegance of their financial flexibility and actuarial creativity or despise them for the gambling they facilitate. They are perceived as rather esoteric financial instruments, so those who love them are few in number – though extremely powerful. They are people in central banks and the back rooms of large corporations and financial institutions. Those who hate them often have less understanding of how derivatives work: after all, you don't need to know the electronics inside a slot machine to know that they are addictive and anti-social. There is a deep sense that 'hedge funds' and 'hot money' must be opposed.

Both are probably right, albeit not necessarily for good reasons. We hope that people with both predispositions will read this book and end up being informed and challenged. For the lovers, there is a need to step outside the formal mathematical logic, and ask what social and historical processes have generated a daily turnover equal to $US1,900,000,000,000 (1.9 trillion) on foreign exchange markets?[4] Surely this is more than a new 'industry' that helps other industries with risk management – it is transforming the way our economic activity is organised. And for the haters, what is actually happening within these $1.9 trillion of daily transactions? Surely it is more than an alternative to a financial game of blackjack or roulette.

Nonetheless, it must be recognised that the popular perspective on derivatives (with the exception of the vast majority of financial economists and market participants) is that derivatives are all about speculation. They are referred to in the context of evaluations of neoliberalism, deregulation, the anarchy of markets, the rise of a regime of finance or a circulation economy, and the loss of nation-state sovereignty over money and finance. But rarely is there concern for the detailed, 'inside story' of derivatives: it is as if they are merely a horror side issue, or an illustration in a debate about speculation, states, markets and regulation.[5] One of our

---

[4] This figure comes from the Bank for International Settlements (BIS) triennial survey of foreign exchange markets. The latest survey was in April 2004.

[5] LiPuma and Lee (2004) is a recent illustration of a book-length analysis, which simply assumes, without question, this sort of perspective.

motivations in writing this book is to challenge the rhetorical, populist and moralistic sentiments that usually lie behind this characterisation. The 'speculation' label is not without foundation, but that cannot be the starting point nor the end point of understanding derivatives. We can build an explanation of derivatives every bit as striking in its implications as the 'speculation' approach, but with a better foundation in a systematic analysis of the new prevalence of derivative markets.

So how do we frame this alternative analysis of the future of capitalism with derivatives? Derivatives have a long history, especially in relation to mechanisms to secure price stability in agricultural products, but there has clearly been a quantum change since the 1980s, which has seen a huge growth in derivatives on a global scale. This has almost entirely involved the growth of derivative products for finance itself as corporations have used them to deal with uncertainty in financial prices (interest rates and exchange rates) and speculators have sought to make money predicting financial market trends. These activities have seen derivatives emerge from obscurity in the 1970s to be, in terms of the value of turnover, the largest economic activity in the world. What has generated this enormous growth in the last quarter of a century?

The most apparent answer is that risk, especially the risk associated with unforeseen price changes, has emerged as a new demon, and derivatives have emerged to deal with it. It's not that the world is inherently more risky than it has formerly been, but there is probably a greater exposure of individuals (especially individual firms) to those risks than there has been for some time. A brief history can set the context.

The post-war period of the welfare state, fixed exchange rates, commodity price stabilisation schemes, industry protection and national capital controls can be (loosely) characterised economically as 'Keynesianism'. With these protections and controls, nation states and a range of national institutional arrangements both absorbed some risks and balanced out a range of other risks within a national territory. Risk about price changes in the future was to some degree socialised. As Antonio Negri (1968: 38) put it so succinctly, 'Keynes's first imperative is to remove fear of the future. The future must be fixed as present. The convention [of removing the fear of the future] must be guaranteed'.

From the late 1960s, however, came a fall in the rate of profit, the emergence of 'stagflation' and, in policy circles, a crisis of confidence in the post-war policy regime. From the 1970s, there emerged a steady dismantling, at different rates and to different degrees in different countries, of many of the pillars of the Keynesian state that had served to socialise risk. The decline of Keynesianism, and its way of managing a range of risks, permitted greater flexibility into price relations, but brought forward the need for means other than the state to fix the future to the present. That role fell in large part to market processes, and the growth of derivatives was the result.

Since the 1980s we have seen a recovery of the rate of profit associated with what are now called 'neoliberalism' and 'globalisation' (both sweeping generalisations with many meanings, but terms with which we must now live). Individuals are now exposed to a greater range of risks that come with connecting across more, and more diverse, spaces. In the economic world, the growth of international trade, investment and finance opens up new exposures for individuals and individual firms. That means more choices in commercial decisions (where to borrow, and in what currency to borrow, where to sell, where to invest, etc.). But these choices also mean exposure to new risks (fears) for business and, in a world of uncertainty this can be commercially dangerous. There can be (retrospectively) wrong choices. You can be caught holding investments in Argentina when a recession strikes, holding Mexican pesos when the peso falls in value, holding a fixed rate loan when interest rates are falling.

In a world of variable interest rates, exchange rates and commodity prices, not to mention political volatility, corporations want some certainty about these critical variables, and they trade in derivative markets as a way of buying that certainty. As their exposure changes in the process of daily business, so they continually buy and sell in these derivative markets to keep their risk coverage in line with their various exposures. Sometimes also, corporations are actually taking a punt on the market – taking on risk rather than laying it off. Sometimes they win; sometimes it goes disastrously wrong, ending in famous cases of insolvency. Either way they all add up to huge trading volumes and the continuing growth of an already very large industry.

The proximate cause of the growth of derivatives, therefore, could be summarised in terms of growing needs of risk management by corporations, and the invention of new (and sometimes bizarre) facilities of insurance (and gambling) in the context of globalised markets.

But financial derivatives are more than just another corporate tool to manage particular contemporary problems. Financial derivatives have moved imperceptibly to the centre of the capitalist economy. Indeed, as a commodification of risk, derivatives are a form of calculation and market transaction that is intrinsic to the logic of a capitalist economy. Perhaps an important question is not so much why derivatives 'took off' in the 1980s, but why they didn't 'take off', but existed only in a minor role, in the two hundred odd years before!

Hence, beyond the *proximate* cause of growth, we pose in this book the *'underlying'* role of derivatives within a capitalist economy: the particular form of capital that derivatives embody. As derivatives have emerged, they are bringing some profound changes to the way capitalism is organised: changes as fundamental as the nature of capitalist ownership, the nature of money, and the process of competition. They are also creating a new exposure to financial crisis. If these changes are indeed recognised, we are entering a period of capitalist development that will be discernibly different from before.

We are reluctant to use terms like 'more intensive' or 'more advanced' capitalism because of the teleological baggage that attaches to these labels. But the frontiers into which market relations can expand never cease to amaze. We have watched, astounded, in the 1980s as state functions were re-configured into commercial processes and then sold off. So remarkable was that process that it was given its own epochal designation: 'neoliberalism'. The pervasive use of derivatives portends more dramatic developments in this direction.

In neoliberalism, the process of competition that has infused so many facets of the social world with a profit agenda was achieved by turning institutions and individuals into competing commercial entities. But derivatives go a giant step further. It is now not just businesses that compete; the assets of these businesses are now being increasingly thrown into a constant and relentless process of competition to verify their 'value'. They undertake this competition not so much on the basis of their corporate designation (say as Coca Cola dollars), but as a price relation between say the Coca Cola share price and the market index, or a Coca Cola bond denominated in US dollars and an Airbus bond denominated in Euros. While no principal or title to ownership needs to be exchanged with derivatives, each derivative contract establishes price relations between bits of capital.[6] They are contracts that exist to configure and reconfigure a corporation's existing risk (price) exposures, and in so doing they are *collectively* as a system of derivatives, performing the anchoring role of pricing all other assets. With the intensified price comparisons that come with derivative markets, intensified competition in capital and money markets is a corollary, with direct implications flowing through to production and the labour process.

The argument we develop throughout this book is that derivatives go to the heart of calculation and competition within a capitalist economy.

---

[6] Dodd (2000: 5) has said for instance in this context that derivatives 'are purely pricing contracts'.

The proximate cause of their new prominence may be explained in the context of globalisation, new risk exposures, communication technology and 'deregulation', but they also have an underlying capacity that goes deeper than these immediate circumstances. Should any of these proximate causes abate, the prominence of derivatives will remain because they have been revealed as quintessentially capitalist products.

So what are derivatives?

We will save a detailed exposition of how different types of derivatives work until Chapter 3. Just a preliminary explanation is required here.

A derivative is a financial contract designed to roll together discrete and often quite different financially related attributes. That sounds vague, because to be more precise will exclude certain types of derivatives. There is a wide diversity of the sorts of attributes that can get linked, and (although we will not consider this until later) a diversity of types of linkage.

Why would someone want to issue or trade such a contract? It is because of what derivatives *do*, not what they *are*. Some illustrations will help to clarify. Derivatives provide a mechanism to link assets in the present to prices in the future (e.g. a tonne of wheat today to its price in 3 months). They also link prices of one asset form to another asset form – for example, interest rates to share prices. Some derivatives involve contriving apparently non-financial things into a financial measure, so that a novel derivative link can be constructed – for example, the Chicago Mercantile Exchange (2005) has constructed a weather (temperature) index, so that (most probably) an energy company can link demand for energy to a financial valuation of the weather. In each case, the agenda of risk management (or insurance) is central. Linking wheat now to future prices gives certainty to current decisions about a future wheat price; linking interest rates to share prices breaks down the stark choice of whether to engage credit or equity markets; linking energy demand to the weather (a weather index) smooths the volatility of energy revenues.

What makes derivatives remarkable is that all these sorts of risks get traded without the underlying asset itself being traded. With derivatives, certain characteristics of a commodity, asset or financial security can be separated out, priced and traded in their own right. The wheat, the shares, the bond, the energy, and, of course, the weather themselves are not traded; just the attributes. Let us say you want to guarantee the price of wheat at some point in the future. Instead of buying wheat now and storing it until when you need it, you can trade wheat futures (that is, purchase (or sell) a contract that entitles you to buy (or sell) wheat on a certain date at a certain price) without having to own any wheat. Moreover, you can trade wheat futures without ever even wanting to own any wheat. Hence also no income as such needs to accrue from a derivative because there is usually no income-generating asset being transacted. Instead, payments may be made or received on derivative contracts depending on the price changes of the instrument(s) it is written on.

A common definition of a derivative, found in finance textbooks, is an asset or 'financial instrument' whose value derives from the value of another asset – hence the term 'derivative'. A wheat option or future is said to 'derive' its value from the current value of wheat; an interest rate option or future derives its value from current interest rates. This standard definition opens up some significant issues for analysis, albeit not those which form the distinctive focus of this book. The issues addressed by the conventional framing relate exclusively to risk management. Here is the essential proposition of that framework.

It is valuable to be able to separate out (and trade in) certain characteristics of an asset or security without trading the asset or security itself. Corporations want to take on some risk, for without risk there will be no profit. But they want to avoid other risks – especially those that relate to unwanted and unanticipated price movements (exchange rates, share prices, etc.). Derivatives permit a separation of the asset itself from volatility in that asset's price. And it turns out that the best way to deal with price risk is often not through actual ownership, but through a separate transaction – this is what derivatives are for. So if what you want to address is the volatility of an asset price, why not acquire (or sell) products that directly address the volatility, rather than the underlying asset itself. Hence, in a volatile world, derivatives are useful: they are used to trade risk. According to how you trade, you can sell off risk or take risk on. Moreover, insofar as risk is to some extent in the eye of the asset beholder, the trading of risk may reduce risk exposure for both buyer and seller (e.g., when an oil producer fears the price of oil going down and an airline fears the price of oil going up, they can both allay their anxiety by purchasing or selling derivative products that have the effect of locking in the future price of oil).

So in the common definition of derivatives, they are paper contracts that entail obligations for the future that serve to relocate risk. But the common definition in terms of a derivative's value deriving from the value of an underlying asset is, however, profoundly limited. It suggests that the thing of 'real' significance is the original asset (a company share, a tonne of wheat, etc.), and the derivative is in some sense secondary or even epiphenomenal. Derivative prices dance around 'real' asset values. Yet in actual derivative markets it is apparent that prices do not in fact 'derive' from the original asset (the price of wheat derivatives does not derive from the spot price of wheat). On the contrary, prices usually run the other way,[7] so that options and futures markets are the places where prices are first formed, and prices in cash markets follow.

This empirical observation, while it may appear minor in itself, signals the need for a whole new perspective on the role of derivatives. This primary role of derivatives in pricing (and price discovery) suggests that derivatives are integral to the operation of financial markets and perform a role in capitalist economies in their own right, which cannot be reduced to techniques of corporate risk management or the facilitation of 'real' asset value determination. We must identify the distinctive, unique role that derivatives perform in their own right.

... And why are derivatives so important?

Our proposition is that derivatives have a combined meaning that is more than the sum of the millions of individual exotic and sometimes even bizarre contracts. Derivatives in combination, as a 'system of derivatives', have two attributes. We will refer to these throughout the book as the *binding* and *blending* roles of derivatives.

Binding: Derivatives, through options and futures, establish pricing relationships that 'bind' the future to the present. Derivatives bind the present to the future. (For example, the current price of wheat and the future price of wheat are mutually determining.)

Blending: Derivatives, especially through swaps (explained in Chapter 3), establish pricing relationships that readily convert between (we use the term 'commensurate') different forms of asset. Derivatives blend different forms of capital into a single unit of measure. (They make it is possible to convert things as economically nebulous as ideas and perceptions, weather and war into commodities that can be priced relative to each other and traded for profits.)

---

[7] Many empirical studies have shown that prices are first formed in derivatives markets (a process called price discovery) and are transmitted back to cash markets, while others have found that this process occurs more or less simultaneously.

To draw implications from later chapters, so that our readers can gain a sense of our project, we contend that three critical developments emerge with the binding and blending processes.

First, derivatives in combination are *capital*. But unlike our traditional concept of capital, these paper contracts need not involve ownership or possession of any underlying asset. A share is a contract that involves ownership of (part of) a company. A bond is a contract that involves ownership of a pile of credit money. But derivatives have no such ownership link, so they are quite different forms of capital. Their distinctive characteristic is the capacity to convert between different forms of capital. The capacity of derivatives to convert any form of asset into any other form of asset means that all assets can be instantaneously compared across time and space. We need to think of derivatives as *meta-capital* whose distinctive role is to bind and blend different sorts of 'particular' capital together. The effect of the growth of derivatives over the last 25 years is, thereby, to give 'capital' a new integration that comes with this blending.

Second, derivatives in combination have characteristics of *money*. Money, of course, is not just notes and coins, but something that performs the functions of unit of account, store of value, or means of exchange, etc. Because derivatives are such liquid forms of capital (i.e. continually adjusting in value and readily tradable), and have as their distinctive role establishing pricing relations between bits of capital, they can also be seen as a form of money. This monetary function is, we argue, at the core of derivative growth in the last 25 years, providing a (flexible) foundation to global currency markets in an era when there are neither fixed exchange rates nor a single money unit such as gold playing the anchoring role.

Third, at a more abstract level, and perhaps most importantly for our analysis, this capacity of derivatives to give one sort of asset the attributes of another is breaking down our conventional distinction between 'money' and 'capital'. The idea that there is a 'real' economy of values separate from financial markets and that financial markets are merely epiphenomenal is made false by derivative trading. Accordingly, our notion of capital and capitalism itself is being transformed by derivatives.

It is important to pause here, for each of the above issues is explored in detail in various chapters to follow. Our objective at this point is not a detailed explanation of the mechanics of derivatives; it is to draw derivatives out of the sphere of esoteric financial management and into wider debates about economic and social relations: to begin to build the argument that financial derivatives are transforming the social and economic world in ways that are only apparent if you first see the momentum that derivatives impart on social and economic change.[8]

How are these issues addressed?

This book is divided into three broad sections:

Part I – Derivatives as Capital (Chapters 2, 3 and 4)
Part II – Derivatives, Money and Competition (Chapters 5, 6 and 7)
Part III – Debating Derivatives (Chapters 8 and 9)

Part I constitutes an analytical and historical introduction to derivatives, seeking to establish their evolution as a particular expression of 'capital'.

In Chapter 2 we look at the rise of financial analysis in the broader social sciences: the range of theories and explanations associated with the rise to prominence of financial markets. Most of them, it must be said, neglect the specific dimensions of financial derivatives. We highlight the issues that are lost by that neglect, argue the necessity of engaging with derivatives, and point towards an alternative approach to derivatives.

Chapter 3 introduces the basic mechanics of derivatives. It is directed to a readership unfamiliar with (and perhaps intimidated by) financial economics. In drafting the chapter, we started with the working title 'derivatives for dummies'. But it turned out to be much harder to write than the working title implied. The difficult thing to explain about the technical characteristics of derivatives is not so much the formal models that make up finance textbooks: there already exist clear explanations of these. It is what we referred to earlier in this chapter as the 'system of derivatives': how derivative markets, and the pursuit of profit, have created forms of calculation that bring into focus all conceivable performance measures on capital and corporations. These include explanations of the 'binding' and 'blending' processes referred to earlier in this chapter.

Along with the technical explanations, an important issue developed in Chapter 3 is the historical evolution of derivatives from the margins of agricultural markets to the centre of finance. This historical analysis is developed in a different direction in Chapter 4. Chapter 4 develops the

---

[8] In this context see especially Maurer 2002.

proposition that derivatives are a new form of capital. By comparison with the formation of the joint stock company in the mid-nineteenth century, we argue that derivatives represent a comparable order of innovation in capital ownership. While the joint stock company separated ownership of capital from the site of production (the 'factory' and its equipment), derivatives separate ownership of capital from the corporation. Moreover, the debates (and especially the apprehensions) that surrounded the formation of the joint stock company are remarkably similar to the same debates that surround derivatives 150 to 200 years later.

Part II (Chapters 5, 6 and 7) draw out the new dimensions to accumulation brought by derivatives – they are a new form of money that now provides an anchor to the global financial system.

In Chapter 5, we show that derivatives now anchor the global financial system in a way somewhat analogous to the role of gold in the nineteenth century, but with an added flexibility gold could never provide. Here, we follow the evolution of the international financial system from the Gold Standard to the present, identifying the class relations that underlie each period. Of the current era, we ask a basic question: if, under floating exchange rates, there is no tendency towards exchange rate stability or a notion of exchange rates backed by 'fundamental value', what is the unit of value in international finance? The answer, we contend, is found in financial derivatives.

In Chapter 6 we develop the idea of derivatives as a new global money produced by the market rather than nation states. It is this transcendence of national money, we argue, that permits derivatives to play their anchoring role. At the end of Chapter 6 there is an Appendix which uses Marxian value theory to present an interpretation of derivatives as new, global commodity money.

Chapter 7 then draws together the implications of the previous three chapters, merging the ideas of derivatives as capital and derivatives as money to show how derivatives have intensified the process of capitalist competition. Derivatives provide a means to commensurate (compare the value of) all different forms of capital across time and space. We argue that this has led to demands for each part of capital (not just each firm or corporation) to justify its value (and contribution to profitability) in an on-going, perpetual process. There are, we argue, direct implications for the labour process, and for labour.

Part III addresses some current debates about derivatives. There are many issues that could be covered here, but we have nominated just those which are most important, but which have not received sufficient attention elsewhere in the book.

Chapter 8 concerns the most widespread criticism of derivatives: their role in speculation. There is an argument that derivatives involve 'hot money', have no purposeful role in accumulation, and undermine nation-state capacities. Accordingly, there is a popular view that derivatives need to be regulated out of existence, and many critics advocate a Tobin tax or national capital controls. In this chapter, we argue a contrary position. There is clearly speculation in derivatives markets, but attempts to shut them down are based on misunderstanding and are probably doomed to fail. Derivatives are too elusive to be easily regulated, and they play a functional role in hedging. There will be unintended consequences on so-called 'real' investment following from policy attempts to isolate and eradicate the effects of derivatives.

Finally, in Chapter 9 we look at the way derivatives are starting to be used in social policy. We can see evidence that derivatives are being used as a model for social relations outside of finance, where new systems of insurance are used to enable individuals to hedge a range of life risks, such as in health and education. The wider social and economic effects of derivatives are still emerging, but on the basis of what we can already see, and on the basis of the analysis established in this book, the chapter attempts to consolidate our position and to 'speculate' on the future that can be seen in the present.

Part I

Derivatives as Capital

A number of propositions in this book are contentious. In the introduction to this, and subsequent, parts, we seek to bring these propositions to the fore, so that the reader may see clearly how they drive our analysis.

This part presents the basics of derivatives. It is designed to address a social science audience unfamiliar with derivatives and highlight both their importance and how they can be understood. It is also designed to address audience already familiar with derivatives, and to open up new, and broader ways of seeing them. The analysis is based on eight propositions:

1. Derivatives, as a 'system of derivatives', are performing a role that is central to modern capitalism. This role is more important than that captured by the hedging-speculation discourse, which has dominated analysis in economics.
2. The importance of derivatives has been insufficiently recognised in the social sciences and, where it has been, technical details of derivatives and derivatives markets are rarely considered.
3. Derivatives have significant implications for the theory of value, and need to be brought into the explanation of value.
4. The growth of financial derivatives has a *proximate* cause in the growth of international finance, investment and trade, and volatility in asset and commodity prices. But they also have an *underlying* cause. Derivatives are integral to the logic of markets in capitalism, and hence need an explanation that is 'deeper' than what can be predicated merely on those proximate causes.
5. In combination derivatives are *capital*. The central, universal characteristic of derivatives is their capacity to focus on the attributes that

different sorts of assets have in common. Derivatives 'dismantle' any asset into constituent attributes and trade those attributes without trading the asset itself.

6. Derivatives need not involve ownership of any underlying asset – they are simply ownership of exposure to some quantifiable attribute of an asset (e.g. exposure to changes in a stock price, but without owning any of the stock whose price is changing).

7. Derivatives present these attributes of any asset (or commodity) in a universally recognisable and generic form, such that the attributes of different assets can themselves be compared and traded.

8. There are close parallels between the historical development of the joint stock company and the contemporary development of financial derivatives. They both represent an evolution in the nature of ownership, and, as such, both have generated the same sorts of debate.

2
A New Perspective on the Role of Finance

Debates about the role of derivatives are only now emerging. Some see them as mathematically elegant tools of risk management; others, as dangerous tools of speculation. These widely divergent interpretations tend to constitute rather discrete and non-interacting analyses, reflecting disparate world-views. In particular, it is hard to find research published in the leading academic finance journals that countenances notions of gambling or engages propositions of social disorder created by 'hot money'. With notable exceptions,[1] few of the outright critics of the impact of derivatives bother with the mechanics.

Our concern here is not to open a dialogue between the lovers and haters (and it is surely not hard to see that derivatives have characteristics identified by both) but to look beyond the polemic and explore the terrain of the impact of derivatives. That is, we want to build the case that derivatives are not just tools of speculation and/or of risk management; they are transforming a wider range of facets of our contemporary economic order.

In this chapter the focus is on how the major discourses of social science have systematically, and no doubt unintentionally, marginalised recognition of the wider transformations that have been brought by the growth of financial derivatives since the mid-1980s. Our ambition is to bring derivatives to centre stage in wider debates about economic change.

The source of the problem, to put it in sharp relief, is that where analysis of derivatives is not tied to mathematical finance and general equilibrium models, it tends to become tied to debates about 'globalisation' and 'economic deregulation' that emerged in the 1980s. In this depiction, a

---

[1] In particular, Partnoy (1997, 2003) and Dodd (1996, 2002b).

generalised role for derivatives can be attributed to the rise of the profitability and power of the finance sector and to a lesser extent to global corporations. It was also associated with the retreat of nation states from regulation in the 1970s and early 1980s that saw exchange rates floating (but inexplicably volatile) and the opening up of globally integrated financial and capital markets. To this we could add the development of computers and satellite technology that permitted speed of calculation, transmission and record keeping, and theoretical advances in valuing financial instruments.

For this style of explanation the growing use of derivatives follows predictably. A global economic crisis in the 1970s saw the state withdraw a raft of economic regulatory practices, including controls over international capital flows, exchange rates, and restrictions on the scope of operation of financial institutions. 'Globalisation' occurred and derivatives blossomed.

In the interpretation of this process, the economists got a head start. From the mid-1980s a new generation of international bankers was emerging with mathematical skills and innovative strategies for packaging finance. University faculties were soon opening up this new area of study and training students in the techniques of risk management. The analysis of derivatives therefore arose (and continues to exist) primarily as an instrumentalist knowledge – how to measure financial risk, how to price options and how to trade derivatives. This seems to have virtually precluded the development of a more critical perspective within the academic tradition of finance and financial economics.

For the other social sciences, including non-neoclassical economics, the explanation just presented is usually told with a negative twist, and generally as a critique of the supposed virtues both of mathematical formalism and neoclassical economics generally, and of the social and political consequences of globally integrated finance. In this counter depiction, focus is on governments conceding control over financial systems under pressures to 'deregulate', the growth of 'off-shore' banking (i.e. outside of national regulation) and the development of a global financial system dominated by globally integrated financial institutions. Derivatives are here associated with debates about losses of national sovereignty, difficulties of governance and the anarchy of global markets.

So as the sociologists, political scientists and geographers started to take an interest in finance, much of it was reactive to this formalistic economic discourse but without entering into the detailed technical workings of derivative analysis. Derivatives have been and remain an analytical 'black box' (Maurer 2002). The critique of neoclassical economic finance was principally a critique of 'deregulation' and 'globalisation': their uncritical deference to market outcomes and their neglect of issues such as the state (or indifference about the role of the state), global economic volatility and growing global and domestic inequality. At this level of critique, the details of derivatives are not seen to matter. Yet, as Maurer (2002: 20) forcefully argues, 'regardless of the mathematical technique's use or efficacy, its being "left aside" allows it to maintain a very privileged status in any account of contemporary derivatives'.

But the technical dimensions of derivatives *do* matter, and in the process of explaining derivatives, it will become apparent that there is far greater significance than is found in the instrumentalist knowledge that dominates the discourse of academic financial theory. In opening the black box of financial derivatives, we hope to engage both an audience familiar with economic theory – who will look for our interpretation of derivatives 'as economists' – and a wider audience of social scientists. This latter audience includes geographers, political scientists and sociologists and others interested in 'globalisation', and even in money and financial institutions, but who tend to steer clear of the mechanics of derivatives. For them, we hope to open the black box not via a quick training in formalistic 'financial economics' but in ways that show how the mechanics of derivatives are essential if we are to engage wider social issues of finance and financial change.

The economics of money and finance: the need for new agendas

The economic analysis of money and finance is clearly dominated by two traditions: the dominant, orthodox tradition of neoclassical economics and the subordinate, heterodox tradition deriving from Keynesianism. (To this, we could add a third – Marxism – which has a clear influence on our analysis, but cannot claim to be a dominant tradition in the area of money and finance.)

In opening up a distinct approach to finance, and one that embraces a broader perspective than what is found in the two dominant financial wisdoms, our objective is not to develop methodological critiques – in the sense of formal refutations – of either, but to set our analytical course in a distinct direction. We wish to state clearly two essential propositions that confront both neoclassical and Keynesian approaches.

First, neoclassical finance, centring on theories of market efficiency and individual optimisation, is of limited use in understanding the broad trends and social significance of financial markets. With a focus on explaining price movements and optimisation strategies, this theory has no claim to be a general social theory. But it has had to extend somewhat in this direction. As a pedagogical device for understanding price movements, equilibrium theories have been challenged by the phenomenon of financial 'bubbles' and by the paradox that markets, which now transmit more and more information at less and less cost, seem to conform less and less to ideas of stable and efficient pricing. The recent development of 'behavioural finance', which seeks to explain volatility and speculative bubbles in terms of the psychology of strategic behaviour, is certainly drawing orthodox finance into new areas.

But in the process of engaging outcomes that were once assumed away, orthodox finance has been undermining the strengths of its own theoretical formalism. Market volatility appears as the critical challenge for a theory that has equilibrium prices at its core. In explaining the reality of financial bubbles, equilibrium theories have to conceive of bubbles as either 'distortions' or as the result of the bounded 'rational' behaviour of optimising individuals. The latter involves the construction of models of strategic behaviours that simulate bubble outcomes, by imputing, for example, certain behavioural responses to imperfect information.

Viewed from outside the discourse, it is apparent that a tautology arises: any outcome – from stability to crisis – is explained via the *ex poste* attribution of the participant strategy that creates the observed outcome. The effect is that all outcomes can be reduced to the market strategies of individuals, to the systematic exclusion of broader social and historical explanations.

Second, Keynesian approaches to money, while capable of recognising these broader social and historical processes, are predicated on the ontological primacy of nations as economic units and as discrete financial centres. This does not preclude engagement with global movement of money (although it is often simply ignored in post-Keynesian analysis), but money and finance are invariably conceived in a system of relations between discrete national money systems. The Keynesian policy aspiration of strong state controls over money and finance, as a central tenet of a national growth strategy, has more recently been extended to the aspiration of global controls on international finance that will serve to re-assert the capacities of state money in a different (global) monetary order (e.g. Eatwell and Taylor 2000). There is here a sustained neglect of analysis of the systematic workings of globally integrated finance (the way in which the operation of finance has transcended the national level) in order to preserve the privileging of nationalist aspirations of creating a world of discrete (Keynesian) national economies. Our argument is not that national economics are in some sense false, but that the dilemmas of globally integrated finance cannot be addressed by asserting the ontological primacy of nations as discrete economic units in the face of evidence that finance has only a limited connection to nations.

Yet we do not wish to caricature these two traditions, for it is apparent that research in both (albeit at the margins) is tentatively probing the boundaries of equilibrium thinking and economic nationalism. For instance, Grossman and others have developed a model of financial market volatility that, following Hayek, is based on the notion that the price system performs a dual role: informing individuals, as well as allocating resources. Standard models of pricing (*vis* the Walrasian auctioneer), do not transmit information, or as Grossman suggests, 'no one learns anything from prices; people are merely constrained by prices' (Grossman 1989: 1). Volatility in stock prices is then understood in this approach as a result of strategic trading by some market participants. Post-Keynesians too are addressing important issues; for instance Toporowski's (2000) historical consideration of the role of derivatives in capital market inflation.

Moreover, Marxism has in some ways been confronted with similar problems to both the neoclassicals and Keynesians. For many Marxists, critical of neoclassical economics, it has been convenient to borrow concepts from Keynesian (and, indeed, snippets of neoclassical) economics. The notion of financial markets as sites of strategic, speculative games; a disdain for finance as disconnected from the so-called 'real' economy, and the notion that the integrity of money can only be secured via state-issued currency, are all borrowed explanations of a deep irrationality of capitalism.

These propositions generally appear as moralistic rather than analytical. They present finance as the vulgar expression of what capitalism is all about – greed, competitiveness, individualism and alienation. The effect of such moralism is the creation of instant opposition to finance, without invoking the need to understand the workings of finance within capitalist accumulation: the specific contradictions embodied in developments in finance.

Conversely, Marxian value theory, as a means to explore the specific economic contradictions of capitalism, has great difficulty in engaging contemporary finance. Marx's focus on gold as commodity money has been seen to leave a theoretical void (although one we seek to fill in later chapters), and his discussion of 'credit money' – an important insight in the mid-nineteenth century, but rather simplistic today – has led many Marxists to a focus on the role of finance in facilitating the tendency towards monopoly, through the debt-funded concentration and centralisation of capital. There are powerful arguments developed here, but none is attuned to engaging this new phenomenon of financial derivatives.

We will return to this challenge later in this chapter and in subsequent chapters. But it is important at this point to recognise that mathematical, neoclassical economists and nationalist Keynesians are not the exclusive students of the economic dimensions of finance or even of financial derivatives, and an evaluation of new insights into finance must accordingly look further afield for inspiration. In the process, a number of conventions will be challenged.

Social sciences: 'new era' explanations of finance

Our review of recent approaches to finance cannot be restricted to the domain of economic theories. There is now a range of social theories and disciplines that take finance seriously. Political science, especially via the emergence of 'international political economy' is extensively addressing the nature and meaning of international finance. There is a long tradition of a sociology of money, with a new, heightened engagement with global money and financial markets. In particular, there is a focus on markets as social institutions (e.g. McKenzie and Millo 2003), the social relations embodied in monetary relations (e.g. Callon 1998; Ingham 2004) and the social behaviours and connectivity of market traders (e.g. Knorr et al. 2002). There is here some real engagement with the mathematics of derivatives (especially the work of Donald McKenzie (e.g. 2004)), but this is exceptional.

Geographers, who have long had an interest in globalisation and in the finance sector, are now probing the development of global financial markets, offshore banking and implications for state capacities of globally integrated financial markets (e.g. Corbridge et al. 1994; Cohen 1998; Martin 1999).[2] Ethnographers too are analysing strategic behaviour, especially in the culture of finance houses' trading rooms (e.g. Zaloom 2003; Stark and Beunza 2004[3]).

---

[2] Martin (1999: 5) makes the claim that 'geography of money' is now firmly established as a new subdiscipline in geography.

[3] See a range of work by David Stark on this topic at http://www.sociology.columbia.edu/people/faculty/stark/publications.html

Moreover, finance appears as the centrepiece of a range of broader, what might be called 'political economy', theories of the current period: the French Regulationists have posited the recent development of a 'financial regime of accumulation'; others, the development of an era of 'financialisation' and 'shareholder capitalism'.[4] The latter contributions will be considered in more detail shortly.

These diverse studies of finance and banking are not devoid of engagement with financial derivatives, and there are some particular germane studies that will be referred to in other parts of this book. But a distinctive feature of much social science analysis of finance is that two analytical agendas predominate which vitiate against an investigation of the calculus of and tensions within the 'black box' of financial derivatives.

One agenda treats finance as a rapidly growing industry, in which the focus is on the expansion of banks, pension funds, etc., as transnational corporations. Here, the analysis is not unlike that applied to the communications industry or information technology. These are the so-called 'new economy': they are rapidly expanding, cutting-edge industries with extensive linkages to other industries, and they are being re-organised on a global scale. In this context, the money-ness of finance is immaterial: it is just another industry. These studies are not a central concern of this book.

The other agenda focuses precisely on the money-ness of finance – the speed and universal reach of its movement. Developments in finance, it is argued, are at the centre of a 'new era' of capitalism. Broadly, we can identify two sorts of new era analyses of finance that have become popular: those that identify finance as the leading edge of globalisation, and those that ascribe a new logic to capitalist economies under the influence of financial innovation. We will look briefly at each, in order to explore the space they open for inclusion of financial derivatives.

Money, finance and globalisation

The globalisation debate opened up in the 1980s with sweeping new era propositions, including a new era of global finance. At one extreme of the spectrum, the 'hyper-globalisers' (as Held (1998) has termed them) tended to emphasise the role of finance as leading global integration because of the speed and ease of movement of finance and the resultant volume of cross-national financial flows relative to both trade and investment. This emphasis includes both those who welcomed the new

---

[4] See especially the special issue of *Economy and Society*, Vol. 28, No. 1, February 2000.

borderless globe (e.g. Ohmae 1990; O'Brien 1992) and those who resisted it (e.g. Strange 1986, 1996).

The advocates saw global financial markets creating global efficiency in resource allocation, with funds facilitating greater choice over the movement of investment to wherever the (expected) rate of profit is highest. National characteristics in markets are simply evidence of 'distortions': progressive policy will see the world move towards a single market in which national borders are irrelevant. For the advocates, financial markets are also the means by which nation states are compelled to adopt policies to facilitate 'pro-market' or 'neoliberal' policies. Thomas Friedman (2000: ch. 5) referred to the 'golden straightjacket' imposed on national governments by the 'electronic herd' of financial market traders who would financially savage 'bad' (i.e. 'not-pro-market') national policy.

The hyper-globalisers also included those with essentially the same analytical focus, but the opposite politics. The argument here has been that the growth of global finance has been a result of weak policy stances by nation states; in particular, the giving up of national capital controls. The result, it is said, is a national exposure to increased economic volatility – for example, Susan Strange's (1986, 1996) depiction of global finance creating the 'retreat of the state' and 'casino capitalism'. Here, as for the advocates, finance is the leading edge of global integration to the benefit of transnational corporations and the detriment of national citizens, especially in poor countries. Occasionally, financial derivatives are placed at the centre of this hyper-globalisation (e.g. LiPuma and Lee 2004).

This polemic was premised on the notion that finance had, indeed, generated a borderless globe and compliant nation states (for better or worse). In both sides of the polemic, derivatives are seen as part of the process (generating efficiency of capital markets on one side, and forums for volatility and gambling on the other) but derivatives do not play a distinctive role.[5]

A slightly later generation of debate challenged that premise. The hyper-globalisation story was seen as an exaggeration. This more recent argument, labelled by Held the 'sceptical position', is that globalisation

---

[5] For example, Kelly's (1995) depiction of derivatives as 'a growing threat to the international financial system' has the simple intention of depicting derivatives, and even hedging generally, as pretexts for gambling, and hence in need of being stifled by (global) regulatory interventions. But there is no attempt to present the way in which derivatives are integral to corporate risk management.

is not new and is generally exaggerated. The polemic shifted from 'globalisation: good or bad' to 'globalisation: fact or fiction'.

The sceptics argue that international flows of trade, investment and finance in the late nineteenth century and up to the First World War were quantitatively comparable to current flows – and nation states are not disempowered. In building this case, Weiss (1998) titled her widely cited book '*The Myth of the Powerless State*'. Hirst and Thompson (1999), from the same general position, argued that corporations still attach to nation states and nation states remain key regulators of accumulation. They contend we have 'inter-nationalisation', not 'globalisation'. It is interesting, and significant, that in both these widely cited works, finance receives scant attention, and derivatives none: the data cited and debated relate almost entirely to trade and direct investment (i.e. transnational corporations).

In this silence, finance is implicitly attributed with two characteristics. First, it is not a part of 'real' economic activity. Real economic activity relates to investment, production and trade, and these can be analysed separately from finance. By viewing 'finance' and 'the real economy' as a dichotomy, the issue of the way in which finance is part of social relations and financial analysis affects economic processes (a process that Callon (1998) calls the 'performative' dimensions of finance) are comprehensively ignored (Mirowski 1999).

Second, to the extent that finance is labelled as 'global', it is understood as having escaped the national economy, and its analytical significance derives from the fact of its escape, not from what finance 'does' on a global scale. For the sceptics, the appropriate role of finance on a global scale is to facilitate trade and long-term investment, and when finance plays other roles, such as in derivative transactions, it must be detracting from trade and investment (i.e. it must be 'speculative'). Implicitly, therefore, there is the assumption that finance is 'naturally' national, and has assumed inappropriate roles on a global scale when it is not at the service of trade and investment. Derivatives are bundled together with other 'short-term' flows as challenges to the appropriate (facilitating) role of finance and of states. A differentiation of 'strong' and 'weak' states (e.g. Weiss 1998) is essentially between nations that are and those that are not vulnerable to international financial raids. Weak states are therefore those that are not resistant to Friedman's electronic herd and its 'golden straightjacket'.

Between the extremes of the hyper-globalisers and the sceptics, Held (1998) identifies an alternative (and for him preferred) interpretation, which he calls the 'transformationalist position'. In this view, there are elements of globalisation and the formation of a single, uniform market, but national territoriality and nation-state capacity remain central. States have not lost out to globalisation, but their role has changed. States have had to adapt what they do and how they regulate accumulation. But they remain integral to the facilitation and management of global integration.

Here, as with the other positions, the analysis of finance has been driven by the national question: specifically, nation-state capacities. Finance is addressed in terms of its articulation with nation states, not by an attempt to understand the requirements of a stable global monetary system, or the role of finance for globally integrated corporations. Indeed, this same framing is central to a range of other analyses that, while not part of the general-theory-of-globalisation debate, are nonetheless addressing the global expansion of finance. A common and abiding theme in this discourse is the ontological primacy of nations and the loss of nation-ness that has come (or is coming) with the expansion of finance. The focus on capital 'flight' (Helleiner 1995; Grabel 2002; Epstein 2005),[6] 'offshore' financial centres (Leyshon and Thrift 1997; Clark 2000), loss of state power to pension funds (Minns 2001) and the end of national (Westphalian) money (Cohen 1998) are all predicated upon money having been once in a state of national grace prior to the fall that was globalisation.

Nonetheless, some potentially interesting debates about the role of financial derivatives do arise in this framework. The role of derivatives in facilitating capital flight and circumventing national capital controls is one that featured in the reviews of the Asian financial crisis (Dodd 2002b).

But the problem with the transformationalist position, probably like all mid-way positions in a polemic, is that it evokes a complex and nuanced reframing (things have changed) but offers few guidelines for specifying the particular nature of those changes. Where finance in general, and derivatives in particular, fit in remains unspecified and therefore a matter of interpretation.

In essence, the problem of addressing finance via the globalisation debate is straightforward. The globalisation debate centres on the role of nation states – whether they are resistant, subordinated or, as some sort of a middle ground, 'transformed' by the growing levels of international trade, investment and finance. The finance question is, thereby, made secondary to the national question, so the dominant framework asks simply whether finance is under or out of national control, and the

---

[6] The issue of capital flight is addressed in Chapter 8.

consequences that follow. Insofar as finance is secondary to the national question and the well-being of national citizens, so finance is subordinated to the 'real' (national) economy as the source of 'well-being'. If finance serves the 'real' economy it is deemed productive, but if it doesn't it is labelled as 'unproductive'. And once it is labelled 'unproductive', explanations of how it works become subordinated to arguments about how it can be contained.

Our alternative approach does not come out of the conventional globalisation debate. The starting point for an analysis of derivatives is not nations but capital, and the way in which derivatives are used by corporations to manage their assets in a world where asset values are individually volatile. Further, our starting point is not the huge volume of financial flows promoted by the finance sector, but the requirements of a globally integrated money system for order and some form of stability. Derivatives are not important because they are large in volume; they are large in volume because they are important. Addressing derivatives from the perspective of capital will require us to transcend the dichotomy between 'finance' and the 'real economy' and between 'unproductive' and 'productive' uses of finance.

New phases of capitalism

At the end of the nineteenth century, in the midst of another phase of rapid 'globalisation', Rudolf Hilferding (1910) observed the growth of what he called 'finance capital': the merging in Europe of big banks and big industrial firms to provide the resources to become ever larger and more dominant. The notion of 'monopoly capitalism' has broadly rested on this sort of tendency.

With the globalisation at the end of the twentieth century, there has also been some parallel proclivity to identify a new, finance-centred phase of capitalism. Three insights warrant particular mention: the identification of a new, short-term focus within capitalism, the Regulationist School's financial regime of accumulation and theories of 'financialisation' and 'shareholder capitalism'. We will consider each, briefly, in turn.

There is a now large literature that reflects on the increasing speed and short-term agenda of globally integrated capitalism. Whether it is called 'flexible capitalism' (Sennett 1998) 'liquid modernity' (Bauman 2000), the 'network society' (Castells 1996) or 'turbo-capitalism' (Luttwak 2000) (to name but a few variations) there is an essential argument that knowledge and technological innovation, economic deregulation and global integration are creating an economic world that is faster and more mobile. The speed of change means that risk and uncertainty are more prevalent, especially for individuals (Beck 1992; Elliot and Atkinson 1998; Gray 1998).[7]

On reading this literature, one is struck by the absence of sustained engagement with financial markets. Finance, in the form of free flows of money and investment appears as a catalyst for this new era, generating sharpened demands for profitability, but the analytical focus is on the interaction between labour, technology and corporate management, with the loss of permanent employment as its principal manifestation and point of concern (Beck 2000). In the role of catalyst, the analysis of finance is generally posed as assertions about 'hot money' and the pursuit of purely short-term profits. Alternatively, finance is presented as a growing industry sector, as a component of 'the new economy'. But the processes of finance themselves, how they have developed and how they operate, are notably absent. Ulrich Beck, for example, has written celebrated books on the growing risk society (1992, 1999) and on the political and cultural challenges of globalisation (2000), but with only passing reference to finance,[8] and no engagement with financial derivatives as capital's tool of risk management.

One notable exception here is the French Regulationist School, which has sought to embrace the new significance of finance. The French Regulationists became recognised from the late 1970s for their characterisation of a shift from a 'Fordist' regime of accumulation (dominant for most of the twentieth century) to one that is now more flexible, based on new technology, short production runs, just-in-time production management, etc. Some recent work in the Regulationist tradition has posed the emergence of a 'finance-led growth regime' as the contemporary alternative to 'Fordism' (e.g. Boyer 2000a; Agleitta and Bretton 2001). The essential theme here is a contrast between a bank-led financial system in the Fordist era and a new, financial market-led regime since the mid-1980s. The bank-led system has its focus on a nationally centred financial system under direct state (central bank) regulation. Finance could, via the central bank, be placed at the service of accumulation under the auspices of the nation state.

---

[7] In this process, there is often reference to Schumpeter's theory of 'creative destruction', although Schumpeter emphasised the importance of monopoly returns as the incentive to innovation.

[8] Beck's (1999: 8) only explicit connection of risk to finance is to the '*social explosiveness* of global financial markets', illustrated by the Asian crisis. This is hardly taking finance seriously!

The new regime, however, is said to be much less subject to state supervision and is not amenable to strong national industry policy. The problem, in essence, is that financial markets have come to place a range of incentives into corporate strategy. These incentives are related to asset price inflation that comes from debt funding and the need to boost share prices in order to stave off takeovers. According to Agleitta and Breton (2001: 434), '[g]rowing financial liberalization has profoundly changed the connections between finance and the rest of the economy'. As a result, at a macroeconomic level, economic growth is constrained by the dedication of profits to protecting the corporations' standing in the market. An accentuation of boom-and-bust volatility is seen to follow.

Yet it is integral to the Regulationist approach that the nation state is central to the regulation of accumulation, and it is no different in relation to this 'finance-led growth regime'. Accordingly, this focus on finance treats finance largely as a leading 'sector' (along with high technology and telecommunications) of the national economy (as manufacturing once was), and so is focused on the positioning of financial institutions rather than on evolving processes within financial markets. Moreover, and consistent with the Regulationist approach, the analysis of a 'finance-led growth regime' is entirely nation-centred and devoid of any real reference to global financial markets.[9]

Perhaps the most developed identification of the processes of finance within a new, 'flexible' phase of capitalism is found in theories of 'financialisation' and of 'shareholder value', themselves derived from the French Regulation School (Grahl and Teague 2000).[10] Shareholder value is purported to constitute a new ideology for corporate governance. It was a management rhetoric that rose to prominence in the 1990s and was taken up by the financial services industry selling investment products like pension plans and superannuation (Lazonick and O'Sullivan 2000: 13).

---

[9] Boyer (2000a: 140–1) concludes his deliberations on developing a model of a finance-led growth regime with the reflection that '[a] closed economy model is not satisfactory in the era of financial globalization'! Aglietta, conversely, whose own work has shifted towards global finance (e.g. 2002), including derivatives, now makes no connections between global finance and Regulation Theory.

[10] We note that Karel Williams (2000: 2), one of the leading figures in critical shareholder value analysis, has emphasised that 'they do not offer prophesy about a new era', and that the claims are of a limited and often localised impact. His proposition is reasonable, although it is probably more a statement about the proclamation of 'eras', for there are indeed claims that 'coupon pool capitalism', the generic basis of shareholder value, represents a distinctive logic of accumulation.

The alternative interpretation (we will call it critical shareholder value) has pursued an analysis of the wider implications of capital restructuring (especially for labour) in pursuit of shareholder value (Froud *et al.* 2000). In essence, this interpretation addresses the way in which the governance of corporations has changed and, in turn, the objectives of corporations have been transformed in order to deliver competitive returns to investors. This change itself is described by the term 'financialisation': a term in increasing use that refers to the new prevalence of financial calculation (and financial institutions) in the private and social world.[11] In the current context, financialisation emphasises the rising influence of institutional investors, especially the pension funds, in the stock market, and their demands on corporations to deliver both a stream of dividends and increasing asset values (Dore 2000; Froud *et al.* 2002; Stockhammer 2004).

Exponents of financialisation and critical shareholder value argue that corporations, especially in the United States, have transformed their traditional policy of retaining and re-investing earnings, which was the foundation of the economic dynamic that generated prosperity, to one of downsizing and distributing wealth to shareholders (Williams 2000: 4). Accordingly, a short-term agenda has been imposed on corporations – to deliver returns, or lose asset value and face takeover. With financialisation, all firms must now compete to meet these new market standards of financial performance (Froud *et al.* 2000). The question the exponents of critical shareholder value ask is whether or not such an ideology of corporate governance facilitates sustainable prosperity. The answers to date are generally mixed and locality- (i.e. nation-) specific (Williams 2000).

'Shareholder value' and 'financialisation' capture an important emerging link between finance and industry, and they point directly to profound implications for labour. The competitive pressure to deliver shareholder value means that corporations place demands on labour for on-going increases in productivity and flexibility.

But while an important connection between recent developments in finance and accumulation are established in this literature, the stock market itself should not be so heavily emphasised. It is, after all, a relatively minor forum for raising funds (Stiglitz 2001; Dumenil and Levy 2004: 121–4). Even in so-called market-based systems such as the United States, United Kingdom and Australia, retained earnings, loans and bond issues are far more important (Herring and Chatusripatak 2000).

---

[11] The term is invariably used in inverted commas, to acknowledge that 'financialisation' is a neologism without a precise meaning. See Henwood (1999).

Moreover, at the core of the shareholder value literature is a focus on the capacity of institutional investors (life offices and pension funds) to exert pressure on industrial capitalists to deliver dividends and share price growth. But here, too, is an exaggerated emphasis. Pension funds rarely if ever play an active role in the managerial decisions of firms. Institutional shareholder pressure on company boards, while an occasional reality, is the exception rather than the norm. And even their capacity to 'vote with their feet' is often overstated. They tend to spread their share portfolios across a wide range of corporate shares, and do not actively sell entirely out of one share and take up equity in another particular corporation on a significant scale.

If the momentum for competitive corporate outcomes associated with financialisation is to broaden beyond the role of the share market, it must take on the phenomenon of derivatives. One (albeit limited) development here is a focus on the growth of executive share options and the way in which their emergence has influenced the pursuit of shareholder value. This form of payment is said to generate the same sorts of tendencies as the pursuit of shareholder value, only internal to the firm and on a more extreme level. When executives are given part of their salary package in the form of share options, they are given the right, but not the obligation, to purchase shares at a pre-determined price (called the strike price). The incentive that follows is for the executive to ensure that the actual share price when the option falls due is greater than the strike price, for then the executive can purchase the shares at the strike price, immediately re-sell them at a higher price, and make an instant windfall gain. The leveraging capacities of derivatives are readily apparent here, and make share options a cheaper incentive than, for example, profit-based bonuses.[12]

A predictable debate follows: do executive share options serve to align the interests of managers more closely with those of owners in running the firm as profitably as possible, or do they tend to encourage managers to focus on riskier and shorter-term strategies of profit making?

While the contradictory incentive effects of share options can indeed be discerned, we are not inclined to give focus to this issue as a significant driver of a new phase of capitalist 'logic'. In part, the shift to share options was driven by the relatively lower taxes usually applied to options compared with other incentive schemes (Murrill and Caputo 2004) and the fact that payment by share options is not recorded in a company's annual profit and loss accounts, so they are payments that

---

[12] Leveraging is explained in Chapter 3 and in detail in Chapter 8.

do not reduce reported profitability. These issues can and are gradually being redressed by changes in taxation arrangements and other national legislation about executive remuneration, and enforcing the full costs of options to be costed in corporate profit and loss statements.[13]

Perhaps also the issue of executive options can be understood in terms of the distribution of profitability between two types of capitalists – managerial insiders and outside owner-shareholders – and debates about corporate time horizons for profitability. But, overall, a focus on executive share options tends to elevate share options beyond what is warranted. The vast bulk of financial derivatives are on or between individual assets and liabilities, and executive options are minor. Their impact is not to be ignored, but there are bigger issues than this that follow from the prevalence of derivatives.

From this short review of shareholder capitalism and executive share options as drivers of capitalism, a central conclusion can be drawn. The inclusion of derivatives involves more than just adding another layer to the critical shareholder value and executive share options story. Executive share options consider only their effects on personal managerial incentives, not the operation of global capital markets. Critical shareholder value retains an entirely national focus, following directly from its Regulationist origins. Proponents of the theory talk in terms of macro (i.e. national) policy agendas to manage the effects of financialisation. They depict the framework as leading directly to 'objects of post-Keynesian macro intervention' (Williams 2000: 12) and especially to state agendas to control asset inflation as a way of regulating this form of finance (Boyer 2000a). Derivatives, as we shall see in later chapters, depict the global integration of finance and challenge directly these sorts of national policy agendas. For this reason, if no other, the analysis of shareholder capitalism needs to extend into financial derivatives.

What general conclusion can be drawn about what is missing in the broad social science literature on recent financial development? The proposition we are developing is that derivatives have a significance that is generally missed in much of the recent social science engagement with finance and globalisation. In part, this is because issues of nation-state capacity have dominated the popular globalisation debate, and derivatives are simply deemed to be part of the package of international finance that is posed as a threat to state capacity. In part also, the

---

[13] See, for example a long sequence of articles in *The Economist*, such as: 'Share options and executive pay', 25th April 2002, and 'Valuing share options', 7th November 2002.

engagement with finance focuses on the institutional connections between the financial services industry and the stock market, leading to a focus on corporate incentives to invest.

So how are derivatives distinctly significant? To answer this question, we need to jump ahead in our analysis, and assert a proposition we will later develop in detail.

Derivatives are distinctly significant because, in combination, they involve a huge market process in which all different forms (and temporalities) of capital are priced against (commensurated with) each other. By this process of commensuration, rates of return on different assets can be directly measured and, in a competitive capitalist environment, there follows a requirement of each asset, across space and across time, to deliver a competitive return. This sort of competitive pressure was identified earlier in relation to the 'shareholder capitalism' thesis. Here we simply note that derivatives help to convey the same pressure so much more intensively and pervasively than is perceived under 'shareholder capitalism', and by a process inherent in capitalist competition, not just contingent upon particular institutional relations between pension funds and boards of directors, or on incentives for corporate managers to deliver shareholder value.

Our proposition that derivatives provide a means to directly compare all different sorts of capital then throws us back to a formally economic issue: the need for a universal measure of value, for this measure is what derivatives are enacting. And here, we have a fundamental rupture with both the neoclassicals and the Keynesians. This is the issue taken up in the next section.

Derivatives as a universal measure

Measurability of commodity value is integral to both economic theory and the organisation of economic activity. As Mirowski has pointed out, 'to forfeit value theory is to abstain from any participation in the inquiry called economics' (1990: 7). Yet, as readers will be aware, there is no universal agreement about the measure of value. There is both a fundamental divide between subjective theories of value (neoclassical utility theory) and objective (or substance) theories of value, the most prevalent being the Marxian labour theory of value. And within each of these, there is intense debate. Moreover, the influence of postmodernism has been to cast theories of value as reductionist. But without a theory of value there can be no theory of exchange, and hence no explanation of the process of commensuration provided by financial derivatives. A theory of value only becomes reductionist when it postures as 'scientific'.

But measurement itself is a social construct. Mirowski (1991: 568) reminds us that, 'there is no one "correct" way for a society to measure a commodity, and (yet) the way its measurement is instituted has important consequences for its subsequent manipulation in various formal mathematical schemes'. Value, he argues (1990: 7), is 'contingent, hermeneutic, negotiable, and non natural'. But rather than reject a measure of value, he argues,

> One must perforce drop anchor at some fixed point, if only to restore a sense of balance and a semblance of rationality amid the giddiness. After all, the actual economic transactors are not paralysed by nausea but seem to go about their business with some degree of equanimity, albeit distracted now and then by some abrupt heave or eddy.

We remain unconvinced by all facets of this depiction of a theory of value, but the issue of contingency is central. It is the contingent nature of valuation that underlies most of the controversies regarding a universal measure.

What is the particular connection between derivatives and contingency? It is that theories of value are generally not good at handling space or time. Can the same good have a different value in different places? Can its value change while it sits in a warehouse? These are difficult questions for a theory of value, but valuation across space, time, and between different asset forms is the stuff of derivatives. Derivative traders do indeed shift financial assets between different forms and they do so in large volumes: they do operate in a world of perceived equivalence but, and this is critical, it is not a fixed equivalence – for if equivalence were fixed, there would be no need for derivatives!

It is not our intention to follow Mirowski's rather tentative 'social theory of value', but his critical insight is important: that there has to be some theory of value even though we are in full knowledge of its contingency. Moreover, we must never forget its contingency. But we should consider how both actual transactors, as well as economic theorists, look to elevate value above its contingency, to give it an objective feel, to take the focus off the reality of contingency so that transactions may securely and coherently proceed.

Indeed, it is because of this contingency that most social scientists prefer to concentrate on the phenomenon of money and prices rather than on 'value'. But this path never ultimately proves satisfactory.

Explanations simply in terms of observed prices are not explanations of underlying determinants, yet the need for a valuation of underlying determinants keeps reappearing. Orthodox neoclassical finance can posit a world of relative prices and develop propositions that market prices gravitate towards equilibrium, but there remains in this orthodoxy the pursuit of a measure of the 'fundamental value' of capital, a measure that lies outside the realm of market-determined prices. When it is said that exchange rates or share values have deviated from 'underlying value' or 'the fundamentals', there is both a notion that price is in some sense both superficial and volatile, and that value has a material foundation: for exchange rates, it is the productive performance of the national economy; for shares, it is the productive performance of corporate assets. The pursuit of a measure of 'fundamental value' arises precisely because price is not a sufficient representation of value. The link between money and price and a material value is ever present, though insufficiently acknowledged.

Derivatives prove critical in this link. Derivatives, by their nature, are a reflection of other assets whose value is contestable. A wheat future relates to the contestable value of a tonne of wheat across time and space; a sterling option to the contestable value of the British pound in different places and over different temporal horizons. Derivatives are thereby the bearers of contestability. So they are crucial to the link between money, price and fundamental value not because they *actually* determine fundamental values (for there are no truths here) but because they are the way in which the market judges or perceives fundamental value. They turn *the contestability* of fundamental value into a tradable commodity. In so doing, they provide a market benchmark for an unknowable value.

Conclusion

While global developments in finance now have widespread attention, financial derivatives are relatively ignored outside of mathematical finance. In much of the social sciences, the black box of derivatives as techniques of risk management is kept firmly closed and analysis too readily diverts into issues of institutionalism (the global structure of the banking industry) and moralism (the dangers of 'hot money').

The constitution of derivatives as a universalising unit of measure presents an issue outside the debates about nation-state capacities, the rise of global financial centres, speculation and unproductive finance. As a new language of money, derivatives are creating new ways of seeing accumulation. Others have suggested this sort of leap associated with derivatives, but their propositions have been more suggestive than elaborated. Pryke and Allen (2000), for example, have referred to derivatives as 'monetised time-space', depicting them as money's 'new imaginary'. This is an exciting idea, but is not developed into a formal exposition of the role of derivatives.

We see in derivatives the language of risk management – that life's contingencies (for corporations and for individuals) can be reduced to commodified risk, for that, in essence, is what derivatives are: commodities that manage risk. And because risk exposure is so changeable, the market for these risk management commodities has acquired a high level of liquidity (volume and mobility) with many of the characteristics of money.

Once we engage the issues of risk management, it becomes apparent that derivatives do something rather basic: they provide a means to convert the value of assets in one form into assets in another form, and so take the risk out of holding any particular form of asset. For the broader social sciences, an important insight follows. If the values of different asset forms can be reconciled, so can the measure of the performance of those assets. A competitive pressure emerges within capital that crosses space and time: the construction of a unit of capital value means that all rates of return on capital can be compared, and pressure is placed on under-performing capital to achieve globally acceptable rates of return. These are considered in more detail in Chapters 3 and 7.

Does this constitute a new era of capitalism? Perhaps, although the pronouncement of 'new eras' is usually more noted for rhetorical effect than substance. The critical issue in 'new era' theories is whether the new era is seen as a complete rupture with the past, or a product of the tensions inherent within the past. Ruptures are too easy to declare: there is no need to explain what generated the changes being identified; it is sufficient to pronounce that the past has been overturned. We argue in Chapter 6 that derivatives constitute a new, private global money. Whether that would constitute a 'new era' is beside the point, but it is only once this development is recognised that we can start to consider the full social significance of financial derivatives and their role in the intensification of competition. That is the task that the remaining chapters of the book seek to begin.

3
Derivatives and Derivative Markets

In this chapter we introduce readers to the nuts and bolts of derivatives. The objective is, however, different from that found in an introductory finance textbook. There are now many good texts on derivatives, explaining how they are priced and strategies for trading them. There is no point in repeating that content. Rather, this chapter seeks to show how derivatives relate to the operation of a capitalist economy and how their impact has changed over time as derivatives have themselves changed and become more pervasive in financial markets.

Central to our explanation are the two functions of derivatives defined in Chapter 1: binding and blending. Some forms of derivatives bind the present to the future by reconciling prices today with prices tomorrow. Other forms of derivatives serve to blend apparently discrete types of assets by creating novel assets with characteristics that are a composite of these (once) discrete types (e.g. a blend of debt and equity, or a blend of stock prices and exchange rates). These binding and blending functions, but especially the latter, have come to play a central role in economic calculation, with direct expression in capitalist class relations. While the analysis of the seemingly technical details of financial derivatives may seem a long way from issues of capital and class, our analysis shows that there are indeed important implications of the rise of financial derivatives for accumulation and class relations.

To draw out these links, it is necessary to confront some of the key technical features of derivatives and derivatives markets: to open the black box referred to in Chapter 1. After some simple explanations of how financial derivatives work, we look at the size of derivatives markets and in what functions they are most important. Finally, the chapter outlines the emerging impact of derivatives in markets as diverse as farm produce, minerals, share markets, foreign exchange markets and credit.

In the process, we introduce many of the issues to be pursued in the remainder of the book.

Defining derivatives

Defining derivatives is now fraught with difficulties. Until the 1980s the definition was generally clear and widely accepted. It was a definition that could explain a history of derivative use, going back to Greek and Chinese antiquity, as specialist contracts used in particular industries to help create commodity price certainty over time and across distances. This same definition prevailed in the 1970s, when derivatives were still dominated by their use in a narrow range of storable agricultural and mineral commodities.

A key characteristic of those derivatives was that parties agreed to a price now for a future transaction of the particular commodity. This is the original sense of the word derivative: the idea that the value of the derivative *derives from* the price of the underlying commodity and was an adjunct to trade in these commodities.

But in the last two and a half decades, derivatives have come to play an extended and qualitatively different role. They are now neither specialist (in the sense of marginal) nor restricted to commodity trade.

Any definition must now encompass a wide range of financial contracts that perform far more diverse functions than had previously been envisaged. From relatively obscure contracts used by a few primary producers, merchants and refiners in the 1960s to lock in future prices, derivatives have now become the largest type of financial transaction in the world (BIS 2005). Quite simply, with derivatives now at the centre of global finance, the old definition is now not only limited, but simplistic and misleading.

But for derivatives to have moved out from under this marginal role, they must have the capacity to do more than lock in future prices. Trying to develop a better understanding of what this capacity is represents a work in progress for economists and, indeed, social scientists in general. Moreover, any definition tends to be a moving target: the range of financial contracts with derivative-like characteristics continues to grow and the range of firms and individuals using derivatives has grown significantly over the last two decades, so that functionalist definitions are continually superseded.

Hence, our object here is not simply to nominate a new definition, but to pose the more nuanced question of how the evolving role of derivatives is to be understood. Of course, how they are understood depends on the questions being asked. Insofar as we are posing different questions from those of a conventional financial economics textbook – questions about the broader social and economic role of derivatives – so we will frame derivatives somewhat differently.

To build towards an appreciation of the role of derivatives, it is helpful to start with the simple definition that applies to the pre-1980s period when commodity derivatives were predominant. We can then watch that definition become superseded by the transformation in the financial system. The development of financial derivatives can thereby be seen to emerge out of the contradictions of the earlier period.

Commodity derivatives

Forwards

Consider how derivatives can be used to assist the operational needs of a wheat farmer and flour miller. Both have an interest in the price of wheat in the future: one as their key output price, the other as their key input price. Both could wait until harvest time and accept the prevailing price. Alternatively, the flour miller may contract directly with the farmer to fix a price for a certain amount of wheat for delivery at a particular place at some agreed date in the future. This is an example of a forward contract, which sets out the terms for a future sale and delivery in advance of the actual exchange of the wheat. The market (or cash, or spot) price for wheat at the delivery date may be above or below the forward contract price, but by fixing the price in advance both parties have gained security.

In this sense, the forward contract appears as a zero-sum game in monetary terms, with any gains from price changes for one party being offset by losses by the other party. This zero-sum dimension underscores both the contingent nature of accumulation at the level of the firm and the intense competitiveness of derivative markets. (It is also, as we will see in Chapter 8,[1] at the centre of the argument that derivatives are purely speculative.)

However, while such derivatives may be a zero sum in monetary terms, in a broader context, they can be seen to involve a positive sum. By permitting the better planning and organisation of production and trade, derivatives may generate positive effects on resource allocation and accumulation (Parsons 1988; Gibson and Zimmerman 1994). The

---

[1] See especially Appendix 8.1.

forward contract allows the flour miller to insulate the milling business against the risk of wheat prices going up. The alternative to such insurance would be to buy wheat now and store it. So by entering into a forward contract, the miller can achieve price certainty without the costs of storage. Similarly, by ensuring a minimum price, the farmer may be better able to calculate returns from wheat and thus plan crop planting more profitably. The alternative to the forward contract may be to plant a range of crops, rather than specialise in the one in which the farmer is most efficient. There are elements of a positive sum game here.

But let us not over-state the possible positive sum nature of such derivative transactions. While they may be real, they are only consequences of the way transactors respond to price certainty; they are not products of the derivatives themselves. This latter notion of a positive sum game does not come until the widespread use of financial derivatives: an issue discussed later.

Futures

There is more to derivatives than forward contracts. Forward contracts can be cumbersome and limited. Although they are specialised to meet the specific needs of, say, a farmer and flour miller, this specialisation may also be a disadvantage. Forward contracts can sometimes involve high search costs to find parties with exactly opposite needs. Further, the contracts usually bind the parties to actual exchange, yet after the contract is entered into this may become inconvenient for either or both parties. The farmer may not have enough wheat to sell, or enough of a particular grade. The flour miller may need less wheat, or more of a different quality. Also, in the case of default or bankruptcy by one party, there may be large legal costs to secure the forward price. So both parties need to monitor each other to ensure that they remain viable and committed to fulfilling their side of the contract.

By standardising the contract terms, such as delivery date, place and quantity, it is possible to make it easier to on-sell such contracts. This is the essence of a futures contract, which is basically a standardised forward contract. With the evolution of specialised markets for trading these futures contracts (commodity exchanges), where the exchange itself guarantees the creditworthiness of market participants, we have most of the key features of a modern futures market.

In futures markets participants do not need to know a flour miller or wheat grower personally to buy or sell wheat futures contracts. Indeed they can trade standardised contracts without even knowing who owns the other side of the contract. Furthermore, once well established, no actual wheat or other commodity is usually delivered at the end of the contract, so market participants do not need to be in possession of wheat at the expiration of the futures contract. Delivery typically takes place in cash as the difference between the futures price and the underlying commodity price (or spot price) at the time of settlement.

Importantly for modern derivatives, the commodity derivative permits the separation of the future price, or other properties, from either actual physical possession, or even rights to actual ownership. This right to participate in, for instance, the future price change of wheat is different from the right to possession or future ownership of wheat itself. This separation of the actual exchange of wheat from its future price permits a greater flexibility in exchange within wheat markets. It also means that futures contracts for (nominally) thousands of tonnes of wheat can be exchanged at relatively low cost.

For a person with exposure to changes in wheat prices,[2] futures provide a cheap means to cover that exposure – a futures contract which gives the right to buy (or sell) a tonne of wheat at a future date costs only a small fraction of the cost of a tonne of wheat itself. Expressed another way, for the cost of directly purchasing a tonne of wheat, a person may be able to purchase futures contracts on 20 or more tonnes of wheat. Accordingly, they are exposed to price movements on 20 tonnes of wheat rather than simply the one tonne. In financial markets, this is known as leverage.[3]

Leverage also facilitates people with no direct interest in wheat *per se* (except the chance to make money on price differences or changes) to become involved in the market. These are usually referred to as traders or speculators. And it is this capacity to obtain exposure to a much greater amount of a commodity, or financial asset, for little investment, and with no necessary interest in the underlying commodity or asset that concerns many worried about their explosive speculative potential. The extra leverage of derivatives is a key reason that Warren Buffet, the US investor at the helm of Berkshire Hathaway, has rather colourfully referred to derivatives as 'financial weapons of mass destruction'. But

---

[2] The term exposure in this context refers to the fact that the change in wheat prices will exert an impact of the person's profitability (or, more generally, well-being).

[3] Leverage is defined by the IMF (Bruer 2002) as 'the magnification of the rate of return (positive or negative) on a position or investment beyond the rate obtained by a direct investment of own funds in the cash market'. The full implications of leveraging are pursued in Chapter 8.

this leverage has another side: it makes it cheaper to secure prices in the future, and easier to make decisions now about the future.[4]

More importantly, this leverage is possible because, through derivatives, aspects of a commodity or financial instrument (especially future prices) can be separated from either the physical possession of the thing itself, or even of ownership rights to it. This separation is a decisive feature of financial derivatives (and will be an issue returned to in later chapters), but within commodity derivatives the full ramifications of such a separation remained quite limited.

Options

Forwards and futures are not the only types of commodity derivatives. Another important form is options.

In some situations, it may be more useful for one party to have the right but not the obligation to buy or sell a commodity at a particular price over a certain period. The flour miller may not necessarily want to be bound to buy a certain quantity of wheat at a certain price, place and date, but would like to have the opportunity, or option, to do so.

In order to induce the wheat grower to enter into what seems like a one-sided contract, the miller will probably need to pay the wheat grower a small amount of money now to hold open such an opportunity to make the purchase in the future. This contract is known as an option and the sum paid to the wheat grower by the miller for the right to purchase is known as a premium. So another way of contracting with derivatives is for one party to buy (and the other to sell) the right, but not the obligation, to undertake a transaction at a particular price over a certain period.

Should the miller decide to go ahead with the purchase, he/she will exercise the option. But should the miller decide not to – because of a decline in the demand for flour, or because it is now cheaper to purchase wheat in the spot market than to exercise the option contract, the miller will not exercise the option. The money spent purchasing the option will be now lost, but at least our miller knew that, had the spot price gone sky high, he/she had protection via the option. As with the futures contract, for a fairly small investment, it is possible via options to acquire access to quite a large exposure to a commodity or asset price

[4] Garber (1998) has observed that, '[t]he problems associated with the rise of derivatives stem partly from the same source as the benefits: the increased ability to separate and market risks means that some counterparties can assume riskier positions more readily than in the past'.

(referred to as leverage), and this makes both hedging and speculation cheaper.[5]

Following these sorts of agricultural illustrations (and a history centred in commodity derivatives), the standard explanation of derivatives within economics posed a very particular relationship between derivative and spot markets. This was the proposition that derivatives were an important adjunct to trade, allowing economic agents to either insure against price volatility or to better exploit perceived price differentials within markets that may be created by such volatility. Some economists countered that the hedging properties of derivatives were often overwhelmed by the destabilising speculation inherent in the greater leverage offered by derivatives. However, even this proposition was consistent with the same basic notion, it was just that, in practice, some derivative markets were seen to have inverted the proper relationship and assumed a life of their own.

This notion of derivatives as an adjunct to trade was also consistent with the general notion that price determination occurs in the cash or spot market, with prices in options and futures said to *derive* from prices in the spot market. This causality is so fundamental that it is the origin of the term *'derivative'*. With 'real' value determined in spot markets, derivatives were accordingly theorised as a form of hedging or speculation for prices in specific markets. Indeed, historically derivatives were an outgrowth of such financial instruments as forward contracts and forms of credit associated with long distance trade (such as letters of credit). Futures markets themselves typically originated within existing commodity markets in trading centres such as Chicago in the United States and Liverpool and London in Britain.

So the stylised facts of derivatives history underpinned their marginal nature. It is not until they had become central to modern finance that it has been necessary to question this story.

From this historical context – centred on commodity market price volatility – the essential function of derivatives came to be defined in terms of pricing contracts that bind the present to the future. By implication, the discourse emerging from commodity derivatives centred on hedging and speculation: the key role of commodity derivatives was

---

[5] It bears noting that Nick Leeson, the Barings 'rogue trader', who lost hundreds of millions of pounds actually engaged in transactions that initially netted cash payments to the bank. He did this by selling options (to cover his earlier losses). Selling options attracts an initial cash amount, known as a premium, even though it leaves the seller exposed to potentially large losses later.

either to lay-off risks associated with volatility (often hedging) or take on risk (speculation).[6] It is from this discourse that we see the popular notion that derivatives are a zero-sum game.

We must also recognise that a theory of derivatives, which uses agricultural markets as its ideal-type, is likely to be anachronistic and limited in its conception, and in the next section we open up the

---

Box 1: Types of derivatives and their uses

There are several ways of categorising derivatives, but a useful way is to distinguish between those with forward-like and those with option-like characteristics.

Forward-type derivatives

A forward-type agreement is simply the agreement to transact or exchange (sale or purchase) at a certain price amount and quality of a commodity at some time and place in the future.

Forward contracts specify a price at which a commodity, financial asset, index or the cash flows from these items are exchanged at some place and at a specified date. They are unconditional in that they oblige both parties to undertaking the exchange. Because both parties are bound to settle, both have a risk that prices at settlement may be unfavourable compared to the cash market.

Forward contracts

These are contracts that commit parties to exchange a specified amount and quantity of a commodity, financial asset or index at a specified price at some place and some time in the future. Forward contracts are typically customised to the specific needs of the parties who enter the contract. Forward contracts are therefore rarely on-sold to others.

Futures

These are contracts that commit parties to buy (or sell) some standardised quantity and quality of a commodity, financial asset or index at some future date and place at a fixed price. Futures contracts are similar to forward contracts but are standardised so as to permit trading on organised markets. A corollary is that futures contracts may be on-sold.

Swaps

These are contracts in which parties exchange a commodity, financial asset (liability) or index, or the net cash flows arising from these for a specified

---

[6] In Chapter 8 we contend that the distinction between hedging and speculation is not as clear as this depiction would suggest. In this context, it is nonetheless a convenient distinction.

period of time. There is a variety of swaps, but two types of swaps are most common: currency swaps where different currencies are swapped for a specified period; and interest rate swaps, where the net cash flows (say interest rate payments) from two loans are exchanged.

Option-type derivatives

Option-type derivatives are similar to forward-type derivatives, except that the owner of the derivative has the *right but not the obligation* to execute the derivative contract. Unlike forward-type contracts, which are unconditional and must be settled, options are conditional contracts, meaning that settlement will only occur if the owner of the option finds it profitable to do so. The element of optionality held by one party means that normally they would pay an amount (known as a premium) to the option seller (or writer). Once the option holder had paid the premium, the option seller is exposed to the risk of price movements.

Options

These are contracts that convey the owner the right but not the obligation to buy (or sell) a specified quantity and quality of a commodity, financial asset or index at a fixed price within a certain period of time. Options come in two forms: put options are the right to sell, while call options are the right to buy. These may be on-sold.

Warrants

These are option-like contracts that are normally written on particular corporate stocks, typically giving the owner the right to buy or sell a stock at a specified price during a certain period. Warrants are often issued by banks or other institutions. As with options, these may be on-sold.

Mixed or combined derivatives

Derivatives or derivative-like features can also be blended either with other derivatives or with commodities or assets.

Convertible bonds

These are debt-like contracts, which contain an option (i.e. the right) to convert a debt (typically a bond) into an equity (share) in the firm over a specified period of time.

Structured notes

These are largely bond contracts in which a variety of cash flows are added so that net receipts or payments may depend on a formula of different prices of several different derivative (and sometimes non-derivative) elements in addition to the principal and interest accruing to the debt. Significantly, it is the leverage or derivative element, rather than the principal or interest payments from the bond of the structured note that may dominate net receipts or payments.

limitations of this hedging/speculation discourse. Nonetheless, it must also be recognised that that commodity derivatives give us almost all the basic derivative categories,[7] summarised in Box 1. What changes with financial derivatives is how these characteristics are put together.

A new role for derivatives

As the role of derivatives has transformed in the last 25 years, so they have moved beyond issues of speculation and hedging. Indeed, current debates that focus on issues of speculation versus hedging can now be seen to be dated and limited to a pre-1980s conception of derivatives.

There are two specific problems with the above depiction, which set the basis for a new role for post-1980s derivatives. First, it treats derivatives as if they operate only within particular product categories – there are discrete derivative products for wheat, cotton, barley, etc., but with limited connections between them and between these derivatives markets and the rest of the economy. Second, it poses derivatives only in the context of markets for storable physical commodities.

But from the 1980s, there was a rapid expansion of derivative products that both cross product categories and apply to non-storable products, especially to financial instruments. Not only did futures and options markets begin to be dominated by transactions on financial instruments, but new types of derivative contract emerged that were, from the outset, financially oriented and could not be understood through the discourse of commodity derivatives. The most important of these was swaps.

Swaps

Swaps use the same basic types of derivatives as applied to commodities, but they emerged to apply to financial assets, especially debt and currencies. Swaps have attributes of both futures and options. Indeed, in one sense, swaps are similar to a series of forward contracts, with several regular settlement dates. With an interest rate or cross-currency swap, two parties raise funds in one form (currency and/or interest rate structure (fixed or variable rate)) and swap repayment obligations. For example, a company may borrow in fixed rate terms in British pounds but, via a swap contract, convert the repayment obligations effectively into variable rate Japanese yen. It will undertake this conversion with another party that has borrowed in variable rate yen, but wants

---

[7] Swaps are a notable exception. They are explained immediately below.

exposure to fixed rate pounds. Why will they do this? Because their asset profile gives them a borrowing advantage in one currency/interest rate structure, but their income and expenditure profile makes repayment more advantageous in a different currency/interest rate structure. By borrowing in one form, and swapping into another form, both parties can gain.

The effect of swaps is also to blend together (or make transmutable) different forms of capital, to create a market of conversion between fixed and floating rate loans, and between different currencies. This permits the calibration of funding to the currency and term structure needs of companies or financial institutions. In so doing, financial derivatives help to blend all interest rates and currencies into a single market. This represents a transformation from the earlier product-specific markets for commodity derivatives.

Take, for instance, the case of a firm seeking to establish operations in a new country or attempting a takeover of a firm in another country. It could use funds borrowed from the company's home market, but this would leave it exposed to changes in the exchange rate between the home and host country. This would create a currency mismatch between the revenues from the foreign operations and the costs of domestic funding. Alternatively, the firm may try to borrow in the market where the new operations are to be located. This provides the firm with what is known as a 'natural' hedge so that revenues and expenses are in the same currency. But a firm may pay more for these funds, either because it is too small or does not have a credit rating in that market.

Swaps offer a different path. The firm may borrow funds at the globally lowest cost in whatever currency and term structure (fixed or floating) it can get its best deal. The firm can then swap the borrowing into the desired currency and term structure that best matches the firm's other exposures. Banks (either directly or as an intermediary) can then find another borrower with the opposite borrowing needs to swap the (net) interest rate payments.[8] Overall, the effect is that by both parties borrowing at the lowest cost and swapping repayment obligations, both parties finish up with lower interest rate costs.

---

[8] Derivatives have thus helped to change the dynamics of institutional performance in banking towards fee-based income, rather than just financial intermediation. In the United States, for instance, fees from financial derivatives transactions now exceed 40 per cent of banks' total non-interest revenues (Bonfim 1999).

Note two implications of this description of a basic swap. First, it is a potential non-zero-sum transaction, and the rapid growth of swaps over the last 20 years is some indication of realised mutual gains. This potential challenges fundamentally the speculation/hedging discourse as a means to understand derivatives.

Second, this swap is not just binding the future to the present; it is also blending different sorts of assets (fixed and floating interest rate loans, in this case). Swaps are prototypical of the capacity of modern financial derivatives to commensurate different borrowing alternatives and forms of money globally.

Changing circumstances, changing attributes

In one respect, the development of financial derivatives represents just an extension of derivatives on storable commodities to new areas. But this is more than just a story of quantitative growth. As is made stark in the case of swaps, financial derivatives perform a role in modern global finance that is much more profound than can be captured by the agricultural derivatives model. It suggests a need to re-think the nature of derivatives. While some of the characteristics of commodity derivatives described above contain a potential for application across a wide range of other economic transactions, this potential was not harnessed for two hundred or more years.

Two questions follow: why did it take so long for financial derivatives to emerge? (and why did financial derivatives emerge so rapidly when they did?); and what are the underlying factors that have permitted financial derivatives to perform such a central role in modern global finance?

The first question has been reasonably widely addressed elsewhere. In essence, it is a story of three concurrent (and related) trends that we have depicted as the 'proximate' causes of derivative growth. They are simply listed here, but will be investigated in more detail in Chapters 3, 4 and 5:

1. Price volatility from the early 1970s associated with two events: the end of the Bretton Woods Agreement, which had regulated capital flows and exchange rates since the Second World War, and the 1970's oil price shocks, and the collapse of many national and international commodity price stabilisation schemes.[9]

[9] On the relationship between commodity price stabilisation sehemes and commodity derivatives, see Gosh *et al.* (1987).

2. The increased importance of finance (especially international finance) in investment and takeovers, typified by the growth of Eurofinance markets.
3. The internationalisation of trade and investment, which saw individual firms become more exposed to international finance and more susceptible to volatility. This was especially seen in the rise of the multinational firm as increasingly the representative form of corporate organisation.

In the conventional history of derivative growth, these proximate causes are often linked to particular discontinuities and market 'imperfections' of the recent period, such as exchange rate volatility. As such, these explanations often get caught up in explaining derivatives purely in terms of market volatility. As we shall see shortly, volatility is a pretty good explanation of the catalyst for the growth of financial derivatives from the late 1970s. The problem with this line of explanation, however, is that financial derivatives have continued to grow in conditions unlike those of the late 1970s. With the growing speed and volume of international capital flows, and what many analysts identify as the increasing efficiency of financial and product markets, derivative transactions have continued to grow exponentially, independently of the level of volatility. This is difficult to reconcile with notions of financial derivatives purely as products of volatility and market imperfections (Ackland 2000).

The second question, therefore, concerns factors beyond volatility and imperfections that explain financial derivatives. Derivatives, we argue, are integral to the logic of markets in capitalism, and hence need an explanation that is 'deeper' than can be predicated merely on volatility. The deeper importance of derivatives is the way in which they link markets: what we have called the blending process. In framing this underlying logic, Henderson and Price (1988: 196) have, in the context of swaps, made a prescient point:

> Swap financing *does not require markets as they now exist; it only requires markets with different characteristics.* ... (they) are the most recent manifestation of the ... trend to turn money into an intellectualised, disembodied force. As the principles of swap financing are fully in accord with the fundamental characteristics of today's global civilisation, they will remain firmly embedded in our financial culture. (emphasis added)

Furthermore, with finance, unlike agricultural commodities, integral to all capitalist accumulation, financial derivatives, too, are now integral to accumulation. As one financier has recently suggested 'the power of derivatives lies in their *versatility and universality*' (Sandford 1999: 5 emphasis added).

It is necessary to explain derivatives in this generic requirement of 'markets with different characteristics', as a means to explain how financial derivatives have become so 'versatile and universal'. This explanation has much more widespread and long-term significance than can be found in theories based on volatility or specific markets for agricultural commodities. It is to this universal potential, which remained latent for most of the preceding two hundred years, that the chapter now turns, albeit to just open up issues to be explored in detail in later chapters.

The central, universal characteristic of derivatives is their capacity to 'dismantle' or 'unbundle' any asset[10] into constituent attributes and trade those attributes without trading the asset itself. For the orthodox finance literature, this dismantling is understood purely as an exercise of isolating particular and different forms of risk, which can then be traded and priced individually. For users of derivatives, risk management is clearly a critical characteristic. But in jumping directly to the pricing and trading of risk, this orthodoxy tends to overlook the very significance of this 'dismantling' process of separating attributes of an asset from the asset itself.

There are two important features that underlie the dismantling process that should be brought to the fore. One feature is that derivatives are separate from possession or ownership of the underlying asset itself. Derivatives are priced, bought and sold without any change of ownership of the asset to which the derivative relates. This is because the derivative is pricing and trading only attributes of the asset, not the asset itself. The significance of this difference is explored in detail in Chapter 4.

The second feature that underlies the dismantling process is that it enables the attributes of any asset to be configured as universally recognisable and generic, and therefore tradable, irrespective of the particularity of the asset itself. A unique asset, for which there may be quite a small market, can be dismantled into generic attributes for which there is a large market. By 'dismantling' assets into tradable attributes, the focus shifts from the particularity of the asset itself to the universality of its attributes. Derivatives thereby focus on what different assets have in

---

[10] For simplicity in this context the word asset will be used to mean commodity, asset or financial instrument, but also non-asset derivatives such as stock market or weather indices.

common (their generic attributes), and the effect is to intensify competition (across space and time) for the attributes of this asset, with direct ramifications for the asset itself.[11]

With financial institutions as major brokers of derivative contracts, and hence at the centre of the 'unbundling' process, they are also key drivers of capital accumulation. As Herring (1994: 3–4), for instance, has noted:

> Financial institutions have introduced a variety of innovations to reduce transactions costs and broaden the range of options available to borrowers in national and international financial markets. In general these innovations have permitted institutions to *unbundle and repackage financial attributes* so that both borrowers and lenders end up with the financial instruments they prefer and risks are redistributed to investors who are most willing to bear them. ...
>
> *The information systems and analytic capacity to compare such borrowing alternatives are formidable; they require virtually instantaneous information about global developments that can be factored into investment, funding and credit evaluation decisions.* But sophisticated international borrowers have come to expect that they can select from an extremely broad menu that includes a multitude of indirect ways to achieve the desired result. (emphasis added)

One critical effect of this development is that corporations can now benchmark the returns of their operations in different countries and in different activities, financed with different amounts and compositions of capital, and with revenue streams in different currencies. The competitive implications of this commensurating process follow directly. This is an issue we develop further in Chapter 7.

Until the 1980s, this capacity to commensurate financial assets and commodities and, critically, for them to commensurate *across* commodities and financial instruments on a more global scale remained latent. While this situation prevailed, the analysis of derivatives markets could remain safely contained within the discourse developed in the context of agricultural commodity markets. The analytical focus continued, therefore, to be centred on the use of derivatives in establishing 'true' prices and price relationships within particular markets. Meanwhile, however, derivatives were beginning to be used in financial markets,

---

[11] Garbade (2001) has referred to this capacity of financial derivatives as facilitating the 'relative value' of assets.

where this capacity for derivatives to commensurate across asset boundaries was much more readily grasped. While it had to wait for certain other historical conditions to come together before this full capacity could be realised, financial derivatives have rapidly become integral to modern global accumulation. We are just starting to come to terms with the importance of this development.

Within the finance orthodoxy the central issue was initially how to 'correctly' price derivatives, in which the Black–Scholes option pricing and binomial pricing models were at the analytical cutting edge The Black–Scholes option pricing theory, for example, was first formulated in the late 1960s, and is now widely credited with permitting the growth of exchange-traded financial derivatives in places like the Chicago Mercantile Exchange and Chicago Board of Trade in the 1970s. At the time, however, the wider implications of this development were not immediately obvious even to its proponents. It took some time before computational techniques necessary for structuring and pricing more complex financial derivatives developed. It also took some time before a generation of managers were trained with familiarity in derivatives techniques and strategies, and so saw their wider potential as a corporate risk management tool.

In part also, it awaited recognition of the wider role of derivatives. Only relatively recently has this wider role been grasped theoretically within orthodox economics, although it rapidly transformed into conventional wisdom. Myron Scholes, one of the originators of options pricing theory, has summarised this new convention succinctly: 'most financial instruments are derivative contracts in one form or another' (1998: 364). Beyond the hubris of this comment is the development of, for instance, real options theory, which poses investment opportunities (and existing assets and activities) as options that can be valued using derivative pricing theory.

Out from the margins

As derivatives have shifted towards financial instruments, the derivative categories identified in Box 1 have not fundamentally changed: futures, options and swaps remain the standard tools.[12] But the scale and scope

---

[12] Ackland (2000) makes the point that the rise of swaps was a product specifically of the globalisation of financial markets and floating exchange rates, and was thus intimately linked to the growth of financial derivatives. This is an important point. Here, however, we seek to emphasise their common characteristics and indeed forwards are the building blocks of swaps.

of their use is remarkable. Some stylised facts and some of the key 'rethinking' of the new position of derivatives should be noted.

1. *The growth of financial derivatives (rather than the traditional commodity derivatives)*

Size and growth *per se* in a diverse industry is difficult to measure, so only a general picture can be created.[13] The most conspicuous development, however, is that virtually all of the growth in derivatives since the early 1980s has been in transactions between different forms of money and finance (financial futures and options, but especially interest rate and currency swaps), not between money and simple commodities (storable commodity futures).

By 1990, market-traded financial derivatives had eclipsed commodity derivatives in size and importance. By then financial futures markets already accounted for over 60 per cent of all exchange-traded futures contracts. By 2000, agricultural derivatives had fallen to less than 20 per cent of exchange-traded derivatives (BIS 2002).

The current scale of financial derivatives can be measured in a number of ways. We can get some indication via two simple measures: foreign exchange market growth and over the counter (OTC) derivative contract growth. (OTC, we shall explain shortly, is the largest medium of derivative transaction.)

In global currency markets daily turnover has grown 50-fold since the early 1980s, and is now about $US1.9 trillion a day. Two-thirds of this is transacted in derivative markets, with three quarters of this derivative trade (half the overall market) made up of foreign exchange swaps (BIS 2005: 5) To put this daily $US1.9 trillion turnover in some perspective, the annual value of international trade is less than $US6 trillion; equal to roughly three days trade in the foreign exchange market.

The most dramatic growth in derivatives has, however, occurred off exchange, through contracts involving direct agreement between two parties, known in derivative speak as OTC derivative markets. (These are

---

[13] Measuring the value of derivatives is done in terms of notional values (of the assets being commensurated) rather than the value of the derivative contract itself. According to Working (1961), recognising that the 'traditional main function of markets, transfer of ownership, is not a significant function of a futures market' required that the activity of futures markets should be measured differently. It was, according to Working, therefore a major advance when futures activity came to be measured in terms of the notional value of open contracts.

explained below.) The value of these markets can be measured in terms of a flow measure (daily turnover) or a stock measure (notional amount outstanding at a point in time).

In terms of daily turnover, the latest figures of the Bank for International Settlements (BIS) measures OTC derivatives at $2.4 trillion (2005: 1). The notional amount of OTC currency and interest rate swaps has grown from $US400 million in 1985 to $US 58.5 trillion in 2000 (Swaps Monitor 2002).[14] Using a slightly different estimation method, the BIS placed the global amount of OTC contracts outstanding at December 2002 at 95 trillion (BIS 2003).

Whether the figure is $58.5 or $95 trillion, this contrasts with the size of global commodity derivatives markets, which were around $1 trillion for the same period (BIS 2003; Swaps Monitor 2003).

2. *The growth of OTC rather than exchange-traded derivatives*

Derivative contracts can be written and traded in two types of markets: on formal derivatives exchanges like the Chicago Mercantile Exchange, or in off-exchange or OTC markets. Agricultural derivatives were traded in formal exchanges, themselves usually an outgrowth of the physical (or spot) markets. When financial derivatives began to emerge in the 1970s, they too were traded in formal exchanges. The development of OTC markets is especially associated with the rise of swaps.

Exchange-traded derivatives are usually standardised in terms of quality, quantity and delivery date and place, so that price becomes the main item being traded. Importantly, standardisation permits trading by strangers, by making the exchange the counterparty to all trades, and reduces search costs for sellers and buyers. In our wheat grower flour miller example, the exchange effectively becomes 'buyer' of the wheat futures contract from the grower and the 'seller' to the miller. In so doing, the exchange guarantees the creditworthiness of each counterparty (acting as a clearing

---

[14] Similar to the conceptual problems with defining derivatives, measuring derivatives is also controversial. Notional values (the face value of the principal of the underlying contract on which the derivative instruments are based) are the most generally used measure. Recall that with derivative contracts the underlying commodity or asset (the notional amount) is usually not itself exchanged. Some therefore suggest that using the notional value overstates the importance of derivatives. They can also be measured by the value of the contract itself (a much smaller value than the notional value). The BIS (2005), for instance, estimated that the market value of derivative contracts at the end of 2004 was $US 3 trillion. Our point here, similar to Partnoy (1999), is that the measurement issue is one of degree; there is no doubt the derivatives market is large and extremely important.

house) and so ensures that transactions will be completed. This normally happens by the exchanges licensing individual traders and demanding them to deposit money with the exchange from time to time as security (known as margin requirements).

Exchange-traded derivatives emerged out of organised commodity exchanges in the mid-nineteenth century in places like Chicago, London and Liverpool, and were the initial way that financial derivatives were often introduced in the 1970s. While exchange-traded derivatives have continued to grow over the last three decades, the overwhelming value of derivatives now occurs in OTC markets.

Over the Counter (OTC) markets are those where buyers and sellers of derivatives contract directly with each other and not through a formal exchange.

It was especially from the early 1980s that OTC products such as swaps took off, in the wake of a period of interest rate volatility that caught many large firms and especially banks off guard (Brewer *et al.*, 2001). From that time, they have dominated financial derivative trade.

OTC contracts tend not to be standardised in size, location or qualities, although they are increasingly so in terms of contractual conditions (ISDA 2002). They require the parties to seek each other out as well as to assess and monitor their counterparty's capacity to fulfil the contract. These markets are therefore best suited to situations where counterparties are well known, or where credit monitoring is being conducted by market agents (such as banks or rating agencies), and where contracts are of a size that may cause significant price changes if they were traded on organised exchanges. For this reason, the average size of derivative contracts tend to be much larger in OTC markets than in formal exchanges. Similarly, because of their roles in credit and risk monitoring, large banks tend to be on at least one side of OTC derivative transactions.

Many OTC derivatives are not necessarily heavily traded themselves, since they are specialised bilateral contracts. But it is easy to enter into other OTC derivatives to reverse or offset an existing position. So 'offsetability' in OTC markets may be a functional alternative to 'tradability' (Heath 1998), and adding to the scale of this market. An effect of this is that these markets have high effective liquidity and can be seen as more liquid than exchange-traded derivatives.

Figure 3.1 provides some indication of that differential growth of exchange-traded and OTC derivatives. It is difficult to compare the size of the two markets, because unwinding positions (by means of an opposite trade) in exchange-traded markets tends to result in a growth in

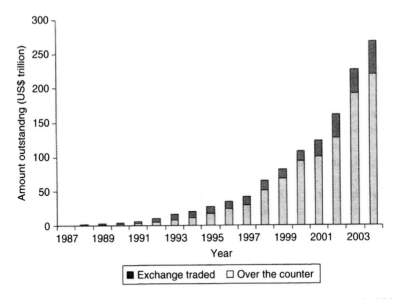

Figure 3.1   The growth in derivatives markets – exchange-traded and OTC markets 1987–2004.

turnover, while in OTC markets it tends to add to the notional principal amounts (Gonzalez-Hermosillo 1994). Bearing this problem of direct comparability in mind, Figure 3.1 shows that from the mid-1990s most growth was in OTC derivatives.

3. *The emergence of swaps (on interest rates and currencies) as the largest form of derivative contract*
Within OTC derivative markets, there are three basic instruments traded: forwards, swaps and options. Of these, swaps are by the far the most important.

The main factors behind the growth of swaps markets are fairly simple. The demise of fixed exchange rates, the growth of global capital markets and their use by corporations for a range of purposes, created a need to structure capital raising in ways that reduce corporate exposure to exchange rate or interest rate volatility. Swaps have not only provided firms with the ability to re-shape their exchange rate or interest rate exposure, they have also been associated with a reduction in borrowing costs.

Figure 3.2 shows the elements in the growth in swaps. Although there has been robust growth in exchange rate (ER) swaps, the main growth has come from interest rate (IR) swaps. The figure shows that while the notional amount of outstanding exchange rate swaps have

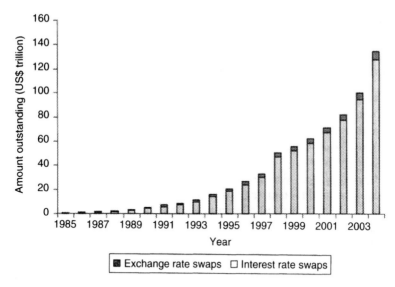

Figure 3.2 Growth in derivatives markets – interest rate and exchange rate swaps, 1985–2004.

grown from about $180 billion dollars in 1987 to $2.4 trillion in 1999. However, it is the growth of interest rate swaps that has been the fastest, from $680 billion in 1987 to $43 trillion in 1999. Interest rate swaps now make up about 80 per cent of outstanding swaps in global markets.

The growth of interest rate swaps from the mid-1980s is due to three factors: the increased demand for large-scale financing to fund the boom in mergers and acquisitions that occurred in the 1980s; the change in financing towards bonds, that allowed debt instruments to be parcelled into (tradable) units; and increased volatility in interest rates.

4. *Derivatives are 'off-balance sheet', but being used by a growing proportion of large and many medium sized corporations to manage their own asset portfolios*

Financial derivatives are becoming increasingly standard ways that large and even small corporations manage various risks. Evidence of this trend is often hard to find in corporate accounts.

Because derivatives normally do not result in a change of either possession or ownership, companies and banks do not normally have to record derivatives trading in their statement of the balance sheet of assets and liabilities. They are 'off-balance sheet' and their immediate impact on corporate balance sheets is often difficult to assess. As the report by the US National Academy of Science's Panel on International Capital Transactions (Kester 1994: 121) noted of financial derivatives,

> Unlike traditional financial instruments, such as loans and deposits, which can easily be defined as assets and liabilities and recognised in accounting systems when they are acquired, derivatives can create either future or contingent financial assets and liabilities. Actual financial assets and liabilities are balance-sheet transactions; contingent ones are off-balance-sheet items.

Off-balance-sheet derivatives have created difficulties for corporate accounting and for banking supervisors, because these large transactions can have significant and different net effects than those being recorded on balance sheets. For instance, a company's balance sheet may show that a firm has a Japanese yen floating rate loan, but because it had swapped this loan, it may in effect have a loan with attributes of a US dollar fixed rate loan. Corporate accounting, like corporate law and finance, is still coming to terms with the challenges presented by the widespread use of financial derivatives.

Nonetheless, we can still get some general information on the use of derivatives by corporations. According to a 2003 survey by the International Swaps and Derivatives Association (ISDA 2003) 92 per cent of the world's 500 largest companies, covering a diversity of industries, use derivative instruments to manage and hedge their risks.

> Of the companies using derivatives, 92% use them to help manage interest rate risk. This represents 85% of the total sample. 85% of the companies (78% of the total) use derivatives to help manage currency risk, 25% (23.5% of the total) to help manage commodity price risk and 12% (11% of the total) to help manage equity price risk.

In other words, not only have financial derivatives become an integral part of the global financial system, they have increasingly become a standard part of corporate finance.

The challenge of derivatives

These four empirical developments create a challenge to the conventional wisdom born of the past era, but still dominant into the 1990s. Three challenges in particular stand out, each of which features prominently in later chapters.

Challenge 1: Derivatives were becoming the largest industry in the world, yet the conventional theory has seen them as marginal.

Until recently, finance theory had cast derivatives in marginal terms. In the hypothesised world of perfect markets, individuals rather than firms were thought to be better placed to undertake risk diversification; and in competitive commodity and financial markets, prices should stabilise so that there would be little or no need for increasing hedging and little or no profit from speculation (Hunter and Smith 2002). This is also consistent with the contention that, in isolation, derivatives are typically a zero-sum game. If the cash price at the expiration of the contract were above or below the derivative contract price, one party or the other incurs a loss and the other an equal gain. As a zero-sum game, derivatives would surely be destined to remain marginal.

Increasingly, however, the empirical fact of derivatives growth has been producing recognition that derivatives are becoming integral to economic and financial processes. For instance, an IMF research paper suggested that

> Arguably the single largest innovation in global financial markets over the past fifty years has been the emergence and spectacular growth of derivative markets in the past ten years. (Vroliijlk 1997: 1)

In a similar vein, US Federal Reserve Chairman Alan Greenspan (2000) has observed that

> [D]erivatives have come to play an exceptionally important role in our financial system and in our economy. These instruments allow users to unbundle risks and allocate them to the investors most willing and able to use them.

But there is a notable absence of substance in such observations: the importance of derivatives to finance may now be well recognised, but, in Greenspan's term, their 'important role in our economy' remains simply an add-on phrase. This importance comes through the capacity of derivatives to blend the attributes of different forms of asset, giving different assets some generic qualities. As we shall see in later chapters, this gives derivatives characteristics of both money and 'capital'.

Challenge 2: Derivatives were becoming integral to corporate financial management, yet many describe them as 'unreal'.

The growth of derivatives has been controversial. We have already seen that, even for market participants (such as Warren Buffet), financial derivatives have been seen as a dangerous development, whereby paper claims, supposedly with no attachment to reality can be used to gamble. The apparent unreality of financial derivatives is particularly associated with the notion of derivatives as duplicate or fictitious capital – that they are just multiple recordings of asset values that net to zero. This notion of fictitious capital builds on the understanding that derivatives markets are separated from trade in real markets, and are an unnecessary distraction from the real economy.

While this perspective is most often associated with left wing radicalism, the notion that derivatives represent a threat to the existing financial order can be found across the political perspective. For instance, Donald T. Regan, former chairman of Merrill Lynch, former US Treasury Secretary and White House Chief of Staff[15] made the following observation about derivative growth:

> These instruments (derivatives on corporate stocks) have combined the worst features of stocks and commodities. They have low margin requirements, practically nonexistent in some cases ... There are those who argue that options and index futures are just like commodities. This statement does not wash with me. Soybeans, wheat, cotton and gold are real. One cannot eat or wear a stock index.

More recently, there has been the concern that institutions, such as hedge funds that specialise in trading derivatives, are engaged in dangerous speculative activities. Hedge funds are investment funds, which typically comprise the savings of very wealthy individuals (minimum investments are normally in the millions of dollars), and are often located in offshore financial centres (or tax havens). Hedge funds use the equity provided by these wealthy individuals to borrow a lot more money, and use financial derivatives to magnify (leverage) those risks in an attempt to make high returns for investors. They may take large positions on say the future price of the Russian rouble (or rouble-denominated assets) compared to the US dollar (or US dollar-denominated assets). Because hedge funds take large investment positions even a small change in relative prices can have a big impact on hedge fund profitability.

The large financial resources at the disposal of hedge funds have given rise to the perception that hedge funds do not just benefit from price volatility, they contribute to it. Hedge funds are indeed anything but

---

[15] Testimony to Senate Inquiry in 1988, cited in Luskin 1992: 13.

passive – they are certainly not hedging their risks as their name may suggest. Instead, they often take big unhedged risks on particular assets. George Soros, perhaps the best-known hedge fund investor was implicated in the speculative attacks in 1992 on several European currencies that forced them out of the first attempt at a common European currency.[16] He was reported to have made tens of millions of dollars out of these 'raids'. Conversely, as we saw in Chapter 1, other hedge funds such as LTCM can use derivatives to make huge losses. Either way, many argue that, in the hands of hedge funds, derivatives compromise the efficiency of financial markets. This is an issue we take up in Chapter 8.

Challenge 3: Derivative markets were increasingly becoming the sites of asset price determination, yet the theory saw derivative prices as derived from the spot or cash market.

By the early 1980s research started to produce evidence that in many markets, even in agricultural markets, pricing was running in the opposite direction to the intuition informing traditional understanding of derivatives. Instead of derivative markets reflecting spot or cash markets, prices were being formed in derivative markets and were then running to cash markets. In commodity markets,[17] Garbade and Silber (1983) concluded that research had shown that, in pricing terms, many cash markets (where actual exchange of ownership and possession occurs) had become 'largely satellites' of the futures markets. A similar process was also observed in financial markets, such as in stock, interest rates and currencies markets (Kwaller *et al.* 1987; Stoll and Whaley 1990; Arshanpalli and Doukas 1997; McDonough 1998).[18] Gibson and Zimmerman (1994: 24) conclude that, in many markets 'it is the cash market which should [now] be regarded as the "derivative" [market]'.

The effect is not just a challenge to orthodox theories of derivatives, but also a challenge to the conventional way of seeing the corporation. It suggests that the financial managers of corporations and the banks that monitor corporate assets via derivatives markets are now at the centre of the competitive process of capital accumulation, for it is they

[16] For a useful introduction to the hedge funds literature, see Eichengreen and Mathieson (1998).

[17] As early as the mid-1970s, it was found that in several commodities with futures markets, price leadership had shifted to the futures market (Cox 1976). Similar conclusions were reached about cattle markets in the mid-1980s; see for instance Ollermann and Farris (1985).

[18] For a recent survey of this process, see Mayhew (2000).

who also play a role in steering corporate assets via their management of asset derivatives.

Defining derivatives (refrain)

The contemporary problem for any analytical approach to the modern functioning of derivatives is that they do not fit neatly within any existing branches of economics, and in fact have rendered many branches of economics unstable. Thus, even the seemingly basic definitional issue of 'what is a derivative?' has no generally accepted answer. Current definitions of derivatives have evolved to absorb changes in derivatives as they have moved beyond the terrain of commodity prices and into finance. For example, in the early 1990s, the *Dictionary of Financial Risk Management* (Gastineau and Kritzman, 1992: 29) defined a derivative instrument or product as

> A contract or convertible security that changes in value in concert with and/or *obtains much of its value from price movements in a related or underlying security, future, or other instrument or index* ... also called a contingent claim ... (emphasis added)

This definition preserved much of the older understanding of derivatives as a second order activity, where derivative prices come out of the underlying commodity or asset.[19] But, as an advance on the 1970s conventional wisdom, this definition did capture the fact derivatives trade was no longer dominated by agricultural derivatives but by money and financial instruments.

By the mid-1990s, the BIS (1995: 8), the so-called central bank of central banks, had established a perspective on the role of derivatives. It defined a derivative as

> a contract whose value depends on the prices of underlying assets, but which does not require any investment of principal in those assets. As a contract between two parties to exchange payments based on underlying prices or yields, any *transfer of ownership of the underlying asset or cash flows becomes unnecessary.* (emphasis added)

[19] A similar definition, but one that emphasises the cash flows associated with the derivative contract rather than the price *per se*, is offered by Arditti (1996: 38): 'The term derivative instrument is generally accepted to mean a financial instrument with a payoff structure determind by the value of underlying security, interest rate or index.'

Importantly, this definition now emphasised how derivatives markets trade in rights not to ownership or possession of an actual commodity or financial instrument *per se*, but to price relativities (normally understood as between now and in the future). In this definition, derivatives are no longer marginal, but move to the centre stage of financial management.

Yet as a formal definition, the BIS depiction remains elusive, and one can only wonder about just how accurately the size of derivative markets and transactions can be quantified in ways that will meet with universal agreement. The issue of quantification has, however, been central to the deliberations of the International Monetary Fund (IMF). Following an extensive consideration of the role of derivatives, including measurement issues for Balance of Payments accounting, the IMF (1998: October 21–23) arrived at a definition of derivatives as:

> any financial instrument that is linked to another financial instrument, indicator (index) or commodity, and *through which specific financial obligations can be traded in their own right* (emphasis added).

Here we see the IMF recognising that derivatives allow different financial obligations to be traded and this helps to open up what sorts of obligations derivatives mobilise, and how financial derivatives are used to shift these obligations within and across commodity and financial asset boundaries.[20]

This list of definitions through time is, of course, far from exhaustive. But it is some indication of the difficulty of pinpointing the essential characteristics of derivatives when their functional forms are rapidly evolving. The shifting definitions also conceal on-going debate (or the need for debate) about what derivatives are beyond a set of pricing techniques and how they should be conceptualised within economic theory. One purpose of our analysis is to contribute to that debate and in so doing to highlight the profound changes in social relations that lie behind these definitional slides.

Conclusion

The unfortunate thing about an explanation of derivatives is that, just as they have become more extensively used, they have become less easy to

---

[20] Indeed, derivatives are often referred to as a 'contingent claim', since they are claims whose pricing and cash flow effects are contingent on movements in the relative prices of other assets (or, in the case of things like weather derivatives, are contingent on certain events).

define. To readers not familiar with the basic categories, we could have left our explanation back in the era of derivative markets for agricultural commodities, with readily comprehendible explanations of agricultural futures and options. We could, accordingly, have taken the reader directly to an argument about hedging and speculation: Are derivatives just speculation? Is speculation bad? Can speculation be differentiated from hedging? We will, indeed, get to these issues in Chapter 8. But they are not the most significant dimensions of modern derivatives, and it is essential to move beyond an understanding of individual derivatives transactions that are seen simply in terms of a zero-sum game.

This chapter has sought to open up the question of the role of derivatives, including an evolving understanding of how they work, and their features that make them adequate for their current role. We noted how this has meant that the analysis of derivatives and even the definition of derivatives are still in some ways embryonic. But we suggest that the capacity of derivatives to separate different aspects of a commodity or financial instrument (such as its price now and in the future) from the actual ownership or possession contained a latent potential to perform a crucial role in modern capitalism: the commensuration of values across time and space. This potential began to be harnessed on a general level only when derivatives began to be used in financial markets. And for this to occur, a range of historical economic factors had to coexist. Once they did, financial derivatives began to be used on an ever-increasing scale.

The alternative way of understanding derivatives is to look at their role in accumulation – the way in which the totality of individual derivative transactions sums to something of wider significance. In Chapter 1, we depicted derivatives as a sort of 'meta capital', separated from ownership of physical assets in which an exchange of derivatives rarely if ever involves the actual exchange of the underlying asset (commodity, share, etc.). It is from this fluidity and self-transforming capacity of derivatives that their wider significance arises.

When each of the technical developments in individual derivative transactions is aggregated, there is a profound social and economic effect. Financial derivatives are integrating financial decisions about the profit-making performance and capacities even more centrally to managerial strategy. The commensuration properties of financial derivatives mean that the logic of capital is driven even more to the centre of corporate policy making. Assets that do not meet profit-making benchmarks must be depreciated, restructured and/or sold. The decision not to do so is now more readily exposed to market scrutiny, as investment bankers use derivatives and derivatives' prices to unbundle the performance of the different assets and liabilities of firms. It is through the capacity for derivatives to commensurate capital in different forms, locations and time horizons that adds greater competitive discipline to the processes of calculation and decision making. While this seems to concern principally relations between different companies, there are direct repercussions for relations between capital and labour.

Perhaps, a reader without a finance background remains confused. The issues developed in this chapter, the claim may be made, involved splitting hairs on technical issues of asset price determination. The big issues of money in capitalism are more prominent – they are about volatility and speculation in money markets, and who has control over money. We beg to differ, not in the sense that these nominated issues are unimportant, but that without an understanding of the mechanics of derivatives, these other issues remain largely rhetorical and moralistic in their claims. The details of how derivatives work matters.

In order to build to that understanding the next chapter considers the parallels between the development of the joint stock company and derivatives, because this story shows several interesting similarities that bear on the analysis of the wider role now being played by derivatives. In so doing, the next chapter explores the role of derivatives in changing the organisational forms of capital.

4
From the Joint Stock Company to Financial Derivatives

The recent growth of financial derivatives has fundamentally transformed the way finance is transacted and the forms in which corporations manage their risk. But derivatives are more than an innovation in risk management. They are also challenging the way we understand what corporations are and what ownership of capital is.

When we think of ownership of capital, two forms have long been understood: private companies, which are generally, though not necessarily, small (family) firms, and public (or joint stock) companies, where ownership is dispersed and transferred via the stock market. Derivatives represent a completely different notion of ownership, which involves neither ownership rights to corporate assets nor of corporate shares, but ownership of financial claims whose value varies with the value of corporate (and other) assets. Indeed with financial derivatives, asset ownership is uncoupled from any necessary direct ownership connection to commodities, financial assets or corporations. Taulli (2003) has referred to ownership under derivatives as 'meta-rights' and in Chapter 1 we termed financial derivatives 'meta-capital': the derivative owner does not have a right to ownership of capital as it is conventionally understood, but they do have ownership rights associated with attributes of capital.

As well as raising interesting legal questions of property rights, this derivative form of ownership changes the way we understand the relationship between capital and ownership. As Blake (1949: 368) contended of the joint stock corporate form, '[e]ven for an economic tendency, it is necessary to seek embodiment in a proper juridical form'. A question we ask in this chapter is what economic characteristics of ownership are embodied in the derivative form of capital?

Our object in this chapter is to explore this question via a comparison between the joint stock company and financial derivatives as forms of capital and ownership. Two important insights will be revealed.

First, our conventional understanding of the connection between capital, ownership and the corporation needs re-thinking, for derivatives involve a form of capital with ownership of the 'performance' of a corporation, but without any ownership of the corporation itself. Capital's attachment to the corporation becomes ambiguous, and with significant consequences.

Second, in their rise to prominence, the joint stock company and derivatives have both, in their different eras, challenged the extant conventions about the relationship between ownership and capital. The parallels in these two histories are developed as a stark reminder that current debates about derivatives are anything but novel.

But there is need for a note of caution here. It took many decades for the meaning and significance of the joint stock company to become apparent and, by comparison, the intrusion of financial derivatives into the lived realities of capitalism is not far advanced. We are, therefore, really opening up a way of framing the relationship between ownership and capital, not making formal decrees of a new epoch within capitalism. Nonetheless, the significance of the formation of the joint stock company for capitalist development is well recognised, and any parallels bear considering.

A new expression of capital

Think of the relationship between ownership of a stock in company X and a stock derivative (option or future) in company X. The value of the latter clearly depends significantly on the former, but the two imply quite different types of ownership. The stock constitutes ownership of a share in the company's profitability (changes in stock value and dividends) and token rights to appoint managers. The stock derivative forgoes the latter, but builds in for the owner guarantees (or degrees of risk) about future prices. With stock derivatives, it is thus effectively possible to trade in equities, and participate in corporate profitability, without ever actually owning a share. It is as if the stock market has gone 'inside' the derivative itself: the derivative is defined so as to spontaneously absorb market calculation.

This apparently minor financial technicality actually transforms fundamentally our understanding of the nature of 'capital', for it signals the evolution of a more abstracted, generalised form of capital now being thrown into circulation as a financial asset. In so doing, derivatives give capital ownership a new flexibility and liquidity, with the effect, as we shall explore in Chapter 6, of converging the categories of capital and money.

But the different forms of ownership are not found simply in the difference between a share and a share derivative. Consider now the difference for company X between raising capital by an equity issue and raising capital by a bank loan or bond issue. The former involves the exchange of a fund of money for ownership of a portion of the legal entity called the corporation, with the owner's right to share proportionately in the profit (or loss) of the corporation. The latter involves no sale of ownership, and hence not exposure to profits, losses, or changes in share value, but gives the lender the right to a guaranteed repayment of principal and interest on pre-determined terms. We have for more than a century operated comfortably with a dichotomy between ownership (equity) and credit as distinct forms of capital.

But what ownership attaches to a form of fund raising that blends the characteristics of debt and equity? A convertible bond, for instance, is a bond with an 'embedded' option to convert to a share. It gives the owner a security with debt-like characteristics, but with the right to convert to a share if the share is performing better than the debt. The derivative element serves to intensify price relations of one form of capital (corporate debt) relative to another form of capital (equity).

Financial derivatives thereby undermine the nexus between ownership and financial exposure to the costs and revenues of an asset or liability. Debt and equity can be exchanged directly, and indeed debt-like characteristics and equity-like characteristics can be combined in different ways. According to Nobel laureate Myron Scholes (1998: 364):

> Standard debt and equity contracts are institutional arrangements or boxes. They provide particular cash flows to investors with their own particular risk and return characteristics. These institutional arrangements survive only because they provide lower-cost solutions than competing alternative arrangements. Competitive opportunities evolve over time with changing frictions and restrictions. ... Time will continue to blur the distinctions between debt and equity.

A conventional notion that equity involves ownership and debt does not is therefore also broken down: financial derivatives have transformed the role of capital as property and as social relation and merged the categories of property and finance. In so doing, financial derivatives are helping to break down the distinctiveness of all particular forms of capital, and serving to bring to the fore the characteristics that all forms of capital within capitalism share in common: the social relations of capitalist competition.

A challenge to the conception of ownership that is raised by the blending of debt and equity appears also as a challenge to the concept of 'capital', for we can no longer presume a direct link between capital and ownership. This issue involves one of the deepest debates in economics, so our objective here is far from comprehensive. It is also an issue returned to in Chapter 7. In the current context, we wish to make the simple point that it has long been difficult to reconcile concepts of ownership with concepts of capital. Financial derivatives represent a special challenge to such concepts.

To build on this point of the specific challenge derivatives offer to our understanding of ownership, we look to historical stages in the evolving relationship between capital and ownership.

Capital and ownership: three degrees of separation

We can identify a shift in the form of ownership of capital from owner-capitalists to the joint stock company to financial derivatives as representing the evolution of major stages in the nexus between ownership and competition. We have called the major points in this evolution the three degrees of separation of capital from ownership, with each separation representing a different imperative to competition. These are presented here as historical phases in the development of capitalist ownership, although with no suggestion that each new separation terminates the imperative of competition established by the previous stage: owner entrepreneurs exist alongside joint stock companies and both continue to exist alongside financial derivatives. There is, however, the proposition that each subsequent separation presents a sharper and more comprehensive imperative to compete because each adds increased liquidity into the concept of ownership and increased competitiveness into the concept of capital.

The first degree of separation of capital ownership involves the process in which the worker is separated from possession and ownership of the means of production so that the owner controls production and capital competes as firms.

Historically, this separation involved proto-capitalist capital becoming separated from labour via the transition from feudalism to manufacture and wage labour. With the enclosure movement and the rise of large-scale factories in Europe, for example, the means of production were no longer in possession or ownership of workers, but now confronted them as under the control of 'the capitalist': the factory or farm owner, typically based around a family business or partnership.[1]

This separation introduced competition into the sphere of ownership because capital (and labour) became more mobile – no longer tied to a particular feudal manor or slave plantation, but with the capacity to move in search of higher rates of return. Accordingly, a surplus was no longer ensured simply by the fact of ownership. The capitalist owner of the factory now had to keep up with technical and commercial innovations as well as strategies of labour management in other factories in order to realise a surplus from labour.

The second degree of separation of capital ownership involves the process in which company ownership is separated from production and capital competes as companies.

Historically, this separation involved the formation of the joint stock company: the separation of ownership from the materiality of 'the factory' and the associated separation of ownership of capital from control over production. Ownership now takes the form of equity in a legal entity called the corporation, with equity investors entitled to 'share' in the firm's performance (and some formal but indirect rights to control). With the creation of the corporation as a legal 'person', capital attains both subjectivity (the firm is the owner of the capital in it) and becomes more specifically the object of economic activity in property (increasing the quantum of value accumulated as the prime goal of the firm) (Kay 1991).

With the first separation, in which the wealthy individual comes to personify capital, it was possible to mix the personal wishes of the owner with the requirements of accumulation. The second separation characterises capital with more ambiguity. Both the owners of capital (as beneficiaries of the private property) and the managers (acting to enforce

---

[1] Within the first separation actual physical separation of labour from possession of the means of production may have been characteristic of European capitalism, such as via the enclosure movement in Britain. But it has not always been necessary. This separation has also been achieved by leaving labour in place and transforming the terms of that labour and the nature of the production and exchange, such as the terms of access to finance, and the way inputs and outputs are mobilised. Cowen (esp. 1976, 1977, 1982) demonstrated this in the context of Kenyan household production. See also MacWilliam (1992).

the interests of capital) are often depicted as the class embodiment of capital, but just 'who' is the capitalist is no longer so clear. Nor need it be, for combined they present a 'logic of capital'. The joint stock company has a single purpose: to accumulate, and responsibility for the control and supervision of that accumulation is shared between owners and managers.

With this single purpose, the historical effect of the joint stock company was to intensify competition in three ways: it articulated a competitive logic, it facilitated an increased scale of operation of capital and it increased flexibility.

Logic: Maximum profitability and share appreciation is not just the self-determined preference of the owner-entrepreneur; it is a driving rationale for corporate managers. Owners receive their rewards from ownership only when they make sure that managers act to maximise the rate of profit. Corporate ownership is now purely a financial claim with no rights to directly obtain any bits of the firm's property or output. Binding managers to the interests of owners (resolving the so-called agency problem) has been the source of a great deal of commercial and academic debate. But mechanisms have evolved that have generally helped to ensure that both owners and managers have a shared interest in accumulation.

Scale: The joint stock form permitted the pooling of capital that was critical for the growth of nineteenth-century industry and commerce. The limitations of the owner/entrepreneur firm in attracting sufficient resources to undertake and profitably manage large-scale activities is well known. As Marx (1867: 780) observed of the joint stock company 'the world would still be without railways if it had to wait until accumulation had got a few individual capitals far enough to be adequate for the construction of a railway'.

Flexibility: The joint stock company required the formation of a secondary market to facilitate ownership transfers consistent with the durability of the corporate entity.[2] Ownership rights became transferable via the stock market. This was also the forum where the profitability of companies could be compared, and the prices of firms established. In this way,

---

[2] The stock market, by providing liquidity to ownership titles, helped overcome what is now termed 'hold up' whereby a partner could undermine the firm by withdrawing capital or services. Creating the firm as a fictional person also helped to encourage what is now known as a 'lock in' of capital, so that the owners are no longer entitled to withdraw their property in the firm, or liquidate it if they decide to get out. For recent discussions see Blair (2003) and Day (2004).

the separation of ownership from the physical form of capital was the means for an additional facet of competition to enter into ownership. Capital itself remained specific to a particular company, and via the stock market *ownership* of capital became a bearer of competition. But, in this separation, capital itself was not the bearer of competition: rights to capital are merely bought and sold in the process of competition.

The effect is that ownership thereby became more liquid and mobile. Even in the early part of the twentieth century, when the joint stock company was still emerging as the generalised form of capital ownership, this liquidity and mobility was referred to by one economist as the development or *abstract property*, defined as rights not to possession of ownership of valuable things *per se*, but to an abstract quantum of value (Watkins 1907: 35–6). Watkins noted that income from abstract property did not require direct participation in production, and that consequently accumulation is not restricted to limitations of individual wealth or managerial talent. Abstract capital in the corporate form was better adapted to the changed needs of capital accumulation of the era, which increasingly required large concentrations of capital and modern systems of management in single firms.

The third degree of separation of capital ownership involves the process by which capital ownership is separated from company ownership and capital competes as itself.

We have already described this separation in its most obvious form: that ownership of a share derivative (option or futures contract) is different from ownership of a share itself. The share derivative (such as a futures contract on a firm or the market index) gives its owner exposure to the performance (price and profitability) of the company (or group of companies) in a form that is more flexible than direct share ownership. But derivatives as a third separation of ownership involves more than the attributes of a share derivative. It is the combining of the attributes of all financial derivatives (and in abstraction) that gives this new form of ownership an impact on competition.

The effect of derivative ownership is that one form of capital (e.g. related to shares) is tied directly to other forms of capital (e.g. related to say interest rates or currency values). Not only does this give derivatives a range of attributes that were once thought distinctive (e.g. equity versus debt), but the value of the derivative varies in a pre-determined way as the values of various underlying assets change. A derivative therefore gives its owner exposure to a selected range of different underlying asset values within the one, combined, form of capital, but, and this is critical to this third separation, *it can provide this selected exposure because it is separated from ownership of the underlying assets themselves.*

Accordingly, with derivatives the very concept of 'capital' and its ownership is separated from the ownership of both direct physical assets (the first separation) and legal representations of those physical assets (the second separation).

To clarify the significance of this third separation, we return to the issues raised in the context of the second separation: the class relations of capital and the competitive processes set in motion by that ownership.

The third separation adds a further layer to the question of the class embodiment of capital. Rather than just owners (the first separation) or managers and owners (the second separation) as the embodiment of capital, it is now also financial market participants such as derivatives traders, corporate finance staff and financial companies (such as international banks and pension funds) that enforce the logic of capital. It is these agents of commensuration that are also now driving the on-going allocation and re-allocation of capital.

Our conception of class relations and class conflict are changed accordingly. We can now say that labour confronts the logic of capital not just as an abstraction (that the essence of capitalism is the pursuit of profit, with the corporation as its institutional expression), but now also as a more tangible concrete reality – that those forces that drive corporate policy are increasingly also being expressed through the mathematical calculations of financial market participants. Their objective is not so much the benefit of the corporation as an institutional entity, but the benefit of capital as value, such that corporations will be forced to revalue, re-organise or divest themselves of assets, indeed of their own recognisable institutional form, if the calculations so dictate.

As such, the process of competition attaching to derivatives is different in this third separation. In the context of the second separation, we identified three characteristics of competition: its logic, scale and flexibility. We can see how these are transformed by the third separation.

Logic: While derivatives are about maximising profits, competition associated with derivatives is not competition between corporations as in the second separation. Corporations are constituted by the concept of ownership, but derivatives do not pertain to ownership in this sense: the legal boundaries of the corporation have little or no meaning to derivatives. Competition in the context of derivatives pertains to the relative valuation of different assets and liabilities between and across asset forms, time and space, irrespective of their ownership. The logic of competition is not of firms or corporations maximising profit, but of assets, everywhere, being continually commensurated with each other on the basis of their profit-making potential. *Derivatives, therefore, represent a form of capital that is inherently competitive, because they embody an intense, market-driven relative valuation of different assets.* Insofar as we commonly think of a corporation's profitability, this is increasingly to be understood as a return on an aggregation of assets, whose values are determined independently.

Scale and flexibility: These are similarly conceived differently in the third separation. While the joint stock company provided a pooling of capital to establish corporations that could undertake large-scale investment, derivatives have a different reach. Their scale is to stretch across (or compress) time and space. Corporations use derivatives, not simply to become bigger, but to secure the value of their assets (and enable their on-going assessment), wherever they may be, and whatever form they take. Their use also allows others outside of the corporation to calculate the relative profitability of the firm's component assets and activities.

Scale in this sense depends directly on the flexibility of derivatives. This flexibility is inherent in the capacity to commensurate one asset with another and to tie one asset form to another. While flexibility in the context of the joint stock company was conceived in terms of the capacity to shift individual ownership from one corporation to another, the flexibility of derivatives is to give the owner of any financial asset the capacity to share in the fortunes of any other asset, but without the need to transfer ownership.

One hundred years ago Watkins (who we referred to earlier) associated the joint stock company with rights not to possession or ownership of valuable things *per se*, but to an abstract quantum of value. We can see that this depiction has been taken to another level with derivatives. Financial derivatives are, in Watkins term, the more comprehensive expression of 'abstract property'. But, we must emphasise, the change is not about actually making capital more abstract. On the contrary, these ownership separations have given to concrete capital the capacities that we have historically been able to consider mostly only in abstraction: the capacities to change form and direction in the search of higher returns. Capital as an owned physical asset and capital as social relation thereby start to merge. That transition is both an important development in the form of capital, and, predictably, an intensely challenging historical process, in which capital appears to take on more universal, and, from the point of view of workers and poorly performing capitals, more threatening capacities.

In developing our proposition, it is not necessary here to consider further the first separation. It is important in that capital is distinctly capitalist, tied to class relations between labour and capital. But the focus of this chapter is the parallels and contrasts, historical and analytical, between the formation of the joint stock company and financial derivatives, so as to compare and contrast them as different stages in the evolution of 'capital'.

The joint stock company

There are several features of the formation of the joint stock company that warrant specific notice: its historical evolution and especially the role of the state therein, the flexibility it gave to 'capital', and contemporary (nineteenth century) debates about its significance.

Evolution

The formation of the joint stock company is often depicted as a quantum leap in the nature of firms and markets. Terms such as the transition from the 'invisible hand' of markets to the 'visible hand' of managerial capitalism (Chandler 1978), the rise of 'the corporate economy' (Hannah 1984) and Robber Barons (Josephson 1934), rise of the 'organisational' economy (Simons 1991) and the 'end of laissez faire' (Keynes 1926) are often drawn on to create the image of a rupture driven by the increased capacity of large corporations to take control over market processes. This image is contrasted with the age of small private firms where the owner/entrepreneur ran the business as a family concern, and so-called 'competitive' markets were the dominant way that economic processes were organised.

Chandler (1978: 16), for instance, comments on the revolutionary nature of the creation of the joint stock company:

> Those institutional changes which helped to create the managerial capitalism of the twentieth century were as significant and as revolutionary as those that accompanied the rise of commercial capitalism a half a millennium earlier.

However, the emergence of the joint stock company was not sudden. It can rather be seen as a slow historical process, often initiated by the state, in which the demands of large-scale production (or commerce), and the associated needs of investor security gradually led to new forms of property in capital.[3]

An important pre-modern form of commercial capital in Britain was the regulated or chartered company, developed under state monopoly privilege. These companies were formed to undertake specific tasks, such as voyages of discovery, or exercise monopoly rights to trade in particular goods or in particular locations. Probably the best known of these firms was the East India Company formed in 1600 (Baskin and Miranti 1997). Chartered companies usually received their legal status in return for providing substantial financial assistance to the crown, and there was, in this form, often no clear distinction between public and private corporations. That distinction was not clearly demarcated until the nineteenth century (Baskin 1988: 208).

Significantly, some of these chartered trading companies were granted the right to issue shares (joint stock), often with the state as a subscriber (Braudel 1984: 444; Baskin 1988). This gave them resources to grow to a size previously unattainable, and generate market power.[4] Initially, these corporations operated as loose partnership frameworks with 'corporate' activities on a venture-by-venture basis. The investment capital of a company was then not permanent and owners had the right to take their capital out of the firm after each venture. Indeed, the term 'capital' (or 'a capital') at this time was used as an accounting term to refer to the investment in each voyage.[5]

From the mid-seventeenth century the chartered companies began to grow in size and take on more durable forms, and the demands for longer-term finance (debt and equity) also began to see financial

---

[3] Rule (1993) has observed of this process that it also involved the changing relationship between the state and markets. He suggested that, 'capitalism and the market economy with their associated relations of production were not created by the eighteenth century state, but capitalism as a system triumphs only when it becomes identified with the state'.

[4] Size was in part also related to the fact that companies were often asked to undertake quasi-state (political/military) functions. For instance in pursuing trade and territorial expansion, the East India Company often built fortresses, and protecting trading routes sometimes required it to form what amounted to a *de facto* standing army.

[5] While the venture-specific nature of these early corporations helped minimise the risk associated with funding activities in which the investor may not be directly involved, the costs of liquidation were often high (such as dividing unsold merchandise).

innovation and the development of secondary markets[6] for trading these instruments.[7] The on-going management of the risk of committing long-term funds to large investments by chartered companies and secondary markets for ownership therefore emerged together – a process that we see, albeit in a different form, associated with the later growth of financial derivatives.

The direct consequence was the establishment of limited liability – a process which required that the company itself exist as a discrete legal entity. With limited liability the capital is owned by a fictional legal 'person' (the company), which is charged with undertaking commercial action on its own account. The firm therefore becomes the owner of the capital invested in it, and can sue and be sued. Limited liability thus involves the separation of the personal interests and liability of shareholders from those of the firm. In so doing, an investor's liability to a firm is limited to the amount of their investment in the firm. Indeed this story of risk reduction for investors in firms is an important way that the early development of the corporate form is explained. We will see that the later development of financial derivatives has also been understood in terms of risk limitation.

The development of the corporate form saw the evolution of the firm as a distinctly capitalist organisation. Braudel (1984: 439) for instance suggests that

> The limited partnerships were associations both of individuals and of capital. The joint stock companies or *sociétés par actions* as they were known in France ... were associations of capital only. This capital or stock formed a single mass, identified with the firm itself.

But these early joint stock companies were inflexible, with a limited management base (Chandler 1979: 13). They still often depended on state-provided monopolies, and were often not well attuned to the growth of competition.[8]

---

[6] Secondary markets were, however, not new in themselves. Secondary markets in securities existed in Amsterdam from at least the early 1600s, and even earlier in Italy.

[7] Eklund and Tollison (1980) make the case that the development of easily transferable shares was at least as important for the growth and spread of the corporation as were the demands of larger-scale investments.

[8] A debate has emerged recently about whether it was the extraction of monopoly rents or the transaction costs of minimising properties of chartered

The joint stock company was quite slow to catch on as a general form of legal organisation. The idea of a share as a separate legal title to the firm, and its transferability, were also slow to develop. As they did, they were often caught up in fraud and speculation. Even during the early transition phase in the late-1700s, economists such as Adam Smith and legal scholars questioned the economic potential of concentrated property and the joint stock company.

In the seventeenth and early eighteenth centuries there had been periodic booms in corporate and stock market activity. At the peak of one notorious boom, in England in the early eighteenth century (1720), the listed capital of joint stock companies had reached 50 million pounds. With these substantial sums of money involved, the development of government legislation, to give greater certainty and regularity to this new corporate form, was essential. The initial catalyst for this regulatory intervention was, however, a major corporate crash. In England, the collapse in 1720 of the South Sea Company, a large joint stock company closely tied to the state, was (eventually) a watershed.[9] But instead of formalising the laws of limited liability joint stock companies, the government's response was to curtail corporate development generally. At this time, political opposition to the joint stock form in the new capitalist order, combined with the general panic over the collapse of such a large organisation, encouraged forms of regulation directed toward a containment of the growth of the joint stock form.

firms that drove the development of joint stock companies. (Carlos and Nicholas 1996; and Jones and Ville 1996). The dichotomy is important, but may be unnecessary for our purposes. The important point here, as Braudel (1984: 443) notes, is that 'the monopolies established by the big [trading] companies have at least two, more properly three characteristics: they were the expression of high-intensity capitalist endeavour; they would have been unthinkable without the privilege granted by the state; and they appropriated for themselves whole sectors of overseas trade'.

[9] The collapse became known as the South Sea bubble. The South Sea Company was a firm established in the early eighteenth century to restructure English public debt, and in return was granted the exclusive rights to trade in Spanish South America. It grew during a period of considerable speculative fervour. With the success of trading companies, public interest in joint stock issues grew rapidly in the early 1700s, and by 1717 the capitalisation of joint stock companies reached 17 million pounds; a four-fold increase in two decades. The collapse occurred after a wave of speculative and often fraudulent company practices, including promoting its own stock price (which increased ten-fold in but a few years) (Frankfurter and Wood 1997).

Accordingly, the adoption of the corporate form as a standard organisational entity was restricted by the Bubble Act of 1720, making unincorporated joint stock companies illegal, and imposing a range of restrictions on firms seeking incorporation.[10] The Bubble Act was never actively enforced, and so the Act slowed, but did not stop entirely, the development of the corporate form. The Bubble Act was not repealed until the early nineteenth century (1825), after which joint stock companies rapidly developed. There remained on-going judicial resistance, but by this time the economic and political landscape had changed significantly. In particular, by the early nineteenth century, it had become clear that the bourgeois order was not going to be compromised by the corporate form.

Resistance to joint stock was nonetheless significant, especially in the context of a comparison with the era of the growth of derivatives. Even after the repeal of the Bubble Act, there was significant opposition to the corporate form, especially to the granting of limited liability. Hunt (1935: 14), for instance, reports that British Parliamentary debates revealed 'not only legal and mercantile opinion hostile to legislative limitation of liability, they reflect as well serious public concern over the difficulty of fixing the responsibility of shareholders in an unincorporated company in the event of financial embarrassment'.[11] Some aspects of these debates are discussed in more detail below.

While partnerships remained the standard organisational form of capital until the middle of the nineteenth century, gradually, and especially with key legislative and regulatory innovations by the state, secondary markets began to consolidate, and the joint stock company became much more widely accepted (Chandler 1979: 36).[12] The advent

[10] The Bubble Act made every new incorporation subject to Parliamentary approval and declared unincorporated joint stock a common nuisance and its promoters subject to prosecution.

[11] Significantly, these debates occurred in the context of considerable social upheaval including sometimes-violent opposition to mechanisation (Luddisim), the repeal of Elizabethan laws of provision, bread riots, the Peterloo massacre, the Cato Street conspiracy, and the suspension of habeas corpus to suppress public meetings and popular organisations.

[12] In particular, there were continuing concerns about the scope for increased speculation and deception made possible by stock markets. Tooke continued to express the view that corporations are rarely if ever run with the same care and skill as private establishments, while McCulloch suggested that corporate balance sheets were worse than worthless, being calculated to deceive and mislead. Senior, Peel and others, on the other hand, argued that limited liability would attract more capital from small investors (cited in Hunt 1935).

of general limited liability was accepted in the United States by the 1830s but did not occur in Britain until legislation between 1855 and 1862 (Baskin and Miranti 1988: 140–1).[13]

In both cases it was the capital and organisational requirements of funding large-scale investment (railroad and canal construction and operation) that made the corporate form, and limited liability in particular, necessary and more widely acceptable.[14] As corporations expanded in scale and scope Chandler (1979: 23) observed that they 'grew and dominated major sectors of the economy, [and as they did so] they altered the basic structure of these sectors and of the economy as a whole'. It was also around these developments that secondary markets for corporate securities became active and were gradually concentrated in major financial centres.[15] Chandler (1979: 58–9) reports that, in the

---

[13] Limitation of liability, like the corporate form itself, occurred gradually. Liability on transfer of shares, for instance, ended in 1834 in Britain, but some authors suggest that courts still interpreted limited liability in restrictive ways in the United States until the early 1890s (Handlin and Handlin 1945). Others have argued that limited liability in Britain did not become really effective until 1897 (Franks and Meyer 2002: 6–7).

[14] Railroad and canal companies required access to vast tracts of land (often granted by state and municipal governments), and with public distrust about stock markets still high, the acceptability of canal and railroad corporations was contingent on being viewed in part at least as a public improvement programme. Indeed, the state was also often the main source of funds for railway and canal developers, and this 'intimate association' increased public trust in canal and railroad investment. For instance, between 1815 and 1860, around three quarters of the almost $200million invested in canals had been financed through the flotation of state and municipal bonds (Baskin and Miranti 1997: 133). In the case of the United States, their acceptability was also underpinned by the fact that the state invested in opening up new areas of land to agriculture and commerce to help create markets for railroads.

[15] Significantly, Chandler also observed that the railroads were the first private business enterprises in the United States to acquire large amounts of capital from outside their own regions, and were critical to the development of secondary markets. 'The great increase in railroad securities brought trading and speculation on the New York Stock Exchange in its modern form. Before the railroads the volume of stocks in banks, insurance companies and state and federal bonds was tiny. On one day in March 1830, only thirty-one shares were traded on the New York Stock Exchange. By the mid-1850s the securities of railroads, banks and also municipalities from all parts of the United States were being traded in New York. Where earlier hundreds of shares had been traded weekly, hundreds of thousands of shares changed hands weekly. In a four-week period in the 1850s transactions totalled close to a million shares' (1978: 92).

United States,

> The unprecedented capital requirements of constructing the American railroad network led to the centralising and institutionalising of the nation's money market in New York. ... From the 1850s until the late 1890s the institutions and instruments of finance on Wall Street were used almost exclusively to finance the railroads. In fact, nearly all the instruments and techniques of modern finance in the United States were perfected in order to fund the construction of railroads and to facilitate growth through merger and acquisition.

So despite the fact that joint stock companies were recognised legal entities from the mid-seventeenth century, it took until the mid-nineteenth century for them to become widely accepted as an organisational form of capital. We conventionally date the impact of the joint stock company to this later period, precisely because its significance lay in its emergence as a new norm for capital.

Corporate 'capital'

One hundred and fifty years ago, our understanding of capital as a class was embodied in the rich, self-funded owner/entrepreneur: the feudal lord or mercantile trader turned manufacturer. Class was personified – the rich capitalist appropriated surplus from the wage labour that was employed in his factory or warehouse.

The formation of the joint stock company shattered that image, and it did this in two ways. First, the joint stock company involved, as Marx put it, the 'transformation of the actual functioning capitalist into a mere manager, in charge of other people's capital, and of the capital owner into a mere owner, a mere money capitalist' (Marx 1894: 567).

Second, the limited liability company changed the concept of 'ownership' fundamentally. As Adolph Berle (1959) observed, the legal entity known as the corporation emerged as the owner of the firm's property. It separated the capitalist (as owner) from the capital invested in the firm and the individual capitalist entrepreneur was transformed into an impersonalised industrial 'capital'.

The development of a separation between ownership claims and control generated a long-standing debate about the tensions between the objectives of managers and owners (growth versus profit), and it must be said that this debate has dominated the interpretation of the

historical significance of the joint stock company.[16] But this focus on
the divergent incentives and interests of managers and owners has
tended to obscure the underlying issue of the changing nature of
property and its connection to competition.

Stockholders now owned monetary claims to a share of the company, not to any specific part of it. Shares could not be converted into
a bit of the corporation's buildings, machinery or work-in-progress.
This de-personalisation of capital ownership allowed owners to sell
shares in the company to others. Company shares came to be bought
and sold in secondary markets, providing both new sources of capital
and, of growing importance, a vehicle for competition between individual capitals (pricing of corporate capital and a market for corporate
control).

A related change was the transformation of private ownership of capital into 'social' ownership, in a process of extending capitalist social
relations. This is the point Marx (1894: 567) emphasised about the joint
stock company. For example:

> Capital, which is inherently based on a social mode of production
> and presupposes a social concentration of means of production and
> labour-power, now receives the form of social capital (capital of
> directly associated individuals) in contrast to private capital, and its
> enterprises appear as social enterprises as distinct from private ones.
> This is the abolition of capital as private property within the confines
> of the capitalist mode of production itself.

Many interpreted this to imply the socialisation of property, but another
interpretation is that the firm as capital was now a more tangible expression of the wider social relations of capitalist society, not simply of the
personal desires of its owner (Kay 1991). The separation of ownership
and control of the corporation meant that, in the workplace, workers
confronted management, not owners and the surplus was extracted
from workers by 'capital' rather than (traditional) owner-capitalists. It
was now less easy to see accumulation as being driven by the personal
motives of the owners or managers; accumulation was now more tangi-
bly an expression of the class relations of capitalism. The class conflict of

---

[16] This literature is extensive, but for seminal contributions see Marris (1964),
Williamson (1964), Alchian and Demsetz (1972) and Jensen and Meckling
(1976).

capitalism became labour's conflict with 'capital' – a system and logic. This logic was driven increasingly by the competitive pressures of corporate balance sheets, with managers having to 'perform' (i.e. to make competitive profits), and, to use a modern euphemism, to 'grow' stock prices (i.e. to accumulate).

Contemporary debates

The development of the joint stock company was an issue of open contemporary debate with close parallels to recent debates about the growth of financial derivatives. The two 'sets' of debates are summarised in Figures 4.1 and 4.2. In the joint stock company debate, two sorts of questions were prominent: would joint stock companies open new scope for fraud and corruption, and would they lead to the demise of small business and the concentration of economic power?

We have already seen that the issue of fraud and corruption was central to the conservative view of capital. The key issue was the separation of ownership from control, and the 'agency problem', as it is now called. Adam Smith's famous comment, that the managers of firms could not be expected to take the same care of 'other people's money' as they would their own, reflected a widely held concern that the corporate form would be an inefficient way of organising economic activity. For Smith and many others it was precisely this de-personalisation of capital that made the corporate form such an unstable and inefficient vehicle for conducting business.[17]

This same point was central to the debate in Britain about the repeal of the Bubble Act in the early nineteenth century. In Parliamentary

---

[17] Smith's (1776: 741) view on this is worth quoting at length here:

> The directors of such companies, however, being the managers rather of *other people's money* than of their own, it cannot well be expected that they should watch over it with the same anxious vigilance with which the partners in a private copartnery frequently watch over their own. Like the stewards of a rich man, they are apt to consider attention to small matters as not for their master's honour, and very easily give themselves a dispensation from having it. Negligence and profusion, therefore, must always prevail, more or less, in the management of the affairs of such a company. It is upon this account that joint stock companies for foreign trade have seldom been able to maintain the competition against private adventurers. They have, accordingly, *very seldom succeeded without an exclusive privilege, and frequently have not succeeded with one*. Without an exclusive privilege they have commonly mismanaged the trade. With an exclusive privilege they have both mismanaged and confined it (emphasis added).

debate in 1825, for instance, Lord Chancellor Eldon, supported by the Tories, opposed repeal on the basis that non-tangible holdings, such as shares, encouraged speculation. They were 'paper' transactions, not real trade, and did not contribute to the nation. On the other side was a group of businessmen and bankers who argued that the joint stock company made possible the development of capital-intensive and publicly beneficial projects such as canals and railways. For the pro-corporate parliamentary group, existing laws of business organisation were an anachronism, and its common law component the accumulated residue of a different (pre-commercial) society. The Bubble Act had been a product of a moment of national frenzy (Harris 1997).

The second point of contemporary debate about the joint stock company concerned the concentration and centralisation of capital. In the United States, Thomas Jefferson and others were concerned that limited liability would benefit wealthy entrepreneurs and offer little to yeomen farmers. Andrew Jackson and others countered that, by allowing a pooling of multiple small investments, joint stock would enable small-scale, talented entrepreneurs to compete with wealthy entrepreneurs on more equal terms (Baskin and Miranti 1997). Both groups saw that only by reconciling concentrated property with individual endeavour was there a basis for social and political support for the joint stock form of capital. One worried that such a reconciliation would prove difficult. The other saw scope for individual co-operation and initiative through the joint stock form.

Both, of course, were correct. The legislative reforms of the mid-nineteenth century helped to re-define property rights in a manner consistent with large-scale production and facilitated the concentration and centralisation of capital. With this transformation, the capacity of large capitals to exercise power in the market became more widespread. This was especially apparent in the US merger waves and sharp business practices of the late nineteenth century, characterised by Josephson (1978) as the age of 'Robber Barons'. There is no doubt that this was not only a threat to 'yeoman farmers', it directly confronted all small, owner-managed capitals.[18] And yet, as Jackson observed, the stock market also gave less wealthy entrepreneurs with a good idea, and a desire for risk, a capacity to raise new capital. What they both reflected was the intensification of

[18] Geisst (2002: 6) notes that during the 1840s and 50s, 'the rural America so fondly recalled by Alexis de Tocqueville was rapidly giving way to the railroad baron and the grain plunger'.

competition: that potentially profitable investments could now better attract subscribers and investment became more mobile.[19]

A further debate occurred about the stock market as an institution, and whether it was encouraging destabilising speculation. During the eighteenth and nineteenth centuries, stock markets were riven with fraud and speculative episodes. For many, such as Jefferson, a distinction could be drawn between investment in land, commerce and joint stock and speculation in securities. Thus stock markets were useful vehicles for raising capital, but also places for unhealthy speculation (Sobel 1988; Gordon 1999). Over time, regulatory regimes evolved not to eliminate speculation, but to harness it (Kindleberger 1989; Geisst 2002; Day 2004). As stock markets have developed, debates over forms of regulation of financial markets have continued. Like the agency debate in the theory of the firm, the appropriate form of regulation of financial markets has never been resolved.[20]

These same themes of debate lasted to the end of the nineteenth century, and it could readily be recognised that both interpretations were historically verified. In *Capital*, Marx referred both to 'stock-exchange gambling' (Marx 1867: 919) and to the formation of joint stock companies facilitating 'tremendous expansion in the scale of production, enterprises that was impossible for individual[ly-owned] capitals' (1894: 567). Weber too saw the stock exchange 'discharging its most important function ... of controlling prices' by arbitrage, but that this function was becoming dominated by speculators. Indeed, he extended this insight into derivatives, contending that 'the advantages and drawbacks of futures trading are almost inseparably mixed' (1895: 374).

By the late-nineteenth century, the development of large corporations in railways, coal, steel and oil produced a second wave of debates

---

[19] Marx (1894: 735) observed at a relatively early stage of this process:

> Even where a man without means obtains credit as an industrialist or merchant, it is given in the expectation that he will function as a capitalist, will use the capital borrowed to appropriate unpaid labour. He is given credit as a potential capitalist. And this fact so admired by the economic apologists, that a man without wealth but with energy, determination, ability and business acumen can transform himself into a capitalist in this way ... much as it constantly drives an unwelcome series of new soldiers of fortune onto the field alongside and against various individual capitalists already present, actually reinforces the rule of capital itself, widens its basis and enables it to recruit ever new forces from the lower strata of society.

[20] For two sides of contemporary debate, see for instance, Day (2004), and Pirrong (1995).

(especially in the United States) about the corporate form, this time about the anti-competitive practices associated with trusts and conglomerates. The concern was that these big monopolistic corporations were undermining competition both in the market place and through their growing political influence. This development saw the emergence of new forms of state regulation of competition, initially through the Interstate Commerce Commission (ICC) in the United States to regulate railroad companies in particular, and then with the growth of other regulatory institutions associated with what Glaeser and Shleifer (2001) recently termed the rise of the 'regulatory' state.[21]

This development was seized on by many on the left, such as Hilferding, Lenin and Kautsky as signalling the rise of a new and mature phase of capitalist development. Hilferding combined this development of concentrated property with the observation that in Germany (at least) the rise of financial institutions as major forms of securing credit was creating a form of finance capitalism. 'An ever-increasing proportion of the capital used in industry is finance capital, capital at the disposition of the banks which is used by the industrialists'. Alongside the growth of large firms, was an increasing presence and control of banks:

> With the development of capitalism and its credit organisations there thus grows the dependence of industry upon the banks. The finance-capital develops with the development of the joint-stock companies and reaches its height with the monopolisation of industry. With cartellisation and trustification, finance-capital reaches the highest stage of its power, while the commercial capital experiences its deepest degradation. (Hilferding 1910: 225)

---

[21] The ICC displaced litigation as a way of controlling business practices (such as disputes about pricing) and was thus a forerunner of a changing system of regulation of capital accumulation. The inefficiency of private litigation and its vulnerability to subversion produced demands for alternative institutional arrangements for the social control of business. Glaeser and Shleifer (2001: 3) contend that, during the three decades following the creation of the ICC, 'regulatory agencies at both the state and the federal level took over the *social control of competition*, anti-trust policy, railroad pricing, foods and drug safety and many other areas' (emphasis added). For an excellent introduction to the changes occurring during this period see McCormick (1981), who describes how 'the government ... began to take explicit account of the clashing interests and to assume the responsibility for mitigating their conflict through regulation, administration and planning'.

The rise of the joint stock company, the growth of monopolistic industries and the rise of finance capital were taken as signals of a mature stage
of capitalism whereby not only are industry and finance merged, but the
institutional ownership and control of capital are concentrated in the
hands of a few large banks. It is at this point, it was contended, that capitalism as a social system becomes vulnerable to the challenge of socialism. As we now know, these developments were part of the institutional
evolution of capitalism, not the beginning of the end of capitalism. And
we also know that the joint stock company was not eclipsed by banks.

In summary, the development of the joint stock company showed a
number of characteristics, which provide important points of comparison with the recent growth of derivatives. As a once-new form of capital
ownership, facilitating new forms of capitalist organisation, the joint
stock company presented itself initially as a radical innovation, undermining conventional notions of ownership as well as of commercial stability and business prudence. We know, moreover, that the conservative
criticisms were well founded. The last 150 years is littered with cases of
fraud and corruption, and periods of extreme, market-wide volatility,
including booms and depressions. Yet, despite this chequered history,
the joint stock company is now the recognised dominant organisational
form of capital as an economic system. This standing, we argue, is based
on the fact that the development of the corporate form of organisation
was integral to the development of capitalism. The generalised adoption
of the joint stock company, and the associated secondary market for
shares (stock exchanges), makes the joint stock company a distinctly
capitalist form of organisation of capital, for it brings competition
directly into ownership and indirectly into the rationale of corporate
management.

Financial derivatives

It is historically too early to summarise the history of derivatives that is
akin to that of the joint stock company, but there are some clear parallels
to be drawn.

Evolution

Just as there is a proclivity to see the joint stock company as an
invention of the mid-nineteenth century that came into being fully
developed, the same is often thought of derivatives: that they are an
invention of the 1980s, and that they emerged rapidly, and with their
'role' in accumulation more or less fully developed.

Derivatives are not a 1980s invention – indeed the history of derivatives is much longer than the history of corporate shareholding – but, as was the case in the history of the joint stock company, it took a range of economic developments and changes in state regulation to bring derivatives to prominence as a dominant form of capital. So just as we date the significance of the joint stock company as a generalised form of capital ownership only from the mid-nineteenth century, we also date derivatives as a generalised form of capital ownership only from the 1980s.

Derivatives in the form of futures and options are almost as old as monetised exchange itself. A potted history of derivatives will note Aristotle referring to options in Book 1 of *Politics*, and of the forward selling of rice in China in 2000BC. It will also highlight the extensive medieval use of futures contracts in rural market places and the role options in the famous Dutch tulip bubble of the seventeenth century.[22]

Specifically organised institutions for trading futures and options however, date from the mid-seventeenth century in Japan, and the mid-nineteenth century in England and the United States. In this way, the first period of derivatives development parallels the generalised emergence of the joint stock company, and at some points their development intersected. The development of stock exchanges in the late eighteenth and early nineteenth century led virtually immediately to the formation of official and unofficial options markets for company stocks.[23] In the United States, for instance, put and call options on stocks were being traded from the 1790s, in the early years of the institution that later became the New York Stock Exchange (Bernstein 1996: 307).

But the predominant history of derivatives within capitalism is found in agricultural markets, which date from the early- to mid-nineteenth century. In 1848 the Chicago Board of Trade (CBOT) established an organised grain market, and some time thereafter began trading wheat forward (for future delivery). Here, as with the joint stock company, the development was associated with the expanding scale of capitalist accumulation. According to Emery (1899), one of the key factors in the development of US grain futures markets was the expansion and

---

[22] For more on the role of options in this event, and on the historical development of derivatives see Swan (2000). For a counter argument about the tulip bubble, see Garber (2001).

[23] In Britain in the seventeenth century options on forms of government debt and private equity were known by such terms as refusals (because the owner had the right to refuse to buy an asset), and puts.

increasing national integration of agricultural production and distribution.[24] With the extension of railways, urbanisation and industrialisation, Chicago emerged as a crucial railway hub and commercial centre for many types of agricultural produce (Gray and Peterson 1974), and it was here in particular that formal agricultural derivatives markets originated. Emery also argued that, with the growth of an increasing international market for grains and cotton, the more severe became the trade risks. Market participants increasingly could not afford to ignore futures markets, and even before the turn of the century it was being argued that 'hedging has become so common a practice that in the main a dealer who does not hedge, that is who carries his own risks is looked upon as extremely reckless. Paradoxical as it may sound, the man who avoids the speculative market is the greatest speculator of them all' (Emery 1899: 48).[25]

The range of commodities that were subject to futures markets grew steadily over the next century. In Chicago, for instance, commodity exchanges like the Egg and Butter Board (which would later become the Chicago Mercantile Exchange) developed futures markets for a range of agricultural commodities, and in New York, an options market on grain began on the New York Produce Exchange in 1877. These became the early bases of exchange-traded derivative markets for agricultural commodities and later financial instruments.

The growth and reorganisation of international cotton trading based around England also generated an important cotton derivatives markets.[26] By the mid-nineteenth century a futures market in the Liverpool Cotton Exchange[27] emerged as a crucial pricing and credit institution for international (especially colonial) cotton trade, and as an important

[24] For instance, between 1854 and 1864 the amount of wheat shipped from the Midwest in America more than quadrupled (Geisst 2002).

[25] Another factor that led to the development of commodity futures markets in the United States was the civil war, which increased price volatility and therefore risks and also changed social attitudes to the accumulation of wealth. This increased speculative activity on the prices of gold and staples. See Geisst (2002) and Rees (1972).

[26] It is worth recalling that in the nineteenth century cotton occupied a central place in international trade. (See, for instance, Marsh 1911.)

[27] Until the late eighteenth century, London had been the main port of entry into England. But with the opening of the Liverpool–Manchester railway, trading through the port of Liverpool became more important. A market in forward prices (known as 'to arrive') emerged as dealers sought to hedge against international price changes (Rees 1972).

source of commercial relations with the Manchester cotton industry. As the Liverpool exchange developed, two distinct markets emerged: one on arrival and the other yet to be shipped, with the derivative market (to arrive, or yet to be shipped) increasingly dealing with rights that were settled less and less by any actual exchange of cotton and more and more in cash (Rees 1972). While for a time the most important business remained spot markets, Marsh (1911: 589) argued that, by the early part of the twentieth century, spot markets had

> ... become subsidiary and ancillary to this main business (of futures trading). It may almost be said that as the main business of banks today is not dealing in money, so the main business of the cotton exchanges is now in credit transactions in cotton, towards which the actual cotton 'on the spot' stands in much the same relation as the money in the banks to the sum total of their transactions in credits.[28]

With the development of cotton futures markets, merchants, banks and other commercial institutions changed and intensified their relations with the cotton industry (Toms 2002). The affinity between derivatives and money, an issue developed later in Chapter 6, was clearly apparent even then.

There were regular revelations of speculation and manipulation of futures and options markets (especially attempts at cornering markets),[29] and some of these episodes helped change market behaviour[30] and public perceptions of these markets.[31] Generally, however, futures exchanges confined their own regulatory activities to contractual enforcement between members and took little or no action to deter manipulation of

---

[28] By the early 1930s Forrester (1931) reports that 'the basis for all the spot cotton prices in England is Liverpool futures'.

[29] Cornering is simply the use of cash and/or derivative markets in a way that permits price manipulation. According to one study of the Chicago Board of Trade, there was at least one corner nearly every year during the period from 1865 to 1921 (Pirrong 1995).

[30] Toms (2002), for instance, reports that in Liverpool one response to the market corner of the September 1889 cotton futures contract was for several individual companies to form the Cotton Buying Company in an attempt to stabilise prices.

[31] Periodic criticism by farmers about price instability in wheat directed farmer opposition to the Chicago futures trading pits, and the Grange movement as it came to be known soon realised that co-operative attempts to stabilise incomes could not prevent price volatility. So they increasingly joined progressive attempts to increase government regulation of derivatives exchanges through parliamentary means (Nordin 1974).

prices (Pirrong 1995; Geisst 2002). Sometimes, but quite rarely, speculative scandals led to changes in existing regulations, ranging from transactions taxes (such as the Capper–Tichner Act of 1921 in the United
States[32]), to attempts to impose controls on short selling (by the 'anti-
optionists' in the United States (Emery 1899)), to outright bans (in
Germany in 1897[33]). From the early part of the twentieth century, derivatives markets in the United States were subject to increasing regulation,
subjecting them to federal supervision, closing some exchanges and
driving others abroad. From the 1920s legislative bodies considered
proposals to tax, regulate and even ban futures trading. While most of
the proposals were defeated, some form of federal regulation of futures
markets existed from 1922.[34]

But while such circumstances that saw the development of the joint
stock company repressed for about a century (in Britain, epitomised in
the hundred-year Bubble Act) there was no equivalent impact in derivatives regulation. There are probably two central reasons for the different
treatment. The first is that, by the late nineteenth century, the question
of containing the rise of capitalism had been almost completely
resolved. Certainly, the ruling class in most nation states were unlikely
to see their interests checked by constraints on the further growth of
derivatives exchanges. Indeed, even critics of futures exchanges con-
ceded that they had quickly come to play an important economic role.
Secondly, derivatives pertaining just to particular commodities were not
transforming the nature of capital ownership in the way that the joint

[32] An earlier proposed tax on futures and options, the Hatch Bill, was passed by
Congress in 1893 but never became law (Geisst 2002).

[33] Weber (1895: 376) contended that it was in the international political interests of Germany that there be policies to control trade on the stock exchange,
including the market for grain futures. His primary recommendation was that
evidence of wealth should be required before admission, and that all transactions
be in cash. The objective was to exclude the small speculators who he thought
were using the leverage provided by derivatives to speculate heavily in the
market.

[34] According to Pashigian (1986) many who opposed futures trading did so
because they felt it encouraged speculation, which was directly analogous to
gambling. But he argues that the primary purpose of successful regulation has not
been to stop speculation *per se*, but directed to eliminating the alleged manipulation of markets by traders. That is, regulation has attempted to make the markets
work better rather than to shut them down. He also shows that areas where opposition by farmers for futures was highest were characterised by grain growing
areas where buyers (such as grain elevators) were thought to be using futures markets to carry out collusive buying (Pashigian 1986). See also Easterbrook (1986).

stock company (or later financial derivatives) did. Single commodity derivatives had helped to establish price relations between the present and future and so reduce certain risks associated with the expanding scale and scope of commodity trade and finance. Commodity derivatives did not, however, become the basis for comparing different forms of capital *per se*. In our terms, therefore, they were not yet elevated to their current role of capital. It was sufficient, at this stage of their development, only to regulate derivatives so as to establish fair market practice between buyers and sellers.

Becoming capital

The generalised growth of the joint stock company related to the needs of large-scale production for both large-scale funds and the spread of the risks of ownership. The generalised growth of derivatives related to parallel concerns in a different historical context: the risks of financing 'large-space' and 'large-time' accumulation.

Critical here was the development of Eurofinance markets in the 1950s and 1960s and then the end of the Bretton Woods Agreement in 1971. These processes will be considered in further detail in Chapters 5 and 9. Suffice it here to note that Eurofinance markets provided cheap credit at interest rates and exchange rates that differed from those that ruled in domestic markets. But there were risks associated with the variability of rates of conversion between the Eurofinance and domestic markets. Financial derivatives emerged to hedge these risks.

With the end of the Bretton Woods Agreement, nationally fixed exchange rates gave way to floating rates and the lifting of national capital controls increased the ease of movement of finance internationally. In the context of increasingly volatile exchange rates the demand for hedging facilities on exchange rates and interest rates grew.

Apart from isolated innovative financial transactions scattered through history,[35] it was not until 1972 that the Chicago Mercantile Exchange introduced the first currency futures contract. It was not until 1975 that the Chicago Board of Trade introduced the first interest rate futures contract. Moreover, exchange-traded financial derivatives did not extend outside the United States until 1979, when the Sydney Futures Exchange issued its first exchange-traded financial derivative contracts.

---

[35] Bernstein (1996: 307–8), for example, refers the Confederate States of America issuing bonds in 1863 that could be redeemed in Sterling or French Francs, or even in cotton. Telser (1986) reports that foreign exchange futures were traded for a short time in the 1920s.

Similarly for options. Prior to the creation of the Chicago Board
Options Exchange (CBOE) in 1973 options contracts were largely negotiated outside of formal exchanges (known as OTC instruments): that is,
contracts privately negotiated between two parties.[36] They were non-
standardised contracts and, accordingly, attracted no significant secondary market. But since the opening of the CBOE, options exchanges have
opened up in all major financial centres.

However, it was really the 1980s when financial derivatives began to
become integral to corporate finance. This marked a critical point at
which derivatives started to become 'capital' so it needs to be explained
institutionally here.

Once financial derivatives emerged, they rapidly changed the face of
derivatives markets generally. Initially, financial derivatives were traded
mostly on exchanges – in the form of futures and options. During the
1970s financial futures markets in the United States grew rapidly. Indeed
in that decade they doubled in size. Between 1970 and 1980 activity
grew seven-fold. In a three-year period in the early-1980s they tripled in
size. As a consequence, financial futures quickly came to dominate
futures trading, surpassing all other futures markets. Whereas in 1960,
foodstuffs, grain and oilseeds accounted for 94 per cent of futures trading activity in the United States, and as late as 1970 they still accounted
for 63 per cent of activity on futures markets in the United States, by
1983 they represented less than a third of trading activity (Carlton
1984).[37] By 1990, futures contracts on financial instruments represented
around 60 per cent of total turnover on US exchanges (Parsons 1999).
But clearest indication of the spectacular growth of financial derivatives
can be found not on futures exchanges, but in OTC markets. This development was explained in Chapter 3.

Corporate 'capital' and derivative 'capital'

The initial use of financial derivatives was as one-off tools for hedging
exposure in commodity markets. In this ad-hoc role, derivatives were
not yet 'capital' in a generalised sense. Even when derivatives first developed in finance, to hedge exchange rates and variable interest rates on

[36] See Chapter 3 for an explanation. From at least the 1870s in Chicago,
options, or 'privileges' as they also came to be known at the time, had been the
subject of bans and restrictions.
[37] This transformation was so great that by the early 1980s some former
agricultural futures markets such as the Chicago Mercantile Exchange had completely given up trading these and had specialised in financial futures, industrial
materials and metals.

particular loans in the context of new exposures in international finance, they were not yet 'capital'. They were still then typically traded in relation to particular, individual financial transactions, closing off individual financial exposures, just as commodity derivatives were generally used to hedge a particular commodity order. They were also circumventing national regulations, and this no doubt motivated much of the early use of derivatives, but they were discrete transactions, without the characteristics of 'capital' we are now identifying.

It was not until derivative markets were sufficiently comprehensive, and could perform the blending role described in Chapter 1, that they could be thought of as 'capital' tied to 'ownership'. The critical development was that derivatives started being acquired for their flexibility and mobility: their capacity to blend different forms of capital with different characteristics into parts of an integrated 'capital'. In this sense of 'capital', we see that this organisational potential of derivatives, like the corporate form, remained latent until their generalised need in accumulation became apparent and, indeed, was facilitated by state regulatory reform, which lifted restrictions on or ratified the growth of these new forms of capital.

How have derivatives changed capital? To answer this, we briefly recall the way this question was answered in relation to the joint stock company. We saw above that the joint stock company initiated two changes in 'capital': it 'socialised' capital (in the sense that it separated the firm from the personal interests of the owner/s) and gave it a legal standing outside of its particular owners (by creating the firm as a distinct legal person). We have also seen how the importance of this transition in the organisational form of capital was gradually recognised by economists. By the 1960s for instance, Galbraith, in his famous *New Industrial State* (1967), identified this transition in terms of the rise to dominance of large corporations. He suggested that power within these large corporations had shifted to the managers and those with specialist knowledge – the 'technostructure' he called them – who provided the technical advice, which framed managerial decisions. Galbraith's technostructure takes the corporation as an institution to be run and expanded.

If the joint stock company constituted the corporation as an 'individual person', and thereby separated capital from 'real' individuals, what have derivatives done? Derivatives have taken the logic of capital beyond the bottom line (annual profit rates) and into the details of each phase of production and distribution, because they permit the corporation as legal entity to continually verify the market value of its component 'pieces' of capital. They have provided a form of capital in which competition has, to use a popular legal phrase, 'pierced the corporate veil'. Rather than a 'technostructure' we see the emergence of a sort of 'financostructure': the back-room financial calculators who scrutinise corporate asset portfolios, and the derivatives traders who continually price and re-price securities. With derivatives, the ability to commensurate the value of capital assets within and between companies at any point in time has been added as a measure of capital's performance alongside and perhaps above the capacity to produce surplus over time. Derivatives then are serving to effectively de-centre the institutional form of capital in the corporation, returning the focus to capital itself.

Derivatives separate the capital of firms into financial assets that can be priced and traded or 'repackaged', without having to either move them physically, or even change their ownership. In so doing they allow scrutiny of the parts of the firm that were pooled by the joint stock process, and so allow a more intensive scrutiny of its capacity for profit making. It has to be noted here that the measures for such scrutiny are still developing, and in part this is because derivatives are undermining normal on-balance-sheet forms of scrutiny and calculation.[38] While there have been several corporate scandals that have exploited this off-balance-sheet nature of financial derivatives (such as Enron and Worldcom), there is little or no sign that restricting the use of derivatives is a serious proposal under discussion. Rather, it is accepted that derivatives are now integral to the accumulation process. In this sense, derivatives are extending and deepening the 'socialisation' of capital that Marx had identified with the formation of the joint stock company.

While the joint stock company transformed private firms into social corporations, they remain(ed) largely 'private' in their internal operations and calculations. The corporation as legal individual makes effectively 'private' calculations in its 'internal' decision making. The stock market attempts to value the effects of these decisions, but because the stock market is not a major way that firms finance themselves, its role is largely to attempt to price whole firms. But derivatives are socialising calculation within and between corporations. There are, in some senses, elements of the return to the form of capital which cohered just for particular ventures, before the joint stock company established the corporation as a large, durable monolithic, administered institution. We have with derivatives a potential akin to a return to (scrutinising, valuing,

---

[38] Currently also, the attention to reporting the financial soundness implications of derivatives has focused especially on financial firms that produce and trade derivatives.

and even running) corporate operations as a temporary and flexible coalescence of assets that can readily be liquidated after each venture.

Contemporary debates

Since the growth of derivatives in the 1980s, and especially derivatives relating to finance, there has been a widespread debate about their contribution to accumulation. Some have hailed them as tools of risk management in an unavoidably risky global market; others have condemned their economic and political role as tools of speculation, accentuating rather than managing risk and volatility.

This debate over financial derivatives is considered in detail in Chapter 8. Here, a simple but central point to be noted is that it parallels the nineteenth-century debate on the growth of the joint stock company. In that nineteenth-century debate, it will be recalled, some saw the joint stock company as a means to secure the expansion of the scale of capital; some saw it as the opportunity for entrepreneurs with good ideas but without wealth to mobilise new capital. Derivatives carry the same characterisation: they permit companies to hedge exposures across numbers of currencies and different forms of capital raising. They also permit smaller companies to insure against unwanted risk, so that their fortunes depend just on their productive capacities.

In the nineteenth-century debate over the joint stock company, claims abounded of the stock market as a site of gambling and manipulation, and the joint stock company itself as facilitating irresponsible management of capital. At the beginning of the twenty-first century, we see the same criticism made of derivatives. Critics of derivatives point to famous corporate crashes, like LTCM, Enron, or Barings as representing the inevitable consequence of derivatives. Indeed, hedge funds are often seen as the institutional expression of twenty-first-century financial derivatives, in the same way that the South Sea Company was seen as the institutional expression of the joint stock firm.

These critics argue for new forms of global regulation to contain derivative growth and prevent systemic risks from creating a global financial crisis. Susan Strange (1998) made the case that the growth of global finance (including derivatives) has been associated with facilities to make it easier for organised crime to transfer money across the globe. She contended that 'the theoretical implication of the closer links between finance and crime, however, go deeper into the structures of power in the international political economy ... (including) the amazingly permissive market for transnational banking services, including the laundering of dirty money'. Proposals to restrict capital flows and impose tighter restrictions on derivatives use follow as a consequence, and these are discussed in more detail in Chapter 8.

Financial derivatives are also now implicated in the agency problem, between managers and owners. It will be recalled that Adam Smith and others expressed concern that with the separation of ownership from management that accompanied the joint stock company, the managers could not be expected to act in the interests of, or with the same diligence as, owners. In the last decade and a half, corporate managers have been receiving an increasing proportion of their compensation in the form of stock options. Indeed, for senior corporate executives in the United States, stock options have become the largest single component of their compensation.[39]

In part, these options are being offered as a form of performance payment, so that if managers run the firm successfully the company's share price will rise and the options will be become valuable. In other words, options are thought to align the interests of managers with those of owners, by giving managers an ownership-like incentive structure. There is some debate however as to whether the use of stock options may result in managers taking on greater risk or greater borrowing, increasing the volatility of corporate returns (John and John 1993). This issue was given some consideration in Chapter 2.

The point to be emphasised here is how the debates about the generalisation of the joint stock company 150 years ago and the generalised role of derivatives today are directly parallel. In their nascent stage, the joint stock company and financial derivatives have been condemned and praised for basically the same reasons. History shows that the joint stock company is now an established and integral part of capitalist economy and the standard organisational form of large units of accumulation. We cannot imagine the past 150 years of capitalist development without it.

It is inappropriate to 'predict' a parallel 150-year future for derivatives. All that we can say at this early stage is that the criticisms currently made of derivatives exist alongside, and with little impact on, their emerging role as an established and integral part of corporate management.

---

[39] This trend to use stock options is extending to salaried employees as well. Hall and Murphy (2000) estimated that, in 1998, salaried employees in around 45 per cent of listed US companies were receiving at least some of their pay through stock options. Even employees compensated on an hourly basis were being offered stock options in between 10 and 12 per cent of public companies.

Conclusion

We are not the first to draw parallels between the transformations brought on by the joint stock company and financial derivatives. Some legal scholars have suggested that financial derivatives are challenging existing concepts of the firm since they challenge the nature of capital ownership and competition (e.g. Krawiec 1998; Partnoy 1999). Partnoy (2000: 2), for instance, has suggested that with the integration of financial derivatives into business practice, 'corporate law has been left in the dust. For the study and practice of corporate law, the consequences of the derivatives revolution are devastating. Many of the traditional building blocks no longer exist.'[40] The argument developed in this chapter has hopefully persuaded readers others than lawyers that this conclusion needs to be taken seriously.

The chapter outlined how the joint stock company has taken 'capital' from the physical form of the factory to a financial claim on the corporation. It developed the case that derivatives have taken 'capital' from that claim on the corporation to a claim on assets that is infinitely convertible (contingent) within and across firms. The result is an increase in the imperative of competition under derivative ownership and that the corporation now potentially faces an on-going market valuation (in relative terms) of each of its assets: its inputs, its outputs and its various financial assets.

The consequences are profound. On the one hand, the competitive pressure that follows is vastly intensified from that faced by capital in the first and second separations (an issue we develop further in Chapter 7). On the other hand, derivatives show that the process by which capital is valued has become increasingly divorced from direct ownership of the means of production.

But derivatives are being widely condemned. The same sorts of arguments that were made 150 years ago about the joint stock company are now being made against financial derivatives. Figures 4.1 and 4.2, present a comparison of the two eras of debate. They are remarkably similar. The concerns about the South Sea Bubble are essentially the same as the contemporary concerns about hedge funds. Derivatives are being widely criticised as a diversion of finance from its key role in funding production; they are widely thought to be driven by speculation and

---

[40] Partnoy also makes the case that whereas in the past it was possible to teach corporate law using almost entirely nineteenth-century railway cases, it is becoming possible today to do so using almost entirely derivatives-related cases.

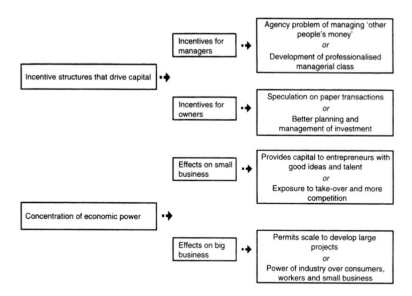

Figure 4.1 Joint stock company debates.

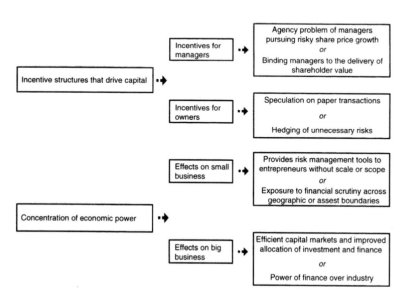

Figure 4.2 Financial derivatives debates.

they are seen as adding liquidity to corporate gambling, and stock options are thought to aggravate the agency problem rather than resolve it. They are, in short, undermining the integrity of capitalist accumulation and should be regulated into insignificance.

In both periods, the arguments have not been without foundation. Since the formation of the joint stock company there have been massive stock market booms and busts and corporate collapses, and, in the short recent history of derivatives, there have also been some significant speculative crises and frauds. But today as we look at the joint stock company, along with an awareness of booms and bust, we recognise it as an epochal change in the way capitalism 'works' and in the nature of capital and ownership. We suggest that the same will be the impact of derivatives. In both eras, the issue of speculation and crisis sits under that recognition.

Part II

Derivatives and International Finance

The next three chapters present an historical analysis that establishes the centrality of derivatives to the operation of current international financial markets. This analysis is based on the following propositions:

1. Floating exchange rates require labour market flexibility as the mechanism of national economic adjustment to the vicissitudes of the global economy.
2. In the context of floating exchange rates, financial derivatives now anchor the global financial system in a role comparable to that played by gold when exchange rates floated freely before the First World War.
3. In performing this anchoring role, derivatives take on the characteristics of global money. They are money that transcends the conventional national system of money.
4. The foundation for derivatives-as-money is not state guarantees, but a commodity basis. The last hundred years has not seen a shift away from a commodity basis to money, but the re-discovery of a new commodity basis.
5. The capacity of derivatives to compare (commensurate) all different types and localities of capital assets is imposing an intensified competition into capital markets, and thereby into all markets.
6. Derivatives generate demands for labour market flexibility. What are widely called 'neoliberal' policies with respect to labour can be associated directly with the ubiquitous impact of derivatives. Via the intensely competitive conditions derivatives create for capital, pressure reverts to labour as the primary area where capital can exert creative discretion in the pursuit of profitability.

5
Anchoring the Global Financial System

Gold once anchored the global financial system and, from the late nineteenth century, the extensive cross-national flow of finance, trade and investment was facilitated by its virtually unassailed role as the global monetary unit. At the end of the twentieth century, there was also a surge in international flows of finance, trade and investment, but without the facilitation of gold, or any other globally recognised single monetary unit. We may identify the role of the US dollar as hegemonic, but it has no formal status, and exchange rates in relation to the US dollar have been anything but stable. So the current era of 'globalisation' is occurring, it seems, without a formal, universally recognised monetary anchor. But does that mean it is occurring without any sort of anchor at all?

This chapter develops the argument that the system of myriad financial derivative contracts is playing the role of a monetary anchor – not a rigid, fixed anchor like gold, but a flexible, floating anchor – and the contemporary global financial system requires that derivatives perform precisely this anchoring function.

This is more than a functionalist argument. While the recent requirements of large and volatile international financial flows may be the *proximate* cause of the growth of derivatives, we have also suggested that there is an *underlying* cause to the growth of derivatives that cannot be reduced to the financial requirements of late twentieth-century 'globalisation'. That latter argument is developed in the next chapter, but it is important at this point to recognise that, in explaining the proximate causes, we are also looking to frame the underlying determinants of the role of derivatives within capitalist calculation.[1] In particular, in this chapter and the

---

[1] Indeed, while we use the term *proximate cause* here, another way of thinking about it may be to say that its initial growth has been *occasioned by* the developments in international financial, production and labour markets. We thank Geoff Kay for this suggestion.

next, we challenge the view, almost universally adhered to, that over the twentieth century the world has moved steadily away from a commodity foundation to money. We argue, to the contrary, that derivatives are not just functional to capital but are also to be seen as a new (commodity) money facilitating a more globally oriented scale of accumulation.

The formal sense in which derivatives constitute money is addressed in Chapter 6. In this chapter the objective is to identify the logical space within which derivatives play a monetary role. Our argument is that, following the decline of gold as global money, capital has gravitated towards an alternative basis to the global financial system, and it shows this tendency for one basic reason: national currencies (be it the US dollar under the Bretton Woods system of fixed exchange rates or, since then, floating national currency exchange rates) cannot meet the requirements of both domestic monetary policy and global monetary stability. The threat of exchange rate instability is on going.

Accordingly, products emerged (financial derivatives) to deliver what pure exchange processes could not. By forming a network of anchors, derivatives are permitting capital and commodities to flow 'as if' there were a single anchor. What is widely depicted as 'deregulation' of finance following the end of Bretton Woods is, at the same time, a process in which the market (or capital) rather than nation states have looked to provide an alternative foundation to global money.

In developing this proposition, this chapter follows the evolution of global finance in the past hundred or so years.

National currencies and global money: the policy trilemma

The problem of nation state money is that the guarantees of stability and security it supposedly provides diminish in direct proportion to the growth of extra-national currency circulation, beyond the territorial jurisdiction of the nation state. This has been argued extensively in relation to the US dollar, and its role from the Second World War to 1971 as the global currency unit – on which more below. But it is not an argument unique to the United States: there are inevitable tensions of money having to serve both domestic and global functions.

Central to the global money problem, therefore, is the difficulty for states in balancing the needs of capital to securely expand, including internationally, and the pursuit of national policy goals. The history of the global financial system had shown that it is possible for states to provide (a maximum of) any two, but not all three, of the following:

- National policies to support labour's living standards,
- Large scale capital flows, and
- Stable exchange rates.

In economics the trade-off between three macroeconomic variables is known as the macro-economic 'policy trilemma'.[2] Any attempt to add the third agenda to the other two existing policies sees at least one of the other spheres thrown into crisis. The history of the financial system is really one of the revolving set of priorities and the different historical ways in which the third agenda gets displaced. This third agenda then can be thought of as the 'swing mechanism' of national economic adjustment, so that this history can be framed in terms of the changing swing mechanism. For example, to secure stable exchange rates and policies to sustain living standards, nation states have to exercise capital controls to regulate the flow of international capital. Capital flows become the policy swing mechanism.

It will be seen that the two great periods of global capital movement – the late nineteenth century to the First World War, and the late twentieth century – have much in common. In both of these periods, where the financial regime is privileging global over parochial agendas, the nation state does not exert direct control over the value of 'its' currency. The material basis of the value of each national currency, and hence all global money, must be found in its capacity to purchase goods and services, not in its guarantee by the nation state.

---

[2] The conventional framing of the trilemma is that an open national economy cannot support all three of:

- Independence in monetary policy,
- Stability in the exchange rate, and
- Free movement of capital

Obstfeld *et al.* (2004a; 2004b) confirm the pertinence of the conventional trilemma to monetary history. However, that trilemma remains purely monetary in its trade-offs. Our argument is that labour, treated as a national attribute in a world of internationally mobile capital, has played a critical role in national policy to secure monetary stability. Accordingly, we have replaced 'independent monetary policy' with the more relevant political/economic variable 'support of labour's living standards'.

Hence the stability of money within any nation has related directly to the conditions of production of goods and services: issues of productivity and production costs, and especially labour costs. Quite simply, in the current era, as under the Gold Standard, global capital movement with stable international finance has required the subordination of labour's living standards to the needs of mobile capital: labour had been the swing mechanism of national adjustment.

We develop this proposition via the historical stylised facts of the global financial system and the major transitions from the classical Gold Standard to the 'Bretton Woods Dollar Gold Standard', and then to the current derivative period.[3]

Early commodity money: the Gold Standard and its contradictions

Capitalism developed on the basis of (pre-capitalist) money: gold and silver. These are forms of commodity money: their integrity in the funding of trade, settling debts, etc., was based on the intrinsic value of the money unit: gold and silver are 'valuable' in themselves.

While the rise of the modern state facilitated the development of inconvertible paper money domestically, and other forms of fiat money, precious metals remained the basis of cross-national transactions. This commodity money worked remarkably well, especially considering that it was anything but well planned.[4] The value of gold and silver varied with their costs and volumes of production, but, while some countries used gold and others silver (and some used both), there was great stability in the gold/silver exchange rate – until the 1870s when silver's price fell dramatically[5] and gold became the (virtually) exclusive international trading currency.

---

[3] In developing the stylised facts the reader is urged to heed Kindleberger's (1973) warning about the Gold Standard that it operated a good deal less automatically than textbook stylised facts often tend to suggest. Indeed, how the Gold Standard and even Bretton Woods regimes played out are not uncontroversial.

[4] Kindleberger (1984: 60) comments: 'Like so much monetary history, fixing the pound sterling in 1717 at a gold price that lasted, with lapses from 1797 to 1819 and from 1914 to 1925, until 1931, was largely inadvertent, rather than the outcome of design'.

[5] The stability is attributed to the existence of sufficient bimetallic countries, which were flexible as to which was used at any point in time. The Australian and Californian gold rushes of the mid-century increased world gold production

The huge growth in international transactions in the late nineteenth century therefore occurred with a stable global currency and hence fixed exchange rates between nations: the classical Gold Standard. Significantly, this stability in exchange rates came not because nation states actively managed currency values (there were virtually no central banks as such), but because the state's role was restricted merely to the provision of a dependable physical currency.[6] On this basis, nations used gold as their currency base and trade imbalances between nations could be settled in gold transfers.[7] Indeed, the need for convertibility of national money units into gold ensured that nation states would not meddle with money too much for fear of creating domestic price instability.

Accordingly, under the Gold Standard, high levels of international capital mobility – in some terms proportionately even higher than they are today – were directly compatible with stable exchange rates (a stable global financial system) because national economic policy subordinated domestic agendas to the stability of the national monetary unit *vis a vis* gold.

Perhaps 'subordinated' is the wrong term, for it suggests a conscious policy stance. As Eichengreen (1998) emphasises, in the major trading and capital exporting countries, there was simply no significant political aspiration or institutional basis for using state policy to pursue social agendas that might result in price instability.[8] Labour did not have the vote, union membership was low, unemployment was not an issue for

ten-fold and pushed down the price of gold. As a result, the bimetallic countries increasingly used gold. As a consequence, silver was released by bimetallic countries on to the world market, pushing its price down. By this flow, the exchange rate between gold and silver remained stable from the beginning of the nineteenth century until the 1870s (Eichengreen and Sussman 2000: 17). However, in the 1870s the expansion of silver production could not be so absorbed, and the exchange rate became unstable (Kindleberger 1984).

[6] But, as Richard Cooper notes, this strength was also a weakness. While the Gold Standard provided a rigid anchor for world prices, no government was responsible for managing fluctuations in the demand for and supply of gold. So the system was prone to sharp global liquidity shocks, and prices for traded goods were also more volatile than under the Bretton Woods regime (cited in McKinnon 1993).

[7] In fact, international monetary relations became robust enough for short-term capital flows to often substitute for gold as the swing variable for balancing international payments (McKinnon 1993).

[8] See also Eichengreen and Iverson (1999). Kay and Mott (1982) provide an excellent account of the transition from liberal to social democracy and its implications for the development of state 'policy'.

states and the state ran minimal social and military expenditure. Moreover, with capital internationally mobile, labour was treated politically as the one component of production costs that was largely national.[9] Wages, employment rates and working class living standards were made flexible on a national scale, and were readily changed to ensure domestic price and hence exchange rate stability.

The Gold Standard was, therefore, not compatible with the rise of the labour movement, and its demands for social expenditure and policies to avert unemployment (DeCecco 1974) – a reality that became stark with the growing social expectations of state expenditure after the First World War. The Gold Standard had shown that it was possible to provide two, but not all three components of the policy trilemma. The Gold Standard had 'foregone' labour's living standards: labour was the swing mechanism of national economic adjustment.[10]

In monetary policy terms, the nation state could not reconcile the domestic demands on finance with the global requirements of currency convertibility to gold. The rise of national central banks in the early twentieth century was associated with growing state management of the domestic monetary system. Gold was progressively withdrawn from circulation as national money and held as reserves by the central bank. National monetary liquidity thereby became a central bank policy issue (and subject to policy conjecture) rather than an automatic (i.e. market-driven) product of international gold flows. Policy conjecture generated scope for speculative positions on exchange rate adjustments because there were not automatic, predictable, market-driven adjustments (Nurkse 1944). Global financial markets became increasingly volatile, and nation states sought, through a variety of mechanisms, to insulate themselves from that volatility.[11]

[9] Labour was indeed quite mobile in some periods of the nineteenth century and the evolution of the modern state can in part be associated with the need to deal with the effects of the emergence of surplus populations, including the threat of its mobility (Cowen and Shenton 1999). We are depicting labour as 'national' in our analysis, because labour was treated 'as if' it were national.

[10] This is not to idealise the 'adjustment mechanism' under the Gold Standard. The price of labour, to paraphrase Keynes, was often 'sticky' downwards. As historians often remind us, attempts to make it less sticky in the nineteenth century varied, but often involved force (Thompson 1963).

[11] Nurkse observed of the period after the Gold Standard, before the Bretton Woods regime that: 'If there is anything that the interwar period has clearly demonstrated, it is that paper currency exchanges cannot be left free to fluctuate from day to day under the influence of market supply and demand' (cited in Gosh *et al.* 2002: 19).

The rise of the national economy as a discrete unit of accumulation and object of national policy, to provide social supports and infrastructure, gradually became incompatible with privileging the stability and scale of the global financial system. Over the next two decades, the Gold Standard steadily unravelled and capital controls (restrictions on the cross-border movement of credit and investment) were increasingly introduced by nation states to provide national insulation from the vicissitudes of globally volatile markets. The era of the Gold Standard was over, although the formation of a new global monetary regime awaited decisive and generally internationally consistent and agreed upon national choices within the policy trilemma.

With the demise of gold as an inherently valued commodity money, there was a range of attempts to re-configure an alternative commodity basis to global finance. One such proposal, which received notable interest, was for global money to be backed by a basket of commodities instead of by gold (Frank D. Graham 1941, 1944; Benjamin Graham 1944).[12] Under this plan, the basket, including upwards of 20 basic commodities, would ensure a degree of stability in the underlying value of money, with stockpiles of storable commodities substituting for stockpiles of gold. This new commodity backing to money was thought to have the added advantage of being useful in times of social hardship, by offering the capacity of running down stockpiles and building them up later.

In the twenty-first century, such a proposal might be thought at best quaint but irrelevant. But in the late 1930s and 1940s, it brought forward significant debate. Divided opinion over the proposal was revealing, for it shows the stark choice between the options of a state-guaranteed basis to a money anchor or a commodity basis. Those who wanted to retain floating exchange rates and keep monetary controls out of the hands of the state, lest they be directed to social programmes or other special interests, were generally supportive of this revised commodity money, at least in principle (Hayek 1943; Friedman 1951). Conversely, those, such as Keynes (1938), who were advocating a central role for the state in building social programmes (requiring fixed exchange rates and capital controls), were strongly opposed.[13] History shows that

---

[12] For a selection of contributions to this debate, see Schwartz 1992. For a full bibliography, see http://www.bufferstock.org/biblio.htm#graham.

[13] Keynes' concern was that the commodity reserve currency, as was also the case with the Gold Standard, would 'confine the natural tendency of wages to rise beyond the limit set by the volume of money'; that is, it would restrict the capacity of nation states to regulate for full employment and

the latter position dominated the global monetary arrangements after the Second World War.

The Bretton Woods regime

With the re-constitution of the global financial system at the end of the Second World War, the new goal was economic certainty and stability and the asserted agenda was nation-centred accumulation, with open international trade gradually being re-established. This regime allowed for the privileging of social programmes and full employment, funded by high (and managed) levels of economic growth. In simple terms, we can associate this with the rise of 'Keynesianism'.[14]

The Bretton Woods Agreement, negotiated principally between Britain and the United States, set the terms for the post-war international financial system that operated from 1944 to 1971. As with the Gold Standard, exchange rates would be stable. However, stability would come not so much because the international flow of money (gold) to settle international debts guaranteed stability, but because nation states would target stability as a policy objective. In the face of external imbalance, the state could invoke fiscal and monetary policies to adjust international financial flows in support 'its' exchange rate. If the imbalance became irretrievable, the state (except perhaps the US state) could announce an adjusted currency value, but such an announcement reflected badly on national policy makers.

In the context of the policy trilemma, with the two policy priorities being stability (of investment, growth and exchange rates) and security (including of living standards) the policy choice required that large-scale capital flows had to be curtailed. Keynes had urged that, 'control over capital movements, both inward and outward, should be a permanent feature of the postwar system' (Keynes 1943a: 185).[15] While labour was the swing mechanism of national economic adjustment under the Gold

---

growth. Indeed, Keynes was opposed to any international monetary agreement that would undermine the autonomy of national governments to manage their own monetary affairs. Thus, as Bernstein notes, the Bretton Woods agreement, 'was intended to provide exchange stability without the rigidity of the gold standard' (cited in McKinnon 1993).

[14] See Radice (1988) for an excellent summary of Keynes' privileging of national over global agendas, especially in relation to money.

[15] Keynes also felt that freedom of capital movements had been an essential part of the old laissez faire (1943b: 185).

Standard, under Bretton Woods the swing mechanism was to be the international movement of capital.

In general, nation-state policies restricted but never blocked entirely the international flow of capital.[16] Some state-approved direct investment and accommodating portfolio and debt flows were even encouraged. Accordingly, national economic policy could target national growth and distribution policy and, by regulating capital flows, secure a stable currency exchange rate (Helleiner 1994). The state aspired to maintaining 'internal and external balance', as it came to be called.[17]

But what was to be the global currency? The Bretton Woods Agreement saw the US dollar as the global trading currency,[18] with the dollar convertible to gold at a rate of $35 per ounce. Other national currencies fixed to the US dollar. Thus there was a commodity backing to global money, but it was a token, symbolic backing: gold itself was effectively 'de-monetised'. The strength of the global financial system lay more in the power of the US economy and the US state within the global economy than in the gold held in the vaults at Fort Knox.

The US dollar-as-global-currency had a certain flexibility and adaptability not possessed by gold.[19] For instance, the US dollar played what is known as a 'vehicle' currency role, allowing parties in different countries to use the dollar to denominate commodity trade even when neither party had any final use for US dollars. Indeed, the status of gold within the new, post-war, money system was contested. Neither Britain nor the United States wanted any sort of return to a Gold Standard, but Britain did not want the US dollar alone to be the global currency,[20] and

---

[16] Nor was it entirely necessary for total control of capital flows, despite Keynes musing on postal censorship. What was critical was that, to paraphrase McKinnon (1993), national capital markets needed to be 'segmented' enough so that macroeconomic policy autonomy (*viz.* control over domestic interest rates) could be pursued.

[17] Some of the key works here are Meade (1948 and 1949), Johnson (1977), Mundell (1962), and Nurkse (1944).

[18] It should not be forgotten how quickly the US dollar rose to pre-eminent global status. According to Broz (1999), as late as 1914, before the formation of the US central bank (the Federal Reserve), the United States was the only major trading country whose currency did not function as an international currency. This he attributes to the fact that domestically the US financial system was highly unstable and volatile.

[19] Hicks (1967) for instance noted that during the 1950s and 1960s the US dollar provided the global economy with alternative secondary liquidity.

[20] Keynes, the leading British negotiator at the Bretton Woods conference, had been quite ambiguous in his attitude to gold in the post-war money system.

the US wanted to utilise the significance of its huge gold reserves. Moreover, given that the world had for so long looked to gold as the major international currency, the thought of administering an international financial system with no gold backing was simply unconscionable. So until 1971 global finance stayed with a form of (passive) commodity-backed money.

But the Bretton Woods Agreement, and the national policies that supported it, were being challenged from the outset – indeed, the Agreement itself reflected the challenge.[21] Within the policy trilemma, the Bretton Woods Agreement worked in providing national social policy agendas and stable exchange rates only so long as the proclivity of capital to expand could be contained mainly to within national borders or directed through international trade. Yet the momentum of capital to expand internationally had not evaporated in 1944, and there was continual pressure on nation states, especially from financial institutions, to facilitate this expansion.

Indeed, the period after 1944 did not see rigid adherence to policies that precluded international capital flows. Amongst others, Eichengreen and Sussman (2000: 31) emphasise that steadily during the 1950s and especially the 1960s virtually all central banks undertook regulatory reforms that enabled the growth of international financial and investment flows and saw the opening up of global wholesale (merchant) banking.

In part, this could be seen as a problem of national imbalances. Growing government fiscal and national balance of payments imbalances created tensions in international payments systems, tensions, which also began to be absorbed in emerging international financial markets (Mendelsohn 1980). The US dollar's role as a 'vehicle' currency started to expand rapidly within these emerging international financial markets, diminishing the association between the US economy and the US dollar.

While he was critical of the theoretical status of gold as money, in his plan for an International Clearing Union, which he started to develop in 1940, he was rather supportive of the status of gold, claiming that, in his proposal, 'the position of gold would be substantially unchanged'. In particular, he emphasised gold's 'psychological value'. His proposed new international bank money was to be defined in terms of a weight of gold, but it would not be convertible into gold (1980: 85, 95, 183).

[21] See Helleiner (1994: esp. 44–50) for a summary of the objections of New York bankers to capital controls and the pressures they brought to the Bretton Woods negotiations, including the effective influence they exerted over the US negotiator at Bretton Woods, Harry Dexter White.

In part also the problem was that governments started to add (or accommodate) the third policy leg of the trilemma. Along with stable exchange rates and policies to support living standards, governments and central banks started to meet the demands of capital for international expansion and to facilitate an increasing scale of international capital flows. As companies began to expand their activities on an increasingly international scale (initially mainly from the United States but then from Europe and other nation states as well), so too did banks.[22] Central here was that a global pool of money balances emerged. They came to be called Eurodollar markets because of their initial location and the fact that the financing was done mostly in US dollar denominated forms. These supra-national money markets for dollar deposits began with the dollar reserves of Soviet-bloc countries and the Chinese government in the 1950s.

One of the initial attractions of Euromarkets to depositors was that they permitted anonymity. The communist governments were keen to disguise and safeguard their loanable reserves from US government sanctions, and placed them with banks in Western Europe to avoid possible confiscation by US authorities. But anonymity was also appealing to 'western' corporations and financial institutions trying to avoid constraints on international capital transactions.

The Eurodollar market began to be used by corporations mainly as an alternative source of cheap and large volume finance, offering interest rates and exchange rates that differed from those under national regulation. Initially, this market was attractive to corporations as a means of trade financing, and later of investment financing. These uses were accentuated in the mid-1960s by attempts by the United States, and later British and German, governments to regulate international capital flows as part of policies to deal with balance of payments imbalances.[23] The Eurofinance market provided sources of credit outside the jurisdiction of those controls, and it emerged as a major international money market, characterised by inter-bank transactions.[24]

---

[22] Multinational firms began to expand offshore, and banks were being pulled into international markets to continue their relationships with key clients.

[23] For the United States, restrictions on capital outflows in the mid-1960s were integral to defending the US dollar/gold parity.

[24] The Euromarkets grew in size from about $20 billion in the mid-1960s to $2,600 billion by the mid-1980s, an annual compound rate of growth of more than 25 per cent (Bryant, cited in Battilossi 2000). Whitman (1974: 556–8) reports that, at the end of 1973, total foreign claims on US residents, both public and private, amounted to slightly more than $90 billion. At that time, the net size

It is at this point that that financial derivatives began to play an important role, not yet in a capacity recognisable as money, but rather for their ability to provide opportunities for regulatory arbitrage – to assist banks and corporations to avoid government controls over capital movement. In the early phase of derivative growth, this enabled, for instance, US dollar-denominated financial claims to be effectively converted into a British pound debt, so that cross-border capital controls could be sidestepped.

But while these developments were outside the formal terms of the Bretton Woods Agreement, they were not eschewed by nation states or their central banks.[25] Indeed, governments became directly involved. Euromarkets were increasingly being utilised by other governments in deficit countries as a cheap source of funds. Moreover, from early on, central banks began to trade in Eurodollar markets as part of their domestic monetary policy, and attempted to influence their structure and direction.

The contradiction here was that Eurodollar markets were an effective means for national governments and their central banks to affect both fiscal and monetary policy, but the overall effect was to undermine the capacity of national monetary policy to deliver its commitments. This showed up most emphatically in the United States, because it was the currency tied directly to gold.

In the face of increasing global capital mobility, the US Federal Reserve had less and less capacity to control either domestic monetary policy or anchor global prices.[26] On the one hand, the US state could pump

of the Eurocurrency market was estimated to be $155 billion, of which almost three quarters, or $112 billion, was denominated in Eurodollars. To put this figure into perspective, Eurodollars were not counted in the money supply of any country but were by then already larger than the money supply of any country except the United States (Whitman 1974). Little wonder then that Podolski considered the development of Euro markets to be a revolution with an impact 'comparable to that of coke smelting in the development of iron and steel, the steam engine in the development of railways, and the computer in information processing' (cited in Battilossi 2000: 160). The origins of the Euro markets are discussed variously in Dufey and Giddy (1978) and Battilossi (2000). For the timing of key innovations in financial markets, see Oxelheim and Rafferty (2003).

[25] See Burn (1999) for an excellent analysis of the development of Eurofinance markets within the City of London in the 1950s.

[26] Cagan and Schwartz (1975) observed that the efficacy of using monetary policy as a tool to stabilise an economy had been the subject of on-going debate from at least the 1940s. One strand of this debate concerned whether financial innovation tended to produce money substitutes, which in turn affected the stability

US dollars into the rest of the world with the imprimatur of gold. On the other hand, it had to defend the integrity of the US dollar even though it was being traded increasingly extensively beyond the regulatory jurisdiction of the Federal Reserve.[27] The effect of global financial expansion was to create US dollar denominated claims that were challenging the convertibility of US dollars to gold at $35 per ounce. The exchange rate regime was becoming unsustainable, and the weak link was not the general stability of national currency exchange rates, but the rate of exchange between the US dollar and gold.[28]

In effect, global expansion had challenged the official balance in the policy trilemma, and policy became unstable and unsustainable. With the development of capital mobility, one of the other objectives – labour's standard of living or stable exchange rates – had to be sacrificed. The most immediate policy objective under threat was stable exchange rates, and the most critical of these was the rate of conversion between the US dollar and gold. This was the first policy to give way.

When President Nixon announced the devaluation of the US dollar in September 1971, the Bretton Woods Agreement was effectively over.

of monetary aggregates. The Radcliffe Report in Britain in 1959, for instance, found that the growth of these money substitutes was impairing monetary policy. As Cagan and Schwartz put it, Radcliffe 'viewed monetary policy as impotent, (when) submerged in a sea of liquidity' (1975: 138). Cagan and Schwartz themselves found that while the growth of money substitutes could be verified, the interest rate sensitivity of money demand had actually declined. Their findings of course bolstered the case for the on-going importance of monetary policy rather than, say, fiscal policy, but the fact that the stability of national money supply was already an empirical issue from the 1950s is surely instructive.

[27] It is something of an irony, therefore, that central banks have emerged as the pre-eminent national regulatory institution. At this time, there was widespread criticism of central bank capacities and it seemed anything but pre-ordained. Harry Johnson, for instance, openly contemplated an increased role for fiscal policy as a counter-cyclical device, but noted that for this to occur, it would require 'either a surrender of some congressional control over the taxing power or a revolutionary change in the methods by which Congress conducts fiscal business' (1970: 640). Johnson thought that the former was the more feasible.

[28] The judgement that the global role of the US dollar under Bretton Woods was not sustainable was not only made in retrospect, but was being argued from the 1950s. See for instance the work of Triffin (1960) and Machlup (1964) who, concerned with the limitations of gold (at least its supply), discussed the importance of the dollar as a way of providing 'secondary liquidity' to international payments, in addition to gold. In the mid-1960s, as early signs of the fragility of the Bretton Woods regime became apparent, the proposal of an international commodity reserve currency again emerged, albeit without significant impact. See Hart *et al.* 1963 and Grubel 1966.

The US devaluation amounted to all other currencies being devalued against gold by a decree from the US state, so there was an immediate termination to a gold-backed guarantee in the international financial system. The hegemony of the US dollar as the world's leading currency survived that rupture; the status of gold did not. Accordingly, the Bretton Woods Agreement ended via a global monetary crisis and the period after 1971 was one of volatile exchange rates as nation states sought to reconcile the protection of labour's living standards with growing international flows of capital.

With the suspension of dollar–gold convertibility, the emerging global financial system began a transition without any clearly defined rules (Whitman 1974). Within eighteen months of the Nixon Government's severing the ties of the US dollar to gold, the Pound Sterling, the Japanese Yen and the combined currencies of the European Union were all in free float. For other countries, the short-term policy answer was to stay roughly attached to the US dollar, or another leading currency, or to a basket of leading currencies. Exchange rates were now the swing mechanism of national adjustment.

After Bretton Woods: the return to floating exchange rates

The termination of Bretton Woods, while ignominious for US monetary authorities and a shock to the political and economic world at the time, was the necessary pre-condition for the massive growth in international trade and investment that followed in the 1970s and 1980s. For the global financial system to develop, it had to throw off the shackles of gold.

But a new financial regime did not emerge, fully developed, from the crisis of the Bretton Woods Agreement. The new regime that would eventually develop was not an invention of the regulatory authorities awaiting its time, or even of inspired market processes, but had to evolve out of market and nation-state practices, to meet the needs of those who use these markets. Accordingly, the decade and some after 1971 lacked financial stability and a clear global financial framework.

For a period, states sought to combine all three components of the trilemma. In the industrialised countries social and labour market policies continued to protect standards of living, and capital flows continued to grow. Indeed, states themselves were becoming increasing players in global capital markets as they sought to reconcile these irreconcilable objectives. Stefan Mendelsohn (1980: 5), who had traded in the Euromarkets before becoming a *Financial Times* journalist noted of the late 1970s:

> The greater part of the market's liabilities ... consist of funds deposited in Western banks by the governments and official agencies of surplus countries and even larger part of the market's assets consist of money lent to the governments and agencies of deficit countries.

Exchange rates too remained the object of policy. For the leading currencies (the Dollar, Deutsch Mark and Yen), there were short-lived, ad-hoc plans for mutually arranged currency realignments.[29] They failed to deliver stability for more than a brief period and, in each country, the domestic policies required to support the alignments met with large resistance.

With high capital flows now 'locked in', nation states (and especially the leading industrial nations) faced a choice: volatile exchange rates or protection of labour's living standards. Highly volatile and unpredictable exchange rates were seen to be incompatible with stable growth in international accumulation. Exchange rates needed to stabilise. In the context of the policy trilemma, the pursuit of (relatively) stable exchange rates along with high levels of capital mobility required that the other policy objective – labour's standard of living – be systematically subordinated to the goals of global financial stability.

Events in the United States were critical. The so-called Volcker shock of 1979–82 was vital to the on-going global hegemony of the US dollar and the stability of global finance generally. While Nixon had sacrificed the global role of the dollar for domestic agendas, Paul Volcker, as Governor of the US Federal Reserve, sought to reverse that effect. He introduced an era of fiscal and monetary austerity (interest rate hikes, and inflation targeting), which asserted anti-inflationary policy above all other national economic policy agendas. Part of this also was an assault on organised labour, to ensure that labour costs would cease to be a source of future inflation. Indeed Volcker later contended that 'the most important single action of the administration in helping the anti-inflation fight was defeating the air traffic controllers strike'

---

[29] Reference here is to such arrangements as the Plaza Agreement and the Louvre Accord, where the central banks of the G3 countries (Germany, Japan and the United States) met openly to negotiate sustainable exchange rates (or at least exchange rate target zones), and occasionally intervened openly in currency markets in concert to reverse short run misalignments. It also refers to the general culture of the early 1980s of international attempts at negotiation of exchange rates between the leading industrial countries (see for instance McKinnon 1993).

(cited in Panitch and Gindin 2004; quoted from Taylor 1995: 778, but see also Volcker 2000).[30]

The intention (and the effect) was to sacrifice domestic growth and living standards so that a stable (i.e. non-inflationary) US dollar could be asserted as the unassailable anchor to global money markets (Volcker and Gyohten 1992). Indeed, Volcker himself contended that the Federal Reserve's anti-inflation policy took on a 'role in stabilising expectations [that] was once the function of the gold standard, the doctrine of annual balanced budget, and fixed exchange rates' (quoted in Johnson 1998: 178).[31]

'Deregulation', 'Thatcherism', 'Reaganomics', 'neoliberalism' and all those other 1980s neologisms that depicted the stripping back of the welfare state, assaults on minimum wages, on employment security and on the power of organised labour, and the increasing autonomy of national monetary policy from democratic pressure, are directly linked to this imperative. These general changes in the nation state in the late twentieth century are now well known, and need no re-telling here. The simple point is that what is called 'deregulation' and 'neoliberalism' has at its core not simply an ascendant ideology of laissez faire (indeed,

---

[30] Further, Panitch and Gindin (2004) note that, on the insistence of Congress, Volcker himself represented the US state in Chrysler's banckruptcy proceedings and that it was he who negotiated with the United Auto Workers, then America's most powerful union, to secure the wage cuts and out-sourcing that the state required before granting Chrysler a bail-out loan.

[31] In an interview with the American broadcasting network PBS in September 2000, Paul Volcker (2000) also said that, as Governor of the Federal Reserve, his actions were geared towards America's international responsibilities:

[1]f we weren't strong economically, we weren't going to be able to carry out what I saw as reasonable responsibilities in the world ... and if anybody was going to deal with this it was going to have to be the Federal Reserve. ... One of the major factors in turning the tide on the inflationary situation was the (air traffic) controller's strike, because here, for the first time, it wasn't really a fight about wages; it was a fight about working conditions. It was directly a wage problem, but the controllers were government employees, and the government didn't back down. And he (Reagan) stood there and said 'If you're going to go on strike, you're going to lose your job, and we'll make DO without you'.

That had a profound effect on the aggressiveness of labor at that time, in the midst of this inflationary problem and other economic problems. I am told that the administration pretty much took off the shelf plans that had been developed in the Carter administration, but whether the Carter administration ever would have done it is the open question. That was something of a watershed.

Thatcher and Reagan were never laissez faire in their policies, especially but not only in their foreign policy) but also the subordination of labour's living standards to the needs of stable global capital flows.

Of course, it was not usually explained to labour in those terms;[32] nor was it rationalised by economists in those terms, as we will discuss shortly.[33] It has almost without exception always been explained by appeal to nationalism: that *we* as a nation cannot live beyond *our* means by running fiscal deficits or importing more than *we* export; that *we* need labour market flexibility to ensure that *our* industries remain competitive and *our* economy competitive. But the result was the same: in the name of 'national competitiveness', a range of attempts were made to force labour to become the swing mechanism of national economic adjustment.[34]

Floating exchange rates then and now

Since the 1980s there has been a notional return to the same policy 'balance' as under the Gold Standard: large scale capital flows at (relatively) stable exchange rates, and with national labour – levels of public

---

[32] The Thatcher Government's assault on the coal miners, and Reagan's victory in the air traffic controllers' strike were an explicit part of union-breaking agendas, with stark messages for the rest of organised labour. The case for floating rates was actually made in economic terms at the time on the basis that exchange rate flexibility would insulate national economies from foreign disturbances (such as inflation), while freeing monetary policy for domestic goals (Obstfeld 1985; Hefeker 2000). Krugman (1999) recently observed however that the US Federal Reserve a decade or so later has become more and more explicit about the role of the state in disciplining labour. He cited a speech that Fed Chairman Greenspan gave to a business lunch in 1999, where he warned that 'labor market conditions can become so tight that the rise in nominal wages will start increasingly outpacing the gains in labor productivity'.

[33] Krugman (1999) interpreted this to mean that

[W]orkers who know that jobs are plentiful will get big raises. And that, Greenspan implied, would be very bad thing. A market economy ... requires that a certain number of people who want to work be unable to find jobs so that their example will discipline the wage demands of those who are already employed. Greenspan, to his credit, tells the truth about what he does, but until now, he has done it in a way that only the cognoscenti can understand. Well, now he has said it clearly. But is America ready to hear it?

[34] We have made the argument elsewhere in greater detail that 'national competitiveness' was used to subordinate labour to capital on a global scale. See Bryan 1995 chs 2 and 3 and, in the context of Australia, Bryan and Rafferty 1999 chs 3 and 4.

consumption and wages relative to productivity – as the swing mechanism of national adjustment. The parallels with the Gold Standard are important, although we are not seeing a direct replication of that earlier regime. Certainly, high levels of capital flows are a close parallel. But to seek to draw too close an analogy between nineteenth-century and twenty-first-century capital flows is inappropriate. Ratios of global capital flow to production, which are widespread in the 'globalisation' literature, tell little about the differing role (and forms) of capital flows in the two periods. But few would disagree that in both periods, domestic agendas have been substantially subordinated to the facilitation of these global flows.

But the differences should also be noted. Under the Gold Standard, labour's role as the swing mechanism was, in effect, automatic. With all countries using gold as both a domestic monetary anchor and trading currency, exchange rate stability was not an issue. Moreover, there were automatic domestic price adjustment mechanisms under that regime that came from cross-national gold flows to settle trade balances. Trade deficits led to an outflow of gold and falling domestic prices. Falling nominal and, via domestic contraction, real wages were the direct consequence.

Today, neither exchange rates nor wages adjust as precisely as under the classical Gold Standard. Today, exchange rate stability is by no means guaranteed, despite the anticipation of the advocates of 'deregulation', and exchange rates are sometimes quite volatile.[35] So in contrast with the Gold Standard, exchange rates are not a systematic mechanism of national economic adjustment: countries retain current account surpluses and deficits for long periods without the exchange rate moving systematically to secure 'balance'. What constitutes acceptably stable exchange rates is therefore a more fluid notion than applied under the Gold Standard. Indeed, current exchange rates are not as volatile as might appear. Standard data on volatility refer to spot prices. Exchange rate derivatives exist precisely to hedge against such volatility. Exchange rates as experienced by individual capitals (i.e. adjusted for hedging) will show much gentler trends than is indicated by spot rates, though still not the rigid stability of the Gold Standard.

---

[35] Obstfeld (1985) concluded that the much-touted insulating properties of floating exchange rates turned out to be quite exaggerated to say the least. This has led many smaller developing countries to what has become known as a 'fear of floating' (Calvo and Reinhart 2002).

Similarly, labour's role as the swing mechanism of national adjustment is neither as automatic nor as nation-wide as under the Gold Standard. For the latter we saw automatic wage adjustment as a more or less direct corollary of the impact of international gold flows on the national price level, and the absence of many wider democratic institutional defences. Today, at least in the advanced capitalist countries, adult electoral franchise and trade unions, wage norms and state legislation on employment conditions continue to mediate the connection between labour's living standards and the conditions of stable global capital flows.[36] Wage adjustments are not automatic.

Nonetheless, from the 1980s, there has been a universal trend for wages to be tied more closely to workplace productivity, at the same time as workplaces themselves are adjusting to engage in productivity competitiveness on a global scale. So while under the Gold Standard, adjustments were simply nation-wide, in the current era labour adjustments are also related to each capital's profitability.

As such, it is not exchange rates that are systematically adjusting to secure national economic stability in a global context, but labour's remuneration *relative to* its productivity. Hence, labour's role of the national swing mechanism of economic adjustment is not an argument of labour's immiseration (either at a national or global level) and falling wages. Rather it is that labour has to keep increasing its productivity to secure on-going globally competitive production. Productivity growth relative to the world market can support wage increases, but where labour productivity cannot secure globally competitive production, wages must fall to compensate for less-than-competitive productivity. It is not surprising, therefore, that so many central banks maintain a close watching brief on labour productivity, and use monetary policy in part to regulate it. A more detailed framework for explaining this competitive pressure is presented in Chapter 7.

---

[36] Obstfeld and Rogoff (1995) are clear about this also. They contend that the main reason exchange rate targeting has not been as binding as under the Gold Standard is not so much that it is technically impossible in a world of global capital markets, but that 'very few central banks will cling to an exchange-rate target without regard to what is happening in the rest of the economy. Domestic political realities simply will not allow it, even when agreements with foreign governments are at stake' (1995: 79). Thus they note that, for many economists, a key to exchange rate stability is to reform domestic monetary policy institutions, such as freeing central banks from democratic control.

The search for a fundamental value of global money

One further and critical point is highlighted by the contrast between floating exchange rates and high levels of capital flow under the Gold Standard and today. Under the Gold Standard, exchange rates floated with respect to gold, but gold itself was a stable, universally accepted monetary unit because of its intrinsic value as a precious metal. What is the new money unit, and how is it secured? What has replaced gold as the anchor of the international financial system?

Our answer is that derivatives have replaced gold as the anchor of the financial system. But that is not the conventional answer. The conventional answer is that exchange rates do not need an anchor. To get to the role of derivatives we must first see what happened to the conventional answer.

Friedman's rational speculation theory

With the decline of the Keynesian welfare state,[37] the new guru was Milton Friedman and his new orthodoxy was dual edged: his monetarist theory and his laissez faire ideology. For Friedman, they were linked via the role each ascribed to the state. His monetarist theory reasserted the nineteenth-century doctrine, which contended that changing the national supply of money does not manage real accumulation; it just impacts on price levels. Keynesian-style fiscal and monetary policies are, he contended, more likely to distort than to promote the rate of accumulation. Hence governments should confine themselves to simply supplying a quantity of money that would grow along with the market-driven growth in 'real' economic activity. Friedman's monetarism was adopted by a generation of policy makers bereft of solutions to the stagflation of the mid-1970s. In the process, there was a return to a fundamental juxtaposition of money and the 'real' economy.[38]

---

[37] Many would immediately respond at this point that post-war national policy was only loosely related to Keynes' edicts, so that if Keynesianism was not tested in the post-war period, nor was it defeated. Our use of the term here is, however, less technically precise than the interpretation that evokes such a response.

[38] While Friedman broke with the Keynesian notion of an active state role in managing accumulation, the quantity theory remains within an orbit of national policy and nationally centred accumulation, via its central notion of a *national* quantity of money. It was partly for this reason Hayek (1978) considered that both the Keynesians and Monetarists shared a basic macro approach to money. McKinnon (1981) makes a similar point about the shared macro approach of the

His laissez faire ideology morally privileged the rights of the individual over 'the tyranny of the state' and his technical economics sought to show that, within this moral code, markets are better allocators of resources than is the state. This provided a powerful 'economic' rationale for eradicating minimum wages and minimising state supports for living standards that were critical to the facilitation of global capital mobility with stable exchange rates.

The laissez faire ideology was also thought to provide the rationale for the determination of all prices, including financial asset prices and exchange rates. This role is critical, for if prices behaved the way Friedman's model predicted, there would indeed be no need for commodity money: asset prices, including exchange rates would be a direct reflection of real conditions in production ('fundamental values', as they were termed[39]), making any 'additional' money commodity superfluous.[40] In this way, money would be 'neutralised' as a source of price instability. Specifically in relation to exchange rates, the view was that flexibility would insulate national economies from foreign disturbances (such as inflation), freeing monetary policy for domestic goals.

Central here was Friedman's (1953) 'rational speculation' hypothesis. This hypothesis contends that markets, including financial markets, free of government intervention will systematically gravitate towards stable equilibria that reflect 'fundamental values'. In this gravitation of prices towards equilibrium, 'speculation' (the activity of rational arbitrageurs) is attributed a central and positive role. The theory argues that if a market price moves away from its 'fundamental' value, then

Keynesians and Monetarists. He observed at the time that, despite their often heated debates, 'neither school disputes the desirability of national autonomy in the field of macroeconomic policy: by implication, both tacitly accept the insular economy as a building block for their macroeconomic schema' (1981: 536).

[39] The concept of 'fundamentals' in relation to exchange rates was discussed briefly in Chapter 2, in the context of the relationship between derivatives and theories of value. The argument there was that even subjective theories of value (such as used in neoclassical economics) have recourse to basic notion of the 'appropriate' value for capital assets, including money. Their notion is that the market, if operating competitively and rationally, will spontaneously gravitate to 'fundamental value'.

[40] Friedman had, we noted earlier, supported the development of an alternative (to gold) commodity money rather than state-guaranteed money. As Friedmanism became the new 'answer' to domestic monetary policy in the 1970s via the notion of national money supply targeting, this earlier support for a new form of physical commodity money fell from significance.

speculators will act to bring it back. Successful speculators will be those who know the fundamental value and position themselves in the market accordingly: they will sell when the price is above fundamental value, pushing the price down, and buy when it is below, pushing the price up. Speculators who do not know the fundamental value, and 'bet' the wrong way will make losses, and, if this continues, will go out of business.

This argument was constructed around rational, maximising individuals participating in markets, which are perfect in every respect except information (speculators gamble on what the value of an asset 'really' is). As tends to happen when assumptions of a model are both hypothetical and rigid, there was a tautology that drove the argument: if markets are in balance, they must reflect 'fundamental' value because, with rational agents, if they do not reflect fundamental value, they would not be in balance! As a corollary, agents who drew a market away from equilibrium could be simply damned as 'irrational', and appropriately punished for their irrationality by making losses.[41]

Around this simple, technical proposition developed an enormous policy wave advocating financial markets (and especially foreign exchange markets) be left to 'market forces' with minimal regulation. Accordingly, global financial markets do not need a formal unit of value: all they needed is relative prices and equilibrating mechanisms.

The problem is that empirical evidence has found no clear relationship between prices and fundamental values in the markets for financial assets. This evidence is critical, for it points inexorably towards the necessity for some 'real' anchor to global finance other than the contrived concept of 'fundamental value': something that would play a role akin to that of gold 100 years ago. In the failure of asset prices to reflect 'fundamentals', the role of derivatives as 'proxy fundamentals' became critical.

Evidence of 'the fundamentals': asset pricing and exchange rate theories

Theories of asset pricing confront directly the question of whether prices reflect 'real', 'fundamental' values. In general, asset-pricing theories

---

[41] McKinnon (1981: 555) argues that most critics of the rational speculation hypothesis of exchange rate determination at the time implicitly accepted the premise of the insular national economy, but attacked the notion that all private speculation was naturally stabilising. In monetary policy terms, therefore, both implicitly or explicitly presumed 'that the demand for each national money is stable and not much influenced by events in the foreign exchange market'.

have been advanced in two broad directions. One approach seeks to determine whether asset prices reflect the capitalised value of future earnings (Gordon 1962; Donaldson and Kamstra 1996; Kamstra 2001). This approach seeks to establish asset prices directly on the basis of 'fundamental' values.

The second approach proceeds on the basis of a more indirect or even agnostic approach to valuation. Instead, it considers markets as information processing institutions, and suggests that, in 'efficient' markets, prices will reflect all relevant information and quickly adapt to the arrival of new information. The efficient markets hypothesis (EMH), as it is known, suggests that in such efficient markets investors cannot make above average returns in the long run on the basis of any generally available information. The implication then is that if above average profits cannot be made by trading, prices must be close to their fundamental values.

While the EMH is not formally an asset-pricing model, its link to asset pricing is two-fold. First, it is implicit in the model that efficient prices reflect fundamental values[42] and, second, when asset prices diverge from fundamentals, it predicts that arbitrage (or what Friedman referred to as rational speculation) would act to pull prices back to fundamentals.

In the 1960s and 1970s, the notion that economic fundamentals drive prices, and that prices in turn reflect all available information seemed increasingly secure as economic doctrine. By the late-1970s a prominent finance theorist was even moved to conclude that no other proposition in economics was supported by such solid empirical evidence as the EMH (Jensen 1978). But this confidence has proven to be quite illusory. Both the Gordon model of fundamental valuation and the notion that markets accurately reflect all available information have been undermined by developments in actual market behaviour over the last 30 years.

Two developments serve to highlight this challenge to fundamental notions of asset prices and any economic notion of efficiency. The first is the growth in the volatility of asset prices (Edey and Hyvbig 1995). More disturbingly still, the pattern of this volatility has been found to be

---

[42] The implicit link between efficient prices and fundamentals is sometimes made explicit. Even Fama (1965), for instance, has said that, 'in an efficient market, at any point in time the actual price of a security will be a good estimate of its intrinsic value'. See however Beechey *et al.* (2000) for the case that efficient markets and asset pricing are related but distinct concepts.

incompatible with any meaningful understanding of fundamentals (LeRoy and Porter 1981; Shiller 1981; Hodrick 1990).

The second empirical observation is that asset prices may be misaligned for extended periods even in highly liquid markets (Summers 1986; Schleifer and Summers 1990; Haugen 1995), and that speculators may not always be able to act to bring prices towards their 'fundamentals' (Pontiff 1997; Schleifer and Vishny 1997).

The evidence that asset prices have been more volatile than could be justified by any fundamentals (Shiller 1991), and that they may diverge from fundamentals for long periods (Summers 1986; Haugen 1995; Schleifer and Summers 1990) has been damaging to the theoretical integrity and coherence of finance theory. And the fact that asset prices have been found to deviate from fundamentals has also been a challenge to which financial theory has devoted much time. The issue remains on-going.

But perhaps more corrosive still has been the evidence that theories of the international determination of currency prices (exchange rates) have also been undermined by the behaviour of foreign exchange markets. In other words, the relative price of the asset money, that is used to measure all other asset prices, has been no more linked to fundamentals than have other asset prices.

Floating exchange rates were expected to encourage real exchange rates to move towards some sustainable fundamental level (Williamson 1983; Obstfeld 1985).[43] But exchange rates have also proven to be quite unstable and appear to move away from anything like fundamental prices for extended periods.[44] Obstfeld and Rogoff (1995: 73) recall the disappointment at the actual experience with floating rates, and its effect on exchange rate economics:

> When the postwar system of fixed exchange rates collapsed in the early '70s, few imagined just how volatile currency values would be

[43] Initially, these movements away from expected fundamentals were labelled 'misalignments', and were thought to be a product of a transitional or at least temporary nature.

[44] Obstfeld (1985) reported that 'short-term volatility of exchange rates, both in real and in nominal terms, has been one of the most striking features of the float'. He went on to argue that such volatility was to be expected in view of the exchange rate being the relative price of two assets, and with the phenomenal increase in international asset trade, capital account transactions now dominate exchange rate determination. But while there had been an increase in real exchange rate volatility, this volatility was somewhat less pronounced than in other asset markets such as stock markets. Edey and Hyvbig (1995) show that a similar pattern of exchange rate volatility continued into the 1990s.

in the ensuing floating rate era. Fewer still anticipated how difficult it would be to divine any systematic connection between exchange-rate movements and underlying changes in economic fundamentals, even at fairly long horizons.

By the early 1980s, Meese and Rogoff (1983) concluded that, during the floating rate period, no model of exchange rate determination could reliably out-perform a no-change forecast. That is, none of the models had any better predictive power than a random model, and were not even very good at explaining movements after the fact. Beechey *et al.* (2000: 19) summarise the findings of two decades of foreign exchange rate theory:

> Floating exchange rates are quite volatile, with two-year movements of about 10 to 15 percent. Economic fundamentals, however, explain almost none of these movements. ... No-one has yet been able to uncover economic fundamentals that can explain more than a modest fraction of year-to-year changes in exchange rates.

In summary, a problem of profound proportions has emerged: if monetary values do not closely correspond to 'real' production values, there are no clear guidelines for the prices at which financial (and non-financial) assets will trade. Neoclassical economists (and post-Keynesians) may construct behavioural stories of 'irrational agents' or 'rational bubbles'[45] to explain the non-correspondence and defend the explanatory power of their theories, but they provide little or no guide to actual pricing decisions that are taken in the market place, nor increasingly for the practice of monetary policy.

Accordingly, with no mechanisms to ensure a stable monetary unit on a global scale (stable exchange rates reflecting long-term 'fundamentals'), it cannot be said that 'floating exchange rates' replaced the need for a commodity basis to global money. Indeed, as Eatwell and Taylor (2000: 13) point out in relation to exchange rates, what 'real' national aggregates constitute the measure of national 'fundamentals' has changed over time. They concluded that what is considered fundamental at any point in time is, in part at least, a matter of fashion.[46] Accordingly, the practice

---

[45] See, for example, Meese (1986), Blanchard and Watson (1982) and Flood and Garber (1980).

[46] Eatwell and Taylor (2000: 13) give the example of the balance of payments current account, which was once considered a 'fundamental' determinant of exchange rates. National currencies were thought to be traded according to the nation's current account performance. But opinion has changed and today a current account deficit no longer produces the reaction it once did.

of financial markets themselves, where ideological debates about exchange rates, behavioural theories of market participants and the 'fundamentals' are of no practical import, the belief that markets gravitate systematically to 'fundamentals' is often not apparent.

Nor, as it turns out, is it necessary. The failure of the ideological alternative (that markets would reflect fundamental values if 'deregulated' to be free from government intervention) was not itself a crisis for capital. While scholars debated the underlying logic of financial markets, and ruminated on the non-adherence to 'fundamental value', the traders themselves kept trading at a rapidly growing rate. There was (and is) nothing unsettling about the contestability of value, except for adherents to mechanistic theories of value. In the market place, capital itself developed means to hedge against monetary instability and provide mechanisms for price certainty in international financial markets: they developed financial derivatives.

Friedman's theory was right, but for the wrong reason – the market has produced a degree of global monetary cohesion not because 'deregulated' exchange rates are stable and move rapidly to reflect 'fundamentals', but because the market has found it profitable to produce products to compensate (as it were) for the fact that they *don't* always reflect 'fundamentals'. To repeat a proposition from Chapter 2, derivatives turn the contestability of 'fundamental value' into a tradable commodity.

Thus it was, from the mid-1980s, as exchange rate agreements between the leading nations were abandoned, and exchange rates floated without global regulation, that financial derivatives emerged as the market's alternative to the ideology of the rule of 'the fundamentals'.

Derivatives anchoring the global financial system

By the 1980s, international capital mobility was accelerating and exchange rates were volatile. One national response, we saw earlier, was in terms of the policy trilemma: to invoke labour as the swing mechanism of national economic adjustment. But the global financial system required not just stable flows of existing forms of money, but a new, more flexible monetary unit. A single monetary unit, be it gold, or the US dollar backed by gold, was not able to meet the multiple and diverse needs of international finance, and floating exchange rates were not (and could not live) up to their theoretical promise as automatic stabilisers.

The central problem of the global financial system is commensuration: how, in the absence of a global value unit such as gold,[47] and stability in relative prices can one form of capital be exchanged for another [all others] at a rate that is predictable and sustainable? How can the market overall create relative prices that are systemically coherent without a single pricing anchor like gold, or a system of international fixed exchange rates like the Bretton Woods system?

The process of commensuration, in which spatial and temporal continuity in the measured value of capital is constructed, is the *raison d'être* for modern financial derivatives. Prices are anchored through the network of financial derivatives. And in so doing they help to provide continuity in the value of capital by trading a diverse range of contracts designed to specify or delimit the rate of conversion of one 'bit' of capital value (whether it be money or commodity and whatever its currency denomination and time specification) into another.

But derivatives do not move prices to stable equilibria – they are not an alternative means of establishing the so-called 'fundamentals' of global purchasing power parity or interest rate parity. Indeed they are predicated on the notion that there are no 'fundamentals' – all asset values have particular temporal and spatial determination, and prices are forever changing, and in unsystematic ways. It is not possible to reduce one locality to another, one time period to another or one form of capital to another; but their values can be, and are, mediated on a daily basis.

Derivatives have also transformed the way that the commensuration process occurs, and they do so in a way appropriate to contemporary international finance. Each derivative product is a package of conversion of one form of capital to another – whether this be a simple commodity futures contract or a complex conversion of a particular currency index to a particular stock market index. When all these products are taken together, they form a complex web of conversions, in which any 'bit' of capital, anywhere and with any time profile, can be measured against any other 'bit' of capital. They are not therefore a fixed single anchor, but a flexible series of many small 'floating' anchors. Critically, they can perform this function because they exist at the intersection

---

[47] It is argued elsewhere that globalised accumulation places an almost impossible burden upon a single commodity like gold, which in any case Adam Smith called so much 'dead capital'. So there is no notion here that financial derivatives are a sort of second best Gold Standard. Indeed, financial derivatives represent a highly developed form of money.

of money and commodities: derivatives themselves are money (they perform a money function in pricing) and commodities (they are traded products) at the same time.

In short, derivatives permit all forms of capital ('moneys' and 'commodities'), at all places and over time, to be commensurated, thereby effectively breaking down the differences between different forms of money (different currencies; different interest rate profiles) and between commodities and money. This new anchor for the global financial system does not rest on intrinsic value (like gold), or on state decree as it did under Bretton Woods. But without the backing of state decree, this new monetary system must be based in a commodity money. There is no logical alternative: money is either state money or commodity money. Derivatives, in their anchoring function for global finance, play the role of a commodity money. While commodity money is usually associated with emphasising the commodity characteristics of money (gold); derivatives also highlight the monetary characteristics of all commodities.[48]

It is this the capacity of derivatives to readily convert one form of money into another and a wide range of commodities into an even wider range of monetary units that is the contemporary financial function equivalent to that performed by gold under the Gold Standard. In terms of the policy trilemma, derivatives at once deliver a significant degree in stability of exchange rates (in a way that spot markets do not) and large-scale capital flows. Indeed, the two are now inextricably linked in a way they were not under the Gold Standard. The effect is to place pressure on labour as the inevitable swing mechanism of national adjustment.

We have already seen how this is playing out. The process of commensuration of capital on a global scale requires labour in each location to deliver 'competitive' rates of wages and productivity to ensure globally competitive rates of return on capital. This – not the value of capital, nor the value of money (both of which are now being resolved and reconciled in global derivative markets) – is the one

---

[48] Hayek, in making the case for private money, or what he termed the 'de-nationalisation' of money, made the point that there is no clear distinction between money and non-money, and, noting Machlup's observation that commodities have different degrees of money-ness, he preferred to say that some commodities or objects had 'currency'. Hicks also suggested that many commodities could be thought to play *partial* money functions. This is an issue we develop in the next two chapters.

available swing mechanism of national adjustment. This competitive process will be explored further in Chapter 7.

Conclusion

There are many monetary histories of the last 100 plus years that depict a shift from commodity money of the Gold Standard, through the post-war Bretton Woods Agreement in which the backing of gold was mostly symbolic, to the current system of deregulated global markets and free capital mobility. Our objective here has not been to retell that history in any detail, interesting as it is.[49] It has been to develop the argument that the world has not shifted steadily away from any anchor to the global financial system, as is commonly argued, but has moved towards a new foundation to global money: financial derivatives. This movement has not been a conscious policy of nation states or a global regulatory authority; it has been a movement created within the market; by capital for capital.

The development of a new anchor for global money has emerged as logical necessity. What is popularly called 'globalisation' places great demands on the international financial system. In the 'globalisation' of the nineteenth century, this demand was met by a truly global monetary unit: gold.[50] Its universal acceptability was based on its value as a precious metal. It was commodity money. But international finance in the 'globalisation' of the late twentieth century has no gold backing; it supposedly has no foundation at all. But a system of variable and at times volatile exchange rates cannot provide a global anchor or unit of value. The notion that money's value is ensured by the state is not sufficient when money must convert between national currencies, states may manipulate exchange rates for domestic policy purposes and, indeed, much trade in financial markets is beyond the jurisdiction of nation-state authorities. So without state guarantees or a single commodity base, the current foundation of the global value of money must be found in mechanisms generated by the global markets themselves.

Derivatives have thereby played a role that is parallel to that played by gold in the nineteenth century. They provide an anchor to the financial system – not a single anchor, but a network of anchors. While the state's monopoly money was gold (gold is a monetary unit designed by a state,

---

[49] But see, for instance, Cooper (1982), Solomon (1977) and McKinnon (1993).
[50] Here we are returning to the narrow requirements of the Gold Standard. The wider political and economic issues were discussed earlier in the chapter.

exercising a money monopoly) the market's monetary anchor is the system of financial derivatives (derivatives are a monetary unit designed by a multitude of self-interested individuals).

Derivatives are not as neat as gold, and are perhaps vulnerable to speculation in a way that gold was not, but they provide a flexibility to systems of commensuration that gold could never provide. And they provide a means for individual capitals to manage their exposure to financial instability and operate 'as if' the global financial system were stable. The current system based on derivatives as the anchor to the financial system therefore provides a flexibility more appropriate to a system of more explicitly globalised capital flows, where individual capitals are also differentially integrated in that circuit across space and time.

But in what sense do derivatives themselves constitute money? We have, to this point, really only asserted their status as a base or anchor for the global monetary and financial system, and the identification of derivatives as themselves money rests on rather different arguments. That is the issue of the next chapter.

6
New, Global, Capitalist Money

Financial derivatives are not usually seen as money. Often, they are not seen at all, but when they are, they are simply classified as financial assets and liabilities, and often as objects of speculation, somehow outside of 'money'. Presumably this is because money has become synonymous with nation-state money, and derivatives are certainly not that.

Yet nation-state money is surely the problem, albeit an unavoidable one, in globally integrated capital markets. Money circulates globally, but, in the absence of gold or some similar money unit, national currencies are the only extant monetary units of account. In order to circulate on a global scale, money has to keep converting between different national currencies, and facing the risk of unwelcome changes in the rate of conversion. The global money system thereby embodies implicit risks for participants. But these risks, while not entirely avoidable, are manageable. We saw in the previous chapter that derivatives perform this function: they unify the money system and, in the process, they are a form of asset holding and even a means of current and deferred payment. They are, in important respects, money.

Some questions require clarification. What sort of money might derivatives be, and where do derivatives fit into contemporary debates about money?

What is at issue?

Is the characterisation of financial derivatives as money any more than a semantic claim? After all, money is one of those nebulous categories that can be defined almost however we want it to be. Why would we want to fit derivatives into the category of 'money'?

The proposition developed here is that it is important to see financial derivatives as money for it gives new insight to the logic of money and its role in global accumulation as it is evolving in the twenty-first century. Many of the confusions about global money start to become clear (at least clearer) once we think of derivatives as a new form of money.

Others have already made propositions that point in this sort of direction. At a macro policy level, where there has been a convention of measuring national money supply, the BIS noted in the early 1980s that, in the face of on-going financial innovation, especially financial derivatives, definitions of money based on the degree of money-ness, or as means of payment for transactions, had become 'virtually insurmountable' (Akthar 1983; BIS 1984[1]). Pawley (1993) also noted that the distinguishing line between money and other financial instruments was fraught with difficulties, and with the growth of financial derivatives, that line was irretrievably blurred.

At a micro level of the individual firm or corporation, Perlod (1995) identified a distinctly money role of derivatives because they are changing the nature of the payments system for firms. The use of swaps in financing or futures in managing future purchases, for example, should be considered in some ways to be 'virtual' cash market transactions. Finally, and significantly, Telser (1986: 5) has suggested that '... the relation between monetary and real phenomena is isomorphic to the relation between a futures contract and the underlying asset'.[2]

It is not that derivatives themselves are new; indeed they are almost as old as money itself. But historically, their role has been marginal and isolated to particular products and localities. It is only in the last 20 years that they have developed a comprehensive monetary role, associated with the growth of financial (rather than commodity) derivatives. (Note that in the remainder of this chapter we will use the term 'derivative' to refer exclusively to financial derivatives.) As we saw in Chapter 3 in relation to the evolution of derivatives and Chapter 5 in relation to the global financial system, it is only in this recent time that there has

---

[1] For the BIS there were two specific problems of the time. One was defining and measuring national money supply in the context of financial innovation and internationalisation. The other was measuring means of payment where measures of derivative transactions on currencies exist alongside cash market transactions.

[2] Telser develops the correspondence between, say, borrowing and lending, and short-and-long hedging. He also argues that futures contracts correspond to bank notes as a sort of private money.

been the combination of both a regulatory environment that has facilitated the operation of global financial markets and a vacuum in the provision of a recognised, stable international trading and investment monetary unit.[3]

So there are two basic points at issue in constituting derivatives as money. First, derivatives are a new sort of money, directly appropriate to the specific conditions of capital accumulation in the current period. With derivatives, money itself comes to be the embodiment of capitalist competition because derivatives embody, in their composition, the competitive computation of relative values, including conversions across discrete, extant forms of money. So rather than being a passive instrument of competitive processes constituted outside the domain of money, derivatives as money internalise the competitive process. That gives a new, more dynamic (and ruthless) edge to capitalist competition. Derivatives are, in this sense, distinctly capitalist money, rather than just money within capitalism.

Second, derivatives constitute a private basis to money, and so challenge the long-held presumption that the integrity of money is based in the authority of nation states. For money to play the role described above, and cross different money forms (including currencies), it has had to come out from under the sanctity of nation states. Derivatives have not replaced national money; nor are derivatives devoid of a national dimension (they are, after all, denominated in national monetary units), but they have effectively transcended the national basis of contemporary money.

For established monetary theory, this casts a profound analytical problem. By convention, a money system can have two possible foundations that ensure its acceptability in the functions of means of exchange, store of value, etc. Either it must have some intrinsic value, which makes people happy to hold money in its own right, or it is token money, which must be backed by some recognised authority which guarantees the convertibility of monetary tokens into real assets. Invariably, this authority is understood as the nation state. Hence these alternative foundations can be understood as the difference between commodity money and state money.

---

[3] This stability does not come, as under the Gold Standard or the Bretton Woods fixed exchange rate system, via state guarantee. Indeed, derivatives are premised on the fact that macro price stability cannot exist in a globalised system of accumulation, when the relationship between different forms of capital is itself the most important requirement of commensuration.

So are derivatives-as-money to be seen as state money beyond the state, or commodity money independent of the state, or as something new: non-state, non-commodity money? The difficulty here is that money has multiple characteristics, and so appears compatible with diverse theories. Advocates of a state theory of money can point to the fact that all derivatives are denominated in particular national currencies (they are not issued in IBM dollars or a unit of currency invented by Chase Manhattan Bank, but US dollars and Japanese Yen). These advocates would contend that a derivative contract is trusted because there is trust in the states of the nominated currencies that appear in the contract.

A commodity money advocate could contend that it is not the nationality of the currency that provides backing to derivative contract: the derivative itself must be seen as a produced commodity, such as gold was a produced commodity money. Or they may argue that the backing of derivatives lies in the commercial integrity of the parties to the contract. It is belief that IBM and Chase Manhattan Bank are trustworthy counterparties (because of their asset backing) that gives agents trust in the purchase of IBM- or Chase-linked derivatives. And perhaps here we could ask whether this latter response constitutes a commodity basis to derivatives as money, or some new basis that can be thought of in terms of an emerging corporate money. Each of these interpretations could be forcefully argued.

We are reluctant to court this corporate money alternative. There are libertarian economists – as we shall see shortly – who have advocated the private issue of money, but it is entirely premature to couch derivatives in these terms. The nation state remains too central to money systems to suggest that their role as the guarantors of money tokens is being challenged by corporations.

Nor, we assert, is it satisfactory to pose financial derivatives simply as state money, for it strips the concept of state money of meaning. It suggests that any liquid asset denominated in a national currency rests on the guarantees of the state of that national currency, even if the state itself has no knowledge of, or regulatory capacity in relation to, that asset. Moreover, this interpretation seems at odds with the wider concern expressed by advocates of state money that assets such as derivatives have reached beyond the regulatory capacity of nation states. Indeed, for many, money's separation from state regulatory capacity and its global reach is the central characteristic of 'neoliberalism', and must be politically opposed (e.g. Duminil and Levy 2004). To call derivatives a form of state money in this context is reductionist and probably wishful thinking on the part of those who seek to keep the nation state at the centre of global finance.

Accordingly, with other possible explanations rejected, we look to financial derivatives as a form of commodity money. While derivatives may not be commodities in the usual sense of the term, they are a type of commodity (a meta-commodity if you will) that is produced to serve explicitly monetary functions. In this chapter, we show how derivatives provide this commodity basis to the international money system.

At this point, however, this is but an asserted argument. In building towards this proposition it is important to pass through some of the central current debates about money and especially state money, before building the conception of derivatives as global commodity money. Our focus here is not the neoclassicals, where the concept of money fails to generate significant debate, but the post-Keynesians and Marxists, where that debate is active. In particular, there are two (often related) conventions that must be challenged: the conception of money as a social relation, as the foundation of a theory of money in capitalism, and the pre-eminence of nation-state money. We will explore these in turn, before building an alternative explanation of derivative, commodity money.

Money as a social relation

There is not much common ground across the social sciences in the analysis of money. Perhaps the most general and important shared observation (with the notable exception of neoclassical economists) is the notion that money is a social relation (e.g., Simmel 1907; Schumpeter 1954; Wray 1999; Ingham 2000, 2004).

Money plays the role of a social nexus between strangers, but it also epitomises alienated social relations – the relations between people appearing as the relations between things. Here the emphasis is on two issues: the social power that money brings, and the trust that lies implicit within complex and temporally and spatially extended financial relations. Both of these have been addressed extensively.

Money as social power

Money as social power emphasises that those who hold money command resources. In its basic form, this is a power over distribution: the familiar argument that people with a lot of money get more than their share of resources. For Marxists, there is a particular focus on command over one particular resource: labour power. From this follows the proposition that command over labour power gives command over surplus value production, command over accumulation, and hence command over the reproduction of social power.

It is an important story, but it must be recalled that it is, in the first instance, a distributional story, in which the resource 'labour' is just a theoretical special case that invokes the sphere of production. And even within this special case, social power over labour is just as much a story of feudalism and of slavery as it is of capitalism: it does not explain a distinctly capitalist form of money. This is not a framing of money that will reveal the role of derivatives.

Money as trust

The second dimension of the social relations of money is trust.[4] Trust, it is said, is what makes money social. The issue of trust in relation to money is generally applied to both the domain of immediate exchange (that the physical money unit is convertible into 'real' goods and services) and the domain of credit (that the institutional money system will convert book entries into physical money).[5]

For the neoclassical economists, issues of trust in exchange are defined individually, but for virtually all other parts of the social sciences, the issue of trust and money is defined at a collective level. Following principally the seminal work of Georg Simmel, author of *The Philosophy of Money* (1907), the issue of trust is associated with the general, unifying, standardising dimensions of money. Exchange creates, in Simmel's terms, 'an inner bond between men – a society, in place of a mere collection of individuals' (1907: 175). For Simmel the principal relations of trust are associated with the credit system. Credit is not a distinctly capitalist relation, but it is clearly pervasive within capitalist accumulation.

But the limitation of 'trust' as the basis for a social theory of modern, capitalist money is that 'trust' is not distinctly centred on money (all arms-length transactions, and, in effect, all phases of accumulation, are contingent upon trust), and the trust dimension of money is not distinctly capitalist: relations of trust are implicit in exchange in mercantile and even feudal societies. While the expansion of the capitalist credit

---

[4] Aglietta (2002) provides a sweeping review of the history and future of money centred on the issue of trust.

[5] This latter domain should certainly be qualified: it is not just credit, but all non-cash forms of money that require trust. We are posing financial derivatives as a form of money, and these, like credit, require trust for their widespread acceptance. The point here is to challenge the association of trust exclusively with theories of credit money.

system no doubt made the relation of trust more complex and institutionalised, it did not create money as a distinctly capitalist social relation.

Moreover (and an issue on which we will expand shortly) relations of trust tend to be defined intra-nationally, and this is of limited value in exploring the social relations of globally circulating money. Since the end of the Gold Standard, money has always been denominated in national units, and the nation has generally been the territorial space within which collective trust in a money unit has been understood as implicit. In the current global economy, money continues to be a social relation (and express social power) but this social relation extends beyond the trust implicit in national territory, law and state.

Social relations beyond the nation

So what is the social relation embodied in money beyond the perceived national limits of trust and community?

Perhaps it is about those essentially territorial notions of trust stretched to an extra-territorial level. In particular, it could be about global trust in the integrity of the US dollar, as the world's major vehicle currency. But that would be to shut down the question, by invoking categories of a nation-centred analysis that are themselves under challenge by the global integration of financial markets. Money is not just inter-national (in the sense of national money systems that articulate with each other) and the integrity of a global money system cannot be reduced to the sum of national cultures of trust. When it crosses national borders, no nation state can guarantee its value. Global money has to rest on more than trust.

The argument we will develop later in this chapter is that derivatives bridge these different and variable national moneys and so add continuity to the global financial system. Where there cannot be trust that a dollar is a dollar is a dollar (because a dollar is not always 0.x of a pound or 1.x of a Euro), derivatives offer a form of conversion insurance. Importantly, this insurance is provided by the impersonal market, not by the state or nationalist cultural ties. So the association of trust with the state does not work for derivatives. They are forms of money designed precisely to transcend national territory and national state regulation (and hence nationally conceived trust) as a precondition for an effective global monetary system.

In this global context, we need to think about the role of money as more than means of exchange, or even credit. We need to think of the diverse roles money plays in international finance and investment and what they all have in common as an expression of social relations. That is, we need to constitute money as 'capital'. Here, issues of social power and trust are insufficient in constituting the global basis of money as capital.

Geoffrey Ingham (esp. 2004), a leading sociologist of money, refers to this role as 'socially constructed abstract value' (2002: 127).[6] It is an appropriate depiction, for the requirement of money in accumulation, as distinct from simply exchange, is that it is flexible – it can be stored, used in accounts and in exchange, and it can be systematically directed to a range of different investment opportunities. It must display generic (or abstract) qualities and capacities.

But what is the substance of this 'abstract value'; what makes it worthy of trust? For Ingham the explanation reverts to the nation state as the guarantor of money. By invoking the state as the bestower of value, Ingham, and other state money theorists have, however, made a critical leap in their argument. There is no necessary reason that it must be the state that bestows value to money and, as a historical proposition, it occludes the possibility that some other basis to value may be emerging. To explore this issue, we stay briefly with Ingham's notion of 'socially-constructed abstract value'. Ingham continues:

> In this conception [of socially-constructed abstract value], money, *regardless of its specific form or substance*, is always a 'token' claim on goods. (emphasis in original)

The problem here is that Ingham is conflating two meanings of the term 'token'. One equates 'token' with abstraction – that abstract money, stripped of its specific forms, must be a token because, by definition, it has no materiality. In this sense, Marx's abstract labour could be thought of as 'token' labour for the same reason. But the second concept of 'token' is specific to money. It contends that, to perform the role of money capital, and the diverse forms that this role implies, the money substance can have no necessary intrinsic value; no commodity basis. It is, in all of its specific forms, a 'mere' token, that is given social meaning only by state guarantee.

The two concepts of 'token' must be seen as quite different. We can accept the first, philosophical meaning – indeed, it is only via abstract money that all particular moneys can operate in a complementary way as 'money' (Fine and Lapavitsas 2000). But we do not accept the second,

---

[6] This concept is familiar to Marxism, but used by Ingham more broadly. Indeed, Ingham (2001) is rather critical of Marxist theories of money.

empirical meaning, which suggests that all specific, concrete moneys are 'mere' tokens, of no intrinsic value.

Empirically, though not in abstraction, the specific form of money *does* matter, because different money forms do money's work in different ways: different forms of money transmit social relations in different ways (just as different forms of labour express different social relations). In particular, what makes derivatives distinctive as a form of money-as-social relation is that they are, by their nature, the embodiment of competitive calculation: they are money that reflects the capacity of corporations for global calculation of the value of all their discrete assets and liabilities.

So in our conception of money as a social relation we can, indeed, recognise the role of trust (though noting trust in economic activity is not unique to the money dimension). We can also recognise the need for a money abstraction – something that all different forms of money have in common. But when these two are reconciled and brought to life by invoking the centrality of the nation state (there is collective trust in state-issued money, and state-issued money is mere token money), it is critical to challenge the implicit nationalism. This framing systematically precludes engagement with conceptions of money that are beyond the nation state, both geographically and administratively – except, that is, by framing this money as being hostile to national policy and untrustworthy.

But this problem is not just with social relation theories of money. It is also apparent with formal economics, especially Keynesian and post Keynesian theories of money, as we shall see. To conceive of derivatives as distinctly capitalist money, we must directly confront the analytical basis of state theories of money.

Money and the nation state: unstated Keynesian presumptions

The connection of money to the state is sometimes posed as explicit and conscious, but it often just appears within implicit nationalist assumptions about money. Once these assumptions have been taken on, analysis leads inexorably to state money, but without the assumptions themselves being scrutinised. We need to observe these assumptions in action to see how an engagement with derivatives as global money is so widely eschewed.

Any standard economics textbook will tell essentially the same simplified story of money as having three essential elements:

- First, money's 'invention' was based upon the impracticalities of direct barter in complex processes of exchange. The selected money must have the characteristics of portability, divisibility, homogeneity and indestructibility;

- Second, money must perform 3 functions: a medium of exchange, a store of value, and a unit of account (sometimes expanded to five, to include means of payment and standard of deferred payment), and
- Third, money can be defined differently according to degrees of liquidity (convertibility into cash).

To make matters confusing, each of the three elements can build quite different and potentially inconsistent explanations of money. When we consider the role of the state in each of these three elements of the money story, a number of points of contestation emerge. For the first element, does the state determine, secure and enforce the selection of the special 'item' to be money? For the second, does the state seek to enforce a monopoly over these functions as a means to manage the national economy? For the third, do less liquid forms of money undermine the state's capacity to determine the quantity and quality of money in circulation? There are no straightforward answers to these questions, for they form the core of a range of on-going debates within monetary theory. But within these debates we find a widespread presumption that money is national, in particular, because it emanates from the nation state. We will identify briefly the foundations of contemporary Keynesian theory in national money and state money before opening up the global dimension.

National money

The one-money-one-nation principle goes back at least to the formation of sovereign nation states and the Peace of Westphalia of 1648 (Cohen 1998 ch.1).[7] In its modern form, national money is associated, at least in the first instance, with Keynesian economics. Money in this Keynesian sense is national not (just) because it emanates from the nation state, but because it is nationally circulating money used for nation-building economic programmes.

Critical here is the capacity to separate the nation from international capital as the precondition for national economic management. Keynes stated adamantly that:

> Economic internationalism, embracing the free movement of capital and of loanable funds as well as of traded goods may condemn this

---

[7] Helleiner (2003) rightly warns that the territorial attachment of money has always been challenged. Reference to Westphalian money as uniquely national is an idealised image.

country for a generation to come to a much lower degree of material prosperity than could be attained under a different system. (1936: 349)

Key to a nation-centred economic prosperity was control over the national money supply so that the state could set a domestic rate of interest that meets the needs of national investment, not the needs of international currency stability:

> In my view the whole management of the domestic economy depends on being free to have the appropriate rate of interest without reference to the rate prevailing elsewhere in the world. Capital control is a corollary to this. (1943: 149)

In the absence of capital controls, money cannot be presumed to be either inherently national or a product of the state.

Hence the analytical framework of Keynesian money as nation state money has meaning only so long as there actually exist the institutional processes that create and sustain distinctly national money: policies that effectively secure capital controls that isolate the national money system from other, globally circulating money. We saw in Chapter 5 that such controls, including those authored in part by Keynes himself (the Bretton Woods Agreement), operated for less than three decades after the Second World War, and from the moment of their implementation they were far from absolute.

Historically, therefore, Keynesian national money was, from its inception, undermining its own conceptual foundations. Yet many contemporary analyses, which take Keynes' propositions as their point of departure, readily conflate their aspirations of discrete national money with current reality.[8] They theorise accumulation *as if* money were territorially defined and constrained (or that the absence of tight territorial boundaries is an aberration to be rectified by national policy). They are theorising how they would like money to be, not how it is. The overall effect is either the neglect of globally circulating finance and

---

[8] Friedman's monetarism utilised this same Keynesian conception of *national* money as subject to direct regulation by the state. His critique of Keynesianism was not its theory of money *per se*, but how money was used for policy purposes. Yet, at the same time, Friedman opposed capital controls and supported the free global mobility of money – which undermined any notion of 'national' money. Little surprise that his money supply targeting strategy, where central banks targeted various measure of money, supply of M1 or M3 did not work, for in the absence of capital controls (e.g. M1 and M3), ceased to be nation-specific.

the role of nationally designated currency circulating offshore, or the treatment of such money as exogenous, both theoretically and empirically, and in need of containment by state (or perhaps global) regulations. Formal, broadly Keynesian, debates such as between post-Keynesians and the money circuit approach remain centred, to this day, on the ontological primacy of the national economy – for many, on the extreme case of a closed economy. The shared position of the post-Keynesians, whether they link money to uncertainty (Davidson 1972) or institutional expansion of credit (Minsky 1982) or the business cycle (Robinson 1956) or bank lending (Moore 1988), is that money is *nationally* endogenous (brought forth as credit by the demands of national accumulation). Similarly, the money circuit approach, which poses money as debt (as the product of bank balance sheets) focuses exclusively on national banking systems.[9]

The problem implicit in the assumed ontological primacy of the national economic unit is that state money, defined as means of exchange, guarantees equivalence only within a national territory. The nation state cannot guarantee equivalence in inter-territorial exchanges, especially those that occur over time. States may try to stabilise national exchange rates and prime interest rates and maintain low inflation. They may also enforce the laws of contract in all exchanges. But they cannot guarantee equivalence in inter-territorial, inter-temporal transactions in the way they can with domestic, spot transactions. Kindleberger (1989: 57) put it succinctly:

> To make a system with two or more monies work well, the relations between, or among, the monies must be fixed. ... But fixed relations among several monies are difficult – some say impossible to sustain.

Accordingly, outside the Keynesian focus on nation-specific exchange, supported inter-nationally by fixed exchange rates, money cannot be nation-specific. Inter-territorial and inter-temporal exchange, and especially those that relate to the store of value and unit of account, can have significant degrees of autonomy from the nation state's monetary security.[10]

---

[9] For a summary of the money circuit approach, see Parguez and Seccareccia (2000). For an excellent collection of contributions to the debates within Post-Keynesianism and between Post-Keynesians and the money circuit approach, see Rochon and Rossi (2003).

[10] In optimum currency area theory, both Meade and more especially Mundell noted that there is no a priori reason for identifying the nation state with the

Recognising a role of global finance as 'money' requires moving beyond these Keynesian precepts of national money.

State money

Monetary nationalism is reinforced by (and no doubt leads to) the apparently automatic attachment of money to the state: that the nation state both supplies and dictates what constitutes 'money' within the nation.[11] Certainly, within a Keynesian framework, national money and state money are one and the same thing. But just as Keynesian national money rests on the presumption of national capital controls, so state money seems to emanate from the presumption that the state will actively manage the supply of money. The policy gives rise to the analytical category. Accordingly, there is a widespread tendency to define money in terms of the state's management function.

A central proposition from Knapp (1924) and adopted by Keynes is that the state's capacity to decree what can legitimately be used for the purposes of paying taxes determines what constitutes 'money', for without acceptability by the state, other 'moneys' will not survive.[12] Convertibility into state-approved money to meet taxation obligations is everything. Accordingly, such chartalist money, as it came to be termed, needs no commodity backing – acceptance by the state is its own legitimacy. Money could thereby be simply state-decreed tokens of value: the term chartalist itself deriving from the Latin word meaning 'ticket' or 'token' (Knapp: 1924: 32).

As chartalism has developed, its adherents have come to see state money not as *a* form of legitimate money, but *the exclusive* form of legitimate money – a position fundamental to Keynes (1930: 3–5) and Minsky (1986: 231) and to those who follow from them. Bell (2001: 161), in summarising this post-Keynesian, chartalist view concludes:

> Only the state, through its power to make and enforce tax laws, can make promises that its constituents must accept if they are to avoid penalties. The general acceptability of both state and bank money derives from their usefulness in settling tax and other liabilities to the

optimum currency area: more relevant are shared economic processes. But a criterion for a currency area is also that it can be subject to a single monetary policy.

[11] Notice also that the notion of the state's 'constituents' begs entirely the question of who makes up its constituents when capital is internationally mobile.

[12] For the Keynesians who focus on state money, it is necessary to distinguish which particular tokens constitute 'money' and which do not. In a closed

state. This ... enables them to circulate widely as means of payment and media of exchange. The debts ['money'] of households and businesses are accepted because of their convertibility (at least potentially) into relatively more acceptable promises. These debts are not accepted at state payment offices and, thus, are not likely to become widely accepted means of payment.

Yet this definition of money in terms of the state requires a rather limited perspective on the textbook notions of money identified earlier.[13] The exclusivity of state money requires privileging the role of money as national (not international), and as means of exchange (not store of value, etc.). Moreover, there is a slide of some proportions when specific acceptability in the payment of state taxes is equated with general acceptability in the payment of a debt. It requires that we define liquidity by reference to state payment offices (notes and coins, cheques), not to convertibility in money markets.[14]

The payment of taxes does indeed require money in exactly these dimensions Bell identified. So if the payment of taxation is the litmus test of 'money', then the other roles and spaces of money and other forms of liquidity (such as provided in derivative markets) are automatically

economy, this reduces to the specification of where to draw a line between money and other tokens, such as train tickets, which are also denominated in national money of account. But the question also needs to be posed in an open economy, where the tokens that contend to be considered as money are not just train tickets, but liquid financial assets (bonds, futures contracts, etc.) and often denominated in another national money of account. In a global financial context, money itself is not inherently either state-based or national.

[13] Ingham (2002: 128) contends that historical evidence supports Knapp's state theory focus on taxation as the basis for the creation of monetary spaces. But there is a neglect here of the role of money across monetary spaces. Gold as money was historically not contingent upon its role in national taxation, and we argue, the same applies in the current era. The point is that monetary 'space' is being redefined, such that different sorts of money circulate in different spaces.

[14] Dodd (1994: 29–30) points out, in relation to Max Weber's analysis of money and the state, a distinction between money's formal validity as a means of payment and its substantive validity as means of exchange. This latter function is associated with the state because 'financial transactions of the state and of the state treasuries in their monetary transactions is of crucial significance for the money system'. Dodd notes that, while the formal and substantive roles of money are assimilated so long as the state dominates the payment system, which it does by raising taxes, the logical possibility of private money is not precluded. Our proposition is that, in global financial markets, states do not dominate the payment system, and what Dodd calls private money is becoming a reality.

deemed 'not-money'. Yet in globally integrated finance such absolute criteria do not apply. Means of exchange is a rather minor role for money – indeed, as many critics of the global financial system point out, the monetary requirement of international exchange (the funding of trade) makes up around half of 1 per cent of annual global financial market turnover. The issue of conversion for national tax purposes is hardly the determining moment in these enormous flows. The requirement to pay taxation in a certain monetary unit only ensures that this money unit remains active: it does not ensure that it is the dominant form of money.

The rationale for privileging state money looks rather weak in this globalised world. At least we need to open up the possibility that the nation state may not secure directly the functions of money as a unit of account (except in relation to the state itself) nor the function of a store of value, especially when these functions must cross national currencies for periods of time and hence at variable currency exchange and interest rates.[15] Indeed, these are precisely the money functions that are being taken on by financial derivatives: they are a market-driven determination of the unit(s) of account and market-driven determination of the units in which value is stored.

Further, the very concept of 'liquidity', conventionally defined by reference to cash as 'liquid' money and other assets defined as less liquid according to their ease of convertibility into cash, locks in a limited and increasingly anachronistic notion of money convertibility. Derivatives are designed precisely to generate convertibility between a vast range of assets without the need to 'pass through' cash. Wheat in the future can be converted into bonds in yen today or in three months, or into any other monetary form at an instantly available rate of conversion formed in derivative markets.

'Liquidity' is what derivative markets are all about. They break down the traditionally conceived liquidity difference between forms of money, financial assets of various sorts and between those assets and traded commodities. Derivatives show the need to move away from a conception of 'degrees of moneyness' or a 'hierarchy of money'[16] (with

---

[15] From within a post-Keynesian approach, Sawyer (2003: 8–12) makes a similar point: that different moneys play different roles, and that the financial assets that define money as a means of payment can be different from the financial assets that define money as a store of value.

[16] Some post-Keynesians and, indeed, Marxists (e.g. Bell 2001; Foley 1987: 249–50) invoke a 'hierarchy of money' within a nation in reference to degrees of liquidity (or different forms of indebtedness/asset holding). Cash, issued by the

state-provided cash at the apex as 'real' money and others as less-moneyed, measured by their distance from cash). All moneys have become readily convertible into each other, and large trade in secondary markets ensures that these conversions are instant and at globally consistent rates.

So the issue we wish to explore is the money functions that exist beyond the nation state, where nation state tokens are not inherently trusted as units of value. It is useful, therefore, to look briefly to the other extreme: theories of stateless money. Our analysis is not advocating the reality or desirability of stateless money, but this does provide an important antidote to the Keynesian presumptions.

Money beyond the false juxtaposition between markets and state

The integrity of money is secured either by the state, or by the inherent characteristics of the particular money items. The latter implies commodity money. Yet it is apparent that those who have opposed the role of the state in determining and supplying money have generally focused not materially, on the particular characteristics of commodity money, but ideologically, on the capacity of the market to provide its own money. Hayek (1978), following Menger (1892)[17] argued that the market, not the state, selects the money commodity. He challenged the direct association of the state with the integrity of money. (It will be recalled from Chapter 5 that Hayek had supported a commodity-based global money after the end of the Gold Standard, in opposition to Keynes' advocacy of nation-state money under the Bretton Woods Agreement.)

state and used as means of exchange, automatically assumes the position at the top of the hierarchy. In global financial markets, where a wide range of assets are highly liquid, degrees of 'moneyness' have to be conceived very differently.

[17] Menger (1892), one of the founders of marginalism, saw money as a commodity selected by the market; not nominated by the state. It is the marketable characteristics of the commodity money (that everyone is willing to hold it) that sets it apart from other possible moneys: a process of 'natural' selection by market processes. Menger contended that it was these sorts of qualities, not state decree, that saw precious metals be nominated as money.

Such anthropologies are, no doubt, partial and extremely limited and selective histories of the evolution of money. There is an almost direct parallel here with those histories that, with equal certainty as Menger, assign the selection of money to the state (e.g. Wray 2000). The point is that there is not, nor need there be, a single history of monetary-based exchange – this is a case of economists contriving simple histories to enhance their theoretical predispositions.

True to his libertarian vision, Hayek opposed the role of central banks as lenders of last resort. He thought the moral hazard problem associated with this function would be unavoidable. He also opposed any capacity for states to create money which could be utilised for government's spending in pursuit of partisan political agendas.[18] Indeed his view was that there need be no connection between state and money. Hayek's preference was that banks privately issue their own currencies, and that these currencies not be nation-specific. There would be global competition in the provision of money, with profitability the incentive for each issuing bank to sustain confidence in its currency.

There is something trivially anti-statist in the libertarian political premises of Menger and Hayek. For Menger's analysis there is need to recognise that the state must always sanction certain moneys as part of enforcing the law of contract. For Hayek's proposal, state corruption in monetary regulation may be averted, but he substitutes impossibly high expectations on individuals to monitor the prudential adequacy of their chosen money supplier.

Nonetheless, these opponents of state money do signal a challenge to the terms of current analysis that seems to be predicated on state money: that market processes can themselves 'select' what will play the role of money in certain circumstances.

In contrast to the libertarians, it is not difficult to concur that chartalist, token money does indeed exist, but Bell's summary cited above shows the slide into the proposition that state token money is the *only* credible money. Two important questions arise which are central to the libertarian agenda, but avoided by the nation-centred chartalists:

1. Is state money the *only* form of money that can be widely accepted?
2. Is token money the *only* form of money in existence?

Menger *et al.* clearly challenge the first. Commodity money challenges the second. We will address each question in turn as a means to summarise our evaluation of Keynesian money.

Money, virtually however defined, and certainly defined to include derivatives, is always denominated in national currencies (Japanese yen; British pounds, etc.). This gives the appearance that all money is state money. Indeed, all money has some links to the state – via reliance on

---

[18] In Chapter 5 it was noted that Hayek had supported a commodity-based global money after the end of the Gold Standard, rather than see the pre-eminence of nation-state money under the Bretton Woods Agreement.

stable national currencies, and on the enforcement of the law of contract. But most of it is not state money as it is conventionally defined.

It was Keynes (1930: 3) who drew the important distinction between 'the money of account' and 'money', in which the former is the description – the unit in which money is denominated (e.g. the dollar or the pound) – and the latter is the thing which answers to the description. Money of account is therefore conventionally in state-designated units, but money itself is something different: it may be state money or it may be commodity money. Money could be, as Hayek argues, a product of markets, and market money and state money could exist side-by-side, both designated in the same moneys of account. Kindleberger (1984: 38), from quite a different position, put the implication succinctly:

> As a unit of account, money is a creature of the state; as a medium of exchange, despite the legal tender question, it is what markets use.

The identification of financial derivatives as state money is simply confusing money of account with money itself.

The other question, whether token money is the only form of money, can be opened up in a similar way. Clearly there *is* token money, and chartalist national money is indeed token money, not commodity money. But it is a moot point as to whether this is the only sort of money circulating globally. Outside the nation-centred theories of accumulation that define the post-Keynesian discourse, there is nothing precluding the re-establishment of a commodity basis to globally circulating finance. Indeed, our argument, opened up in the previous chapter, is that where the popular credibility of money does not rest on state guarantees, it must have some other material basis: it must in some sense be commodity money.

But this does not 'prove' the existence of non-token, commodity money: it just contends that if money is *defined* exclusively by reference to the state, then the proposition that all money is token money ultimately rests on a tautology. Alternatively, we are looking to re-open the possibility that global finance is dominated by commodity money ... if only we know how to recognise it! We know emphatically that this commodity money would have none of the characteristics of metallist or bullionist commodity money, for history showed that these are not appropriate to advanced capitalism. Maybe the money commodity need not be a *physical* commodity at all!

Derivatives as commodity money

Derivatives, we argue, have the attributes of a commodity money, and hence a commodity foundation to global finance.

So in what sense are derivatives 'commodities'? Clearly, if derivatives are commodities, they are a different sort of commodity from those we conventionally think about. They are commodities in the sense that insurance can be a commodity, or information can be a commodity: they are a production process within a circulation process.

Financial derivatives are produced (as contracts) and offered on the market as products of the labour of financial institutions and operatives that stitch up the deals. That they may be re-traded at variable prices and for speculative purposes is a secondary matter and true of most commodities anyway. Indeed, the fact that OTC derivatives (an agreement between two pre-determined parties usually made over the telephone and not mediated through an official exchange) now far exceed the number and value of (arms-length) exchange-traded derivative contracts is some testimony to this primary function.[19]

In clarifying this perspective, two propositions warrant explanation. First, the proposition is not that the full value of a derivative contract is the product of the labour of financial intermediation, any more than transport produces the full value of a relocated commodity. Derivatives are commodities whose primary function is the commensuration of other commodities.[20] Accordingly, the value created in derivatives can be specified in a number of ways: it could be posed by individual capitals as 'security' (the adjustment of risk), but more generally, we frame the value created by derivatives in terms of the active computation and commensuration of the value of other commodities.

We have earlier argued in relation to futures contracts that one effect of derivatives is to reconfigure commodities as (also) money to emphasise their money-ness. The argument here is simply the converse, that financial assets are also commodities. Combined, the effect is to merge the categories of commodity and money – in short, to make apparent that all commodities are forms of capital. Herein lies the importance of derivatives as commodified finance, providing a system of universal

---

[19] See Chapter 3 for an explanation of exchange-traded compared with OTC derivatives.

[20] There are, however, exceptions. For example, some derivatives, especially stock options, are being used as a means of payment for senior executive salaries.

equivalence, but not, as with gold, a commodity contingent upon the limited universality of one particular commodity.

Second, the commodity value of a derivative is to be defined in terms of what a derivative does, not what it represents. What it represents is merely a book value of an asset; what it does is provide 'designer' mechanisms of risk conversion, for which the trader is prepared to pay. Take, for example, a $100 fixed interest debt that is entered into an interest rate swap. The swaps 'represents' a value of $100, but the intrinsic value of the interest rate swap is what that swap 'does': it gives the holder of a $100 fixed rate debt token the capacity to have interest paid, in terms of a variable rate of interest, in yen or Euros, rather than at a fixed rate in dollars. That ownership is fundamentally different from holding a $100 token from the US Federal Reserve.

There is, perhaps, a temptation in the context of commodity derivatives to pose the value of a derivative in terms of the value of the 'underlying' commodity (e.g. that the value of a wheat futures contract is somehow linked to the value of a tonne of wheat). But this does not capture the value of a derivative itself as a commodity. The commodity basis of derivative money is not in the reduction of money to some other commodities, but the commodified role of commensuration that derivatives perform.

Given the above, and following Kay (1999: 272–6), we find it useful to draw a distinction between basic, or simple, commodities (wheat, iron, cars, etc.) and *meta-commodities*. The former, being historically prior and the products of labour, are 'productive' and correspond with our standard conception of a commodity. *Meta-commodities* come historically later, with the initial purpose of hedging the conditions of production and circulation of simple commodities. They absorb value discontinuities across time and space. As these meta-commodities have grown in importance, particularly since the 1980s, they have come to provide commensuration across time and space between diverse simple commodities as well as between different forms of money and finance.

So the essential characteristic of derivatives as commodities is that they are *products of circulation*, not significantly of labour, and accordingly their value is defined in exchange and not in consumption. These meta-commodities are therefore always 'capital', for they never 'leave' a circuit of capital so as to be consumed. In that sense, they are more intensively capitalist commodities than simple commodities, for the latter are merely *produced within* capitalist relations, while meta-commodities are *products of* capitalist relations.

A way in which derivatives may be posed as commodity money within Marxian value theory is posed in Appendix 6.1.

Conclusion

We concluded Chapter 5 with the proposition that derivatives are now anchoring the global money system in a way that bears some key parallels with the role played by gold in the nineteenth century. This opened up the question of derivatives as a new global money and whether, as money, derivatives must be seen as a new form of commodity money. We can now pose these issues in summary.

In what sense are derivatives 'money'? The simple answer is that in the world of global finance they are used as money, and have the characteristics of money – albeit not money as means of exchange. Something that functions as money *is* money.

In what sense are they commodity money? There are two answers. First, they logically need to be. They are not state money, and are only minimally guaranteed by states (via their utilisation of nation states' units of account, state stabilisation of exchange rates and enforcement of the law of contract). Yet they are used extensively in global money functions. They therefore must have a material basis to sustain their use as money.

Secondly, unlike many other forms of money which are simply titles to ownership, financial derivatives actually do something: they are computations, not merely statements of equivalence, and they are valued because of their in-built computations. In this sense, they are products (commodities) as well as money.

If derivatives are, for better or worse, market-created money without formal nation-state guarantees, what anchors secure the stability of this new money system? Derivatives show that there are commodified links that bind the financial system. Derivatives are themselves commodities to be bought and sold, and they are distinctively capitalist commodities that arise and terminate exclusively within the sphere of circulation.

It follows that financial derivatives are now a pivotal aspect of competition between capitals. The centrality of money capital to the whole accumulation process sees derivatives disciplining the terms on which (and the locations in which) money capital is transformed into productive capital and the terms on which the output of production is transformed back to money capital. The competitive discipline in the sphere of money capital asserts direct pressures on capital in production, and thereby in the labour process, because all capital, everywhere, needs to be (and is being) actively compared for its on-going profitability. This competitive commensuration is what makes derivatives distinctly capitalist money, and it is the issue we address in Chapter 7.

Appendix 6.1: a Marxian interpretation of financial derivatives as commodity money

Marxian value theory can address money from two principal directions:

1. Money as the equivalent form of value
2. Money as a form of capital in the circuit of capital

From the first comes the notion of money as a commodity – that in an equivalent exchange of value from commodities to money to commodities (C-M-C), money is of the same value (measured in embodied labour time) as the commodities being exchanged.

From the second comes the notion of money as a part of total capital, providing the capacity to purchase means of production and commodity outputs, and acquiring profit in the form of interest. Here also is the notion of the difference between production capital and circulation capital. Circulation involves both finance and buying and selling as opposed to the production of goods and services, with the critical analytical distinction being that surplus value is created only in the sphere of production.

From this second direction comes the category of 'finance capital' – a term which seems to have loosened its meaning from the time of its creation by Rudolf Hilferding (1910) at the beginning of the twentieth century to now loosely refer to the co-operative connections between finance and industry.

From this second direction also comes the distinction between productive and unproductive labour, directly linked to, but not reducible to, the distinction between production and circulation. It is this path into the question of money that is clearly dominant in contemporary Marxist analyses of finance. Essentially, the interpretation starts with the proposition that the finance industry is 'unproductive' (of surplus value). It may be a necessary component of accumulation, in the sense that there can't be accumulation without money capital advanced, but it creates no new value. Accordingly, it is an argument that lies behind much Marxist opposition to the expansion of finance from the 1980s – that its scale is out of proportion to its necessary role of facilitating production (e.g. Dumenil and Levy 2004).

It is not the object of this appendix to enter the minefield of the 'unproductive labour debate', except to make a single comment. The interpretation of Marxian theory through the productive/unproductive distinction proves stifling of an understanding of changes that occur *within* finance. If the premise of analysis is to identify finance as unproductive (but necessary) and the object of analysis is the question of whether finance has increased its share of surplus value at the expense of the share of productive capital, the subject of finance itself becomes highly simplified. All that is required in the productive/unproductive divide is that money exists as credit (i.e. accrues a rate of interest) and that the question to ask of money is whether it is or is not being directed to the funding of production. Developments within finance, such as the enormous growth of financial derivatives, fail to receive direct analytical attention. This depiction of finance as 'unproductive' readily slides into more pejorative labels such as 'speculative'.

Our own object, however, is precisely to understand the role played by derivatives in capital accumulation. Our path into this issue is not advanced by an entry through the productive/unproductive debate, but via Marx's own analysis of the contradictions that lie within a distinctly commodity money.

This is certainly not a fashionable path. Marx's own writing on commodity money, and the role of a distinct commodity (or set of commodities) in assuming the role of 'money', is generally dismissed as anachronistic and trapped in the nineteenth-century practices of the Gold Standard. The Gold Standard, with its implicitly fixed exchange rates that came from all trade being transacted in the same money commodity, meant that Marx never had to pose the currently pressing question of variable exchange rates.

Here we develop an alternative explanation of money in the era of globally integrated financial markets, where currencies circulate freely outside the nation of their designated account and comprise money issued both by states and by private organisations such as in the form of bonds and other debt instruments. Our argument, contrary to the dominant view, is that Marxian analysis is not impeded by a reliance on a commodity theory of money. On the contrary, it was Marx's particular designated commodity money, restricting the money commodity to gold, which obstructs a more creative understanding of the nature of capitalist money in the twenty-first century. Derivatives, as traded commodities, hold the foundations of a more general theory of capitalist money as commodity money.[21]

Marx's commodity money: a brief background

Marx addressed money in two broad contexts: money and alienation (money as fetishised social relations), and money and accumulation. We will have reason to combine these two dimensions, but it is appropriate to start with the latter. In this context, Marx introduced money in a not dissimilar way to the economic orthodoxy. In the exchange of commodities of equal value (defined in terms of socially necessary labour time) a particular commodity that plays the role of the universally equivalent form of value emerges. It is designated as money. Money is thereby defined by reference to its role as means of exchange, and inherently as commodity money – the money unit embodies the same amount of socially necessary labour time in its production as do the two commodities whose exchange it facilitates. Historically, it was precious metals that performed the money function. As commodity money (the representation of social labour) this money is always the bearer of social relations.

Money entered Marx's theory of capitalist accumulation as a single commodity: gold. In capitalism, the commodity gold is produced under the same competitive processes as are all other commodities: the logic of profitability. The value of money is therefore always bound up in a tension between the socially necessary labour time involved in the production of gold and the general level of

---

[21] We are drawn to Fleetwood's (2000) explanation of the necessity of commodity money to the integrity of Marx's theory of value, but not to his (tentative) conclusions that the abandonment of commodity money means the end of a universal equivalent form of value. Nor is there the question of why nation states have abandoned the universal equivalent and the value form. This appears a rather instrumentalist approach to value theory, and, more critically, fails to open up the terms on which Marxism can understand new forms of money.

prices associated with the ratio of commodity gold to all other commodities.[22] That tension is difficult for value theory to absorb, and Marx spent considerable time in the *Grundrisse* and in Volume III of *Capital* trying to resolve an effective technical formulation. No one claims that he succeeded, and the global scale proved the most difficult part.

With gold as international currency (the spatially universal equivalent), but produced under specific, nationally delineated costs of production, there was always a tension between value determination on a national and a global scale, and an ambiguity as to how cross-national transfers of gold 'equilibrate' the value system. There was no basis on which the value of gold as produced commodity and the value represented by gold as the equivalent form of value would be systematically commensurable. Indeed, the problem is not specific to gold; it applies to all commodities and hence doubly to gold.

The fact that gold was produced under capitalist relations of production therefore appeared as a source of Marx's problem. Conversely, with derivatives it is precisely their distinctly capitalist conditions of production that permit them to operate as money.

But Marx was not a bullionist: the pre-eminent status of gold was based, he contended, in superstition, and he considered that economists' obsession with gold as the natural form of money as little more than 'educated superstition'. His concern was more with the determination of equivalence between different commodities in an M-C-M (money-commodity-money) or C-M-C (commodity-money-commodity) exchange, and in this regard gold was an inferior representation of the equivalent form of value. In the context of money as capital – money capital – he largely took for granted the equivalence of money to other forms of capital.

The problem posed

The problem is that the nation state is not a satisfactory way to explain the basis of global money, yet there appears no commodity unit that forms an alternative basis. If we start with a national notion of money, the state's role in the provision and guarantee of symbolic money immediately intercedes, and analysis is swept away from (re)conceptions of commodity money, but without ever really exploring the contemporary relevance of a commodity basis to international money. Conversely, if the money commodity is an 'ordinary' commodity required to 'double up' as money, we cannot reconcile its own cost of production with its role in establishing equivalence in exchange between other commodities.

Marx's instincts about money were probably more astute than his analysis. His instinct was that money had to have commodity characteristics, but it had also to be abstracted from the characteristics of a particular commodity. The problem of gold was that it is, indeed, but a particular commodity among many; albeit one that could, for a long time, 'double up' as the special money commodity. Moreover, gold was never distinctly capitalist money – it is pre-capitalist, even ancient money cast (literally) into a capitalist role. And for the most part under capitalism, it has laid idle in bank vaults while paper tokens represented it in virtually all money functions. There is nothing more absurd in a capitalist context than having

---

[22] See Foley (1998) for an interesting analysis that includes consideration of changes in the socially necessary costs of production of gold.

abstract labour lying idle so that its form (gold) can symbolically play the role of the equivalent form of value. Distinctly capitalist commodity money would be a living part of accumulation, not a congealed, dormant, labour numeraire!

How is this problem to be framed within Marxist theory? As well as money being a produced commodity like other commodities, it has to be a commodity that can guarantee value, but without reliance on the imprimatur of the state. This money commodity has to resolve temporal and spatial variability in value: it has to, in itself, resolve the problem of conventional state money, that a process of exchange of equivalent values is always expressed at a given time and in a given monetary unit.

For conventional state money, this means that there are volatile exchange rates and a range of interest rate regimes for each currency: the equivalence of exchange cannot be verified. There is, in Marxist terms, a spatial and temporal problem in the commensuration of value: there is a discontinuity in the measured value of capital in different forms and at different locations, and this discontinuity needs to be reconciled.[23]

The new commodity money has to have the capacity to absorb that discontinuity into itself as (one of) its defining characteristics, so that money can, indeed, secure equivalence (commensurate value) across time and space.

This process of commensuration is what Marx attached to the function of money: money is the means by which '[different] commodities become magnitudes of the same kind, of the same unit, i.e. commensurable' (Marx 1939: 143). But how different moneys are commensurated within a theory of value, and what it means to commensurate packages of financial assets whose underlying value is not itself being exchanged were questions not posed by Marx, nor since Marx. It is this issue that brings financial derivatives to the centre of a Marxist theory of capitalist money.

Marx's theory of money: its link to financial derivatives

The investigation of the rudiments of a theory of money consistent with financial derivatives must look beyond the form of gold. It is to Marx's earlier writings, particularly on alienation, that we look for conceptual propositions about the nature of money and finance.[24] For example, reviewing James Mill's *Elements of Political Economy*, Marx (1844) emphasised the importance of contingency in relation to 'laws' about money and the essential role of money as a mediating process. Here Marx goes on to explain the basic characteristics of capitalist money, and it warrants citing at some length:

> The essence of money is not, in the first place, the property alienated in it, but that the mediating or movement ... is estranged from man and becomes the attribute of money. ...
>
> The personal mode of existence of money as money – and not only as the inner, implicit, hidden social relationship or class relationship between

---

[23] The concept of discontinuities is explored in detail in Chapter 7.

[24] Marx's writing at this time, being strongly influenced by Feuerbach, is drawing on parallels between money and religion and both as alienated forms of social relations.

commodities – this mode of existence corresponds the more to the essence of money, the more abstract it is, the less it has a natural relationship to the other commodities, the more it appears as the product and yet as the non-product of man, the less primitive its sphere of existence, the more it is created by man or, in economic terms, the greater the inverse relationship of its value as money to the exchange value or money value of the material in which it exists.

Hence paper money and the whole number of paper representatives of money (such as bills of exchange, mandates, promissory notes, etc.) are the more perfect mode of existence of money as money and a necessary factor in the progressive development of the money system. In the credit system, of which banking is the perfect expression, it appears as if the power of the alien, material force were broken, the relationship of self-estrangement abolished and man had once more human relations to man.

The important point Marx was contending above is that the more money is 'lifted above' direct commodity relations by 'losing' the characteristics of other commodities, the more 'perfect its mode of existence' because the social relations of capital, expressed in commodity production, are not being contaminated by the particularities of the chosen money commodity.[25] Gold is, in this regard, an extremely primitive form of capitalist money: indeed, we know it historically as pre-capitalist money. Financial derivatives, on the other hand, as advances beyond promissory notes and bills of exchange – contracts that are man-made and having no 'natural relationship' to the products from which they derive, appear as a highly advanced form of money.

Nonetheless, the requirement for a global monetary system is precisely as Marx conceived of it in the abstract – a role for commodities that are both part of other commodities, but also discrete commodities in themselves. But gold is a single (or at best dual) dimensional commodity.[26] There are too many types of discontinuities in the global financial system to be reconciled by a single commodity in the role of money. The multiple forms of risk-exposure, reflecting the range of possible inter-temporal, inter-spatial, inter-financial-instrument price relativities requires intermediation in a form that is itself flexible and able to reflect the range of possibilities in these relativities. Gold does not meet this requirement, especially in an era when money capital increasingly takes the form of different types of credit money and other financial assets. Derivatives, on the other hand are commodities produced and traded for precisely this purpose.

Derivatives: commodities commensurating monetary discontinuities

We have seen that, in terms of Marx's benchmark of the 'progressive development of the money system', derivatives meet the requirement of a more 'perfect mode

---

[25] Notice also that Marx could contemplate an association of 'perfect money' with something as basic as the credit system and paper representations of money. That now seems a rather low bar for depicting perfection.

[26] The duality relates to Marx's emphasis that gold never traded at its costs of production.

of existence' by being abstracted from 'a natural relationship' with other commodities. But are derivatives themselves commodities, and how can Marx's conception of money reconcile the need for commodity money, yet for commodity money to appear as 'not the product of man'?

Marx's conception of commodity money was both advanced and constrained by the Gold Standard within which it was conceived. It was advanced by recognition that money must have a commodity basis if it is to be an integral component of capital accumulation and not just a numeraire.

But Marx's conception was also constrained by the then widely held belief that one commodity, gold, could act as a universal equivalent form of value and furthermore, that the robustness of its status resided in its defined and finite quantity. In Marx's time, the expectation was that one particular commodity (gold) could traverse and reconcile all the discontinuities within the money system.

Derivatives, however, confront that image. Any single unit of measure such as gold can represent only a balance of multiple processes of commensuration, and thereby actually reconcile perhaps none at all. Derivatives, on the other hand, are literally thousands of types of commodities whose specific characteristics are designed to secure commensurability between different forms of capital and their spatial and temporal characteristics. If money is defined by its role in the process of commensuration (or, as Marx also put, it in the 'mediating' process), there is no logical preclusion that a range of 'commodities' could not fulfil the function of the equivalent form of value when there are clearly articulated mechanisms of commensuration between the various monetary commodities.

7
Global Competition

It is now commonplace to identify 'globalisation' with a growth of competition. International trade generates spatially extensive competition between buyers and sellers. International investment sees corporations shifting to more profitable localities. There is competition between localities to attract investment, and competitive pressure on 'local' producers to be cost-competitive. This global mobility of investment and goods then has implications for labour. Some contend a productivity race, creating development and higher wages. Others see a race to the bottom, as low wage countries set the benchmarks to which wages in richer countries must gravitate. Clearly, competition is the central driving force of the global economy, for both capital and labour.

In these various connections between globalisation and competition, finance itself is not generally seen as a driving force. It is the passive conduit. This chapter builds the connection between finance and competition, showing that finance, in the form of derivatives, intensifies the process of capitalist competition. It argues that financial derivatives, through their roles in commensurating capital across the globe, impose a direct competitive pressure on capital to perform at globally recognised rates of return, or be devalued. Accordingly, we argue, the pressure is placed on labour to ensure that capital does indeed achieve this acceptable rate of return. Where capital is not achieving this rate of return, pressure reverts to the sphere of production, and particularly labour to deliver higher profitability, be it by higher productivity, longer working days or lower wages. Through competition we identify a direct causal connection between finance and labour.

This argument must, however, cut a path through a rather extensive literature on competition and on 'capital'. Once these concepts are defined in ways that are mutually clarifying, the role of derivatives in the intensification of competition becomes apparent.

Competition: a contested concept

Competition can be described simply as being what capital does. It does not follow rules, or adhere to market structures depicted in textbooks. It is the strategic process by which capital pursues profit. The connection to financial derivatives is that derivatives escalate the nature of competition, and hence intensify what capital does. To explain this process, it is important to clarify this concept of competition in such a way that makes it easy to use when it comes to explaining derivatives.

In its neoclassical version, competition is idealised, and given moral status through a hypothetical model of 'perfect competition' – a contrived set of behavioural and institutional assumptions sufficient to ensure that market processes are seen to meet their goals: optimisation for every market participant, efficiency in the overall allocation of resources, and maximisation of social welfare – the best of all possible worlds. But outside that hypothetical world, the nature of competition is quite a different matter.

From the 1920s, neoclassical views were transformed by internal critics: monopoly and oligopoly started to be theorised in the name of realism, but nonetheless retaining a rigid set of behavioural and institutional assumptions which ensured that monopoly and oligopoly could be theorised on the same analytical terms as perfect competition. Monopoly and oligopoly, were, thereby, to be defined by their inefficiency; their deviation from perfect competition. So while there was a shift to realism about market structure (recognition that some market participants do, indeed, have power), the a priori formalism (that market power can be understood through a simple variation of the assumptions of perfect competition) remained intact.

It was not until the development of game theory, at the margins of economics from the 1950s and at the centre from the 1990s, that competition could be understood as a dynamic, interactive process where apriori assumptions did not specify market outcomes and where it was formally recognised that firms have to take their rivals' actions into account. Yet here, everything is contingent and a focus on individual strategy replaces any notion of structural determination.

Despite debates that have emerged in the evolution of this theory, all variants of neoclassical theory share a framework based on the moral superiority of individual rights over collective endeavours. This is, after all, the defining characteristic of a neoclassical discourse, so the above statement is virtually a tautology.

There is always a proclivity to slide into the hegemonic neoclassical discourse of competition. It is as if the neoclassicals define competition, and other economic and social theories explain why that conception is hypothetical, not 'realistic', not ethical, etc, but, in the process, the neoclassicals set the definitional benchmark. The consequence is that those of us who are not neoclassical economists can find ourselves contending that the economy is not 'competitive' when we are really just attesting that the world doesn't work according to neoclassical precepts. Yet any notion that the economy is not competitive is absurd – competition is inherent to a capitalist economy, albeit not neoclassical 'perfect competition'.

But this neoclassical discourse is not the only way of characterising competition. Several alternatives warrant noting. For the radicals,[1] competition has been a fairly straightforward inversion of the neoclassicals' conception, framed in the harsh realities of imperfect markets. Drawing on Marx's proposition about the concentration and centralisation of capital, many radicals have emphasised the power of monopolies and oligopolies, including international corporations. In the first instance, this emphasis simply invokes the neoclassical model of monopoly; only asserting it as the market norm rather than, as the neoclassicals claim, an exception. But for both radicals and neoclassicals alike, monopoly is a distortion. For the neoclassicals, the distortion takes the form of inefficiency in resource allocation; for the radicals, the distortion takes the form of inequality in market power and hence market outcomes. This radical alternative often thereby falls into the absurdity of claiming that capitalist markets do not engage in competitive activity, because they are dominated by powerful monopolies! The inversion of the neoclassical position embodies its own entrapment into the notion that competition and monopolies (or large corporations in general) are antithetical.

A clear alternative, that we would now identify with a post-Keynesian and social democratic position, emphasises the need for state involvement in market relations. Within the formalism of the neoclassical framework, they highlight technical cases of failures in market signals (externalities and public goods) that require the state as an active enforcer of property rights. Of itself, this remains consistent with a neoclassical discourse (Coase 1960) but in historical application, the post-Keynesians pose that

---

[1] We use the term 'radical' here to depict analytical positions adopted in the name of immediate resistance to capital on the grounds of moral or ethical judgements.

markets may fail to equilibrate, or may equilibrate at points that do not meet broader social needs. For Keynes in the 1930s, this un-met need was full employment, and the role he attributed to the state was directly associated with addressing the volatility that generates unemployment and the hardship endured by those in unemployment. Today, those needs could also be posed in terms of the environment or global inequality. But whatever the social objective which the market cannot meet, it is the state which must step in to regulate and over-rule markets. Clearly, this subordinates (to some degree) markets to social policy agendas, but it preserves at its core the notion of competition as a relation between optimising individuals interacting in the market. It just contends that this competitive process is insufficient on its own.

The analysis developed below sees competition outside the discourse of individualism and efficiency on the one hand and the role of the state in over-riding markets or correcting market failures on the other. It centres on the way in which capitals seek to cut costs and increase revenues faster than can other capitals, to gain a (often temporary) profit advantage.[2] This emphasis on 'capital' leads the analysis of competition in very different directions from those identified above. Unfortunately, however, the meaning of this proposition is open to wide interpretation.

Capital with many meanings

What makes the depiction of this alternative conception of competition difficult is that this concept of 'capital' gets defined so many different ways. Worse, many of these ways lead to useful analysis, so it is not a matter of giving a 'correct' definition of capital and labelling all others as 'incorrect'. Indeed, given that the term 'capitalism' is so comprehensively accepted as the umbrella depiction of the last 200 years of social and economic history, it is hardly surprising that the root term 'capital' can mean all things to all people. These multiple concepts of capital have given rise to periods of intense debate about the meaning of capital.[3]

We can identify four senses in which the term capital applies within the context of competition: two reflect static conceptions that are components of the competitive process (the objects of competition);

[2] See, in particular, Clifton 1977, Semmler 1984, Weeks 1981, 1999.
[3] See Fisher (1904) for a review of the field at the end of the nineteenth century, and for the debate in the 1960s see Harcourt (1969).

two depict the dynamic nature of the competitive process (the subjects of competition). It is useful to first identify them:

K1   Capital as a stock of means of production, as in 'capital equipment'.
K2   Capital as a stock of wealth, as in 'the investment of capital'.
K3   Capital as an 'individual capital' in reference to a single process of production and exchange.
K4   Capital as 'social capital' – a social relation, in reference to the capitalist system of property ownership and surplus appropriation.

Our proposition is that these four definitions can be combined in a general understanding that changes significantly with recognition of the role of derivatives. We will first identify the common interpretation before adding derivatives.

K4 defines capitalist competition as a class-based process: it is the assumed starting point or context of competition (i.e. we are dealing with competition under capitalist social relations) and it is reproduced by competition (i.e. the competitive processes involving all K3s serve to reproduce capitalist social relations).

K3 defines the units of accumulation controlled by the individual capitalist (notionally firms or corporations), which compete with each other. This is usually thought of as the 'real' site of active competition: firms competing in the market.

K1 defines the capitalist's productive inputs into K3. In the absence of K4, these are merely pieces of machinery etc. It is K4, expressed through the activity of K3 that realises these pieces of machinery as 'capital'.[4]

K2 defines the fund of money advanced for the operation of K3. In the absence of K4, this is just a fund of money. It is K4, expressed through the activity of K3 that realises this fund of money as 'capital' or 'money capital'.

Within this depiction, K1 and K2 (productive inputs and funds) are social because of K4, but they are nonetheless passive inputs into K3. They are used in competition by K3 and/or they are a produced output of K3. They are what competition seeks to manipulate or act on, but they are not intrinsically competitive items. They are 'bits' of capital. For K1 these 'bits' are blast furnaces, computers, coffee bushes etc. For K2

---

[4] Marx (1849: 159), in a famous reference, made a similar point: 'A cotton-spinning jenny is a machine for spinning cotton. It becomes *capital* only in certain relations. Torn from these relationships it is no more capital than gold in itself is money or sugar is the price of sugar.'

these 'bits' are dollars and pounds in cash or other claims like credit. Indeed, from the perspective of K4, K1 and K2 are really the same thing – one in the physical form, the other in the money form. But, and this is critical, they are not themselves an active part of the competitive process. They are the objects of competition; not its subjects.

The role of financial derivatives can now be specified. Derivatives have served to bring K1 and K2 directly into the dimension of competition, discrete from their role in K3. K1 and K2 cease to be passive 'bits' of capital whose use is defined by their input into an accumulation process – these 'bits' are themselves now being constituted competitively and at the centre of the accumulation processes. K1 and K2 are being transformed from being objects to subjects of competitive practice. The effect, we will show, has profound effects for the way we understand K3 and, by implication, K4.

In developing this proposition, it is necessary to further elaborate K3, the individual capital, before we start to consider how it is being reconfigured by the role of derivatives in transforming K1 and K2.

Individual capital is something akin to a firm, or corporation, though it is actually not necessarily the legal entity called the corporation: it is rather a unit of accumulation. The difference between an individual capital and an individual corporation or firm is that a corporation (as an institutional unit of ownership) may undertake a number of discrete production processes (or investments), while an 'individual capital' identifies each of these processes discretely (though recognising their interconnections). A large corporation, producing many items at many sites, could be thought of as multiple 'individual capitals', though the boundaries between these individual capitals may not always be clear. The concept of 'individual capital' emphasises that it is not legal entities, but the processes of accumulation that engage in competition.[5]

A seminal essay by James Clifton (1977) made stark the difference between an individual capital and a firm or corporation in relation to competition. Clifton pointed out that capitalist competition is not for market share or sales, it is competition for profit, and profit is earned on investment. Hence the key strategic decision of the capitalist is what to invest in and the defining characteristic of capitalist competition is the mobility of investment – mobility over space and between different commercial/financial/industrial activities.

---

[5] It was seen in Chapter 4 that it is important not to define the process of accumulation simply with reference to legal entities.

Competition means that where the rate of profit is low, investment withdraws; where it is high, new investment enters. (There are, of course issues of barriers to mobility and entry, but we can leave these aside for the moment.) Clifton then makes a key point. It is large corporations, with diverse investment activities, that have come to show the greatest mobility. Those who administer these corporations face choices as to which of their diverse operations to expand, which to contract, which new areas to enter and which to withdraw from. They will attempt to choose systematically to expand profitable activities and contract unprofitable ones.

Competition (in terms of the mobility of investment) is, therefore, something that occurs *within* corporations, between its various investment options as well as between them. It is competition between what we have called individual capitals. Small firms (the neoclassical ideal type), on the other hand, have no such choice – their administrators can know and act on only a few kinds and sites of investment. Their investment decisions are, therefore, not directly based on their capacity for mobility. Accordingly, while neoclassicals (and radicals) think of large corporations as the antithesis of competitiveness, and small firms the ideal image, Clifton argues, if anything, exactly the opposite.

The point for our analysis is that it is investments, or units of accumulation, or, as we have called them, individual capitals, that are the key to competition; not corporations or other legally defined entities. This framework is important for our analysis, for derivatives serve the role of facilitating the monitoring of asset values in any location, any sector, at any point of time. They are therefore critical to the practice of competition between individual capitals. But we will develop this argument more systematically shortly.

Competition and the circuit of capital

At this point there may not appear a direct connection between the ideas of competition and capital and the mechanics of derivative markets. But the gap can be closed readily via one brief elaboration of the theory of the individual capital.

Think of a circuit of individual capital, as set out by Marx in Volume II of *Capital*. It is a circuit that, albeit stripped of its Marxist meanings, is often seen in economic geography texts. The circuit:

$$M - C \cdot\cdot P \cdot\cdot C' - M'$$

describes the process by which capital (a store of value) in the form of money (M) is converted into commodity inputs (C) (labour and capital) which are combined in a process of production (P) to produce commodity outputs of expanded value (C'), which are then sold and thereby converted back to money of expanded value (M'). What makes this a circuit is that the M' at the end of the circuit is now available to acquire commodity inputs and undertake a new act of production. The operative word here is 'available', for it may be so directed, and the expanded value of M may see the next 'round' of the circuit on an expanded scale. Conversely, M could be directed in all or in part to other uses.

Notice the blending of the four concepts of Capital in this circuit. There is the circuit of individual capital (K3) as a discrete process of accumulation. There is capital as a store of value in the form of money (K2) and commodity inputs (K1). Giving context, it is all part of social capital (K4) – the conflicts between labour and capital in production, and (though it isn't explicit above) between various claimants on the surplus being created in production.

The circuit is a visual characterisation of accumulation as a process of (expanded) reproduction. It could easily be read as a mechanical statement of perpetual growth. Yet the 'dashes' that link the circuit are each points of negotiated settlement – there is nothing pre-determined about any of the rates of conversion around the circuit. Each point of negotiated settlement in the conversion of capital from M to C and C' to M' is determining the distribution of surplus between the constituent components of the circuit – money lenders, suppliers of commodity inputs (including suppliers of labour), industrialists and merchants. Who gets what is expressed by terms of exchange within the circuit: by competition.

When thought of in more institutional terms, there are at least three contiguous processes of competition depicted in the circuit:

1. There is competition between labour and capital over the conditions of employment and work, manifesting in the rate at which inputs are converted to outputs, depicted in C-P-C'.
2. There is competition in each of the transactions within the circuit. There is competition between capitals (financial and industrial) over the direction and terms of the advance of M for the purchase of C (and hence where and in what proportion surplus in M' at the 'end' of the circuit accrues and who it accrues to). There is also competition between commerce and industry over the price at which C' is sold wholesale (and hence what proportion of surplus value in C' accrues to commerce).
3. There is competition for market share between circuits that use the same inputs (C) or produce the same outputs (C').

Within these processes, (3) is the focus of the neoclassicals and post-Keynesians. For Marxian competition, (3) is both a form of competition in itself and adds intensity to the competition in (2) and (1), for it constrains the size of the surplus to be fought over. Process 2 shows that all capitals compete with each other for a share of surplus: competition is not just, as in (3), in output markets. Process 1 emphasises the size of the surplus, and hence what is left for the industrial capitalist after (2), and process 3 depends on the capacity to extract surplus from labour in production.

This depiction is useful as far as it goes, but it obscures the intensified dimensions of competition that come with financial derivatives. The institutional framework sees competition as a temporal sequence of completed transactions: M-C is resolved via the determination of a loan agreement for the purchase of inputs; then C-P-C' is resolved via a labour contract and other production agreements; then C'-M' is resolved via a selling agreement between producer and purchasers.

The underlying problem that we seek to address here, ironically, is that a perfect competition assumption has crept into the circuit, unannounced, via this 'sequence-of-transactions' conception that is part of the institutionalist interpretation. There is the presumption that as capital moves around the circuit, the value of capital is maintained – that the value of capital in the money form (M) is equal to the value of capital in the commodity form (C).[6]

But this circuit is not a series of discrete, sequential, arms-length resolutions except in a narrowly legal sense. From the perspective of accumulation and the overall process of competition, these 'resolutions' keep getting re-calculated.[7] Rather than thinking of the process of recalculation as a retrospective validation (or not) of an initial valuation (for example that the value of output is validated (or amended) when it eventually sells in the market), derivatives make the process of validation and amendment simultaneous: the value of output to be sold in the future can be validated now via a futures contract. The value of M (e.g. a stock of Canadian dollars) gets re-valued over time, and especially across

---

[6] Of course, surplus created in production expands the value of capital, but the point here relates to the process of circulation and the exchange of equivalents.

[7] In the context of circuits of capital, Marx (1885: 133) emphasises that money capital, commodity capital and productive capital are not independent varieties of capital and distinct branches of business, but 'simply particular functional forms of industrial capital, which takes on all three forms in turn'.

space as this M gets converted to other currencies in foreign exchange and interest rate futures markets. The value of C (a tonne of wheat) is in a continuous process of calculation as the wheat futures market keeps amending wheat prices. Hence, the terms of movement from M-C etc. are constantly being recalibrated. Indeed, by this on-going recalculation, derivatives make C and M themselves competitively determined.

A problem of continuity in the circuit: what about time and space?

We can look at the problem of not following this proposed path. C and M in the circuit (K1 and K2 as we have termed them) have different values in different times. A stock of money increases at the rate of interest. Capital equipment will not only deteriorate over time, but its replacement cost will change with innovation in its method of production and its site of production. Innovation in production technology also means that commodities produced at different times embody different internationally competitive production costs. The same concern applies to space. Space is not uniform, and the commensuration of capital in different sites and forms is a moot point. Does a machine in Paris have the same value as that machine in Hanoi, where notions of necessary production costs are different from those in Paris? In the context of globalisation there is the additional question of how we know that the value of capital is preserved in an M-C-M transaction when the two 'Ms' may be different currencies.

The problem, stated simply, is that there is no unique 'M' and no unique 'C' in the circuit: the value of M and C is always contingent, and always in need of mediation, or as we have called it commensuration. This is where derivatives come in, so the point warrants clarification.

Explaining K1 commodity capital

Conventionally, we explain the values of different commodities only in the present, at a particular site. The explanation is in terms of internationally competitive, or market-determined 'necessary' production costs. But how do we deal with space and time? Transportation across space is productive (but only if it is deemed necessary by competitive norms), so that commodities have different values in different locations. How we compare those different values – at what spatial point – is a difficulty. For example, if the well-head value of (identical) oil in Indonesia and Kuwait were the same, the transportation of Kuwaiti oil to Indonesia would not see the value of the Kuwaiti oil higher than the value of the Indonesian oil because the transportation did not constitute socially necessary labour. On the other hand, if there were a shortage of oil in Indonesia, and oil had to be shipped in from Kuwait to Indonesia, the value of the *Indonesian*-produced oil would have to be recalculated to include the costs of shipping Kuwaiti oil to Indonesia, for the latter process is part of competitive production costs in the provision of oil in Indonesia. Hence the problem: in which location is the value of commodity oil being measured?

Transportation over time poses an identical problem. Storage constitutes necessary production costs. But it does so only when the stored commodity meets the norms of necessary production costs in the future. In our oil case, technological change in exploration and drilling may (and indeed has) reduced the necessary production costs required for the production of a barrel of oil. Oil stored from the past, being identical to oil produced in the present, has a value only equal to the necessary production costs required to produce oil in the present, even if that barrel was produced in an era of higher necessary production costs. But if we do not know the value of oil in the future, what is the value now of oil being stored for the future? Hence the problem: what is the time at which the value of commodity oil is being measured?

Explaining K2 money capital

If exchange rates do not adhere to the law of one price (purchasing power parity) and if financial assets generally cannot be explained by reference to 'fundamental market values' – and they emphatically do not – there is a discontinuity in the value of 'M'. We have to ask what does our concept of capital make of M having a different value (in terms of commodity equivalence) in different currencies? When different currencies have different interest rates, the future value of M has a double discontinuity. There is, essentially, the same space and time problem as there is for 'C' (K1), but with extra layers. Indeed, the fact that the dominant form of swaps contract is not between commodities and money but between different forms of financial assets, is some signal that reconciling different forms of financial asset is more complex than reconciling the value of different physical assets.

In summary, these discontinuities between different sorts of money and different sorts of commodities at different localities and in different times are an irresolvable problem for a concept of capital at least as it is generally understood, yet they are resolved explicitly in practice by derivatives contracts. The huge growth in financial derivative products over the past decade is a reflection of just how many bridges there are to cross in mediating the complex representations of value on a global scale. The simple point to be made is that derivatives provide a means for the value of Ms and Cs (or K1s and K2s) to be compared wherever they are in the circuit, wherever they are in space and wherever they are in time. This is the process by which our abstracted assumption of the equivalence of value around the circuit is empirically verified.[8]

Consider the standard interest rate swap, which involves a contract between two or more parties where they agree to exchange (or swap) future interest rate payment commitments on debt contracts. These swaps are often linked to different exchange rates as well, so that if the difference between the reference short- and long-interest rates change, or if exchange rates change, the parties to the swap will have to make payments to the swap counterparty. The net effect of the swap contract is to set the overall cash flow obligations of the debt obligation for the life of the contract. This is important to economic calculation because it allows for a finer calibration of investment and financing decisions by individual capitals, and by extension greater scrutiny over K1 and K2 forms of competition.

Rethinking competition

The abstract version of K3, which assumed an equivalence of value as capital moved round the circuit, can now be thought of as an empirical reality but not, as in the abstracted version, because of the assumption of a spaceless globe and uniform time. Rather, it is an empirical reality because there are systematic mechanisms, in the forms of derivatives contracts, to bridge discontinuities in space and time.

This process leads us to reconsider the process of competition. Derivatives permit any form of capital at any place and time to be compared in value with any other form of capital at any place and at any time. They help to show 'at a glance' when any form of capital in any place at any time is over- or under-valued.

Returning to our four conceptions of capital, we see that their relation as depicted earlier is transformed by the operation of derivative markets. K1 (commodity capital) and K2 (money capital) cease to be just 'bits' of capital that are utilised in a competitive process (K3). K1 and K2 are now themselves integral parts of a competitive process in an on-going way. It is important to be clear here. In the conventional version of the circuit, K1 and K2 were always acquired via a market transaction – itself a

---

[8] Perhaps a less assertive term than equivalence is thus needed, and a better notion would be continuity of value.

competitive process. But this was a 'one off' competitive process – once the money or commodity inputs were acquired, or the commodity output sold, they were no longer themselves subjects of competition; they become quarantined property of the owner – objects of competition (bits of capital) in the individual circuit of capital (K3). The importance of derivatives in competition is summarised in Table 7.1.

The introduction of derivatives to this analysis shows that C and M (K1 and K2) continue to be subjects of competition throughout the circuit of capital. Futures, options and swaps transactions reveal that the value of M and C is not quarantined by a single act of acquisition, but is being continually negotiated and, in the process, benchmarked against other assets. M and C are now available to be actively engaged in driving calculations about the profitability of K3.

With K1 and K2 now understood as perpetual elements of competition, several consequences follow for an understanding of the nature of capitalist competition. The interactive engagement between K3s (individual circuits of capital) now appears too limited a conception of competition: each form of capital (M, C, P) is itself an on-going site of competition. Clifton, as we saw earlier, highlighted that competition be seen as a process *within* corporations – a competition for rate of return on investment between different activities of the firm. We called this competition between individual capitals. We now identify an additional competition *within* individual capitals – where the values of C and M as forms of assets are constantly being recalibrated.

Profit, then, shows up not just as an end-of-year account, but as a continuously adjusting account. Corporate strategy follows directly. Underperforming assets can more readily be identified and transformed or sold. Competition between capitals thereby intensifies – it is a daily exercise of verifying the value of every form of asset against every other form of asset through time and across the globe. The result is that many of the traditional sources of monopoly profits are being traded away in derivatives markets: the profits of circulation are being undercut.

Conclusion

Social capital (K4), the class relations between labour and capital, has so far in this chapter been something as a context category – a reminder that the process of competition takes place within and is specific to a particular system of class relations. We can now observe how the operation of derivative markets impacts on our understanding of class relations generally. This is set out in Table 7.1.

Table 7.1 Competition with and without financial derivatives

	Competition without financial derivatives	Competition with financial derivatives
K1 means of production	Value determined by necessary production costs (for Marxism, this is socially necessary labour time) at a particular location and at a particular time	Value being continually benchmarked and re-calculated against other K1 and K2 across all locations and across time. There is competition in determining the value of K1
K2 money	Money capital advanced of particular value at a particular time in a particular currency (or at a fixed rate of currency conversion)	Value being continually benchmarked and re-calculated against other K1 and K2 across all locations and across time. There is competition in determining the value of K2
K3 individual capital	A 'unit' of competition. Sometimes thought of as a firm, but more generally a discrete investment (process of accumulation). Capitalist competition occurs between different individual capitals producing the same product and between individual capitals as their circuits intersect	As before, but with the addition that all points of the circuit are continually being re-calculated. Monopoly rents in circulation disappear or are capitalised and traded away, so that competition now focuses directly in the sphere of production: competition to cut costs of production and increase productivity
K4 social capital	The class relations of capitalism that are articulated through K3 and reproduced by the competitive interactions of K3s	This is no longer just the social context of competition: the changes to K3 make stark the centrality of the labour process as the source of profits

Finance and class relations in production have appeared analytically separated – 'casino capitalism' and 'the working poor' have become distinct issues. This chapter has sought to show how finance and financial markets are not only providing the means for commensuration across the differences that define the global economy, they impose the imperative for such commensuration.

With financial derivatives, the boundaries between individual capitals have been blurred, the differences between forms of capital (debt and equity) made less important, locational differences in activities made easier to compare, and the nature of assets with different time horizons made less incompatible. Financial derivatives show that all these distinctions are reconciled within the unity of capital as a social relation of accumulation (K4), but they do so in ways that we are still trying to understand.

Derivatives are now continually deployed in re-calculating the monetary values of capital throughout the circuit and in this way financial derivatives have intensified competition and drawn the different notions of capital together. Accordingly, competitive pressure returns to the labour process. The capitalist faced with intense, generalised competition in money and commodity markets must look to the sphere of production (C-P-C') as the one site where it is possible to 'get a jump' on competitors. This is not a case of the 'race to the bottom' of wages and conditions nor the 'race to the top' of productivity. It is a race for profitability – a process that includes both those tendencies. Labour that cannot deliver globally competitive levels of productivity must compensate, as it were, for its less than frontier productivity by accepting longer hours and lower wages. The effect is to draw labour indirectly into the same mode of calculation as applies to other production inputs. The widely documented intensification of labour over the past two decades, centring on flexibility in skills and working conditions, longer working hours and wage increases less than productivity, follows directly.

Herein lies the direct connection between developments in finance in the past 25 years and the resurgence of capital's assault on organised labour. Many have simply thrown the label of 'neoliberalism' over this era and noted the coexisting resurgence of finance and the shift of income from labour to capital. But the connection is made purely at a ideological level – neoliberalism's pursuit of 'free market' policies. Here we present the connection as an integral part of capitalist competition.

Part III
Debating Derivatives

Insofar as derivatives have become a central component of capitalist finance and calculation, there are many contentious issues for consideration. In the next two chapters we raise just a selection, which strike us as being important in current debates.

The key propositions of these chapters are:

1. While derivatives are frequently associated with speculation (and often thereby judged pejoratively), it is virtually impossible to identify a discrete set of activities that are 'speculative'.

2. Attempts to regulate so as to reduce the speculative role of derivatives cannot be successful. Not only will any controls impact also on 'virtuous' transactions, but derivatives enable undesired financial transactions to be disguised as 'virtuous' transactions.

3. Accordingly, policies such as a Tobin tax or national capital controls to prevent 'capital flight' are likely to have large unintended and undesirable consequences.

4. Whilst many see derivatives as part of a product of 'deregulation' they are more usefully seen as part of a new, though undoubtedly vulnerable, system of regulation.

5. The 'formula' of derivatives is now entering into wider social policy, as a way of converting social responsibility into individual responsibility and personal misadventure into personal financial mismanagement. It is a frightening scenario.

8
Speculation, Derivatives and Capital Controls

Those concerned with levels of economic growth, investment, employment, wages and the like frequently look at data on financial markets with bemusement. Why do global financial markets turn over each year about 100 times more than is needed to fund international trade? What goes on in these financial markets, and is it necessary if they are not supporting the 'real' activities of production and investment?

There is a widespread belief, in both popular debate and in some academic circles, that derivatives are permitting highly leveraged positions and thereby facilitating excessive risk taking. Derivatives markets are forums of widespread, costly and often destructive speculation, generating market volatility and potential major crises, without contributing much to 'real' production and investment. Of course, the issue of speculation predates derivatives, and is certainly not limited to the realm of derivatives. But with financial derivatives now at the centre of global finance, contemporary debates about speculation and global financial instability cannot exclude consideration of derivatives.

The problem is that in some circles, derivatives are synonymous with speculation: the issue is not about how an understanding of derivatives might transform an age-old debate about speculation, but about an age-old disdain for speculation being used to judge derivatives.

In this chapter, we seek to challenge that prejudice. The objective is not a moral defence of derivatives, but to build the case that many of the judgements about speculation are ill considered in the light of derivatives. Moreover, the importance of this issue shows clearly when these judgements are taken to the level of policy. The chapter shows that any attempts by governments, individually or collectively, to control capital movements or exchange rates must now include a strategy regarding derivatives. This strategy has to be not just the inclusion of derivatives into old policy programmes dating from the 1970s and before, but an engagement with derivatives as a new form of money and capital. These regulatory policy proposals need to be understood as a confrontation not just with aberrant and opportunist profiteering, but with capitalism itself.

Clarifying the case against derivatives

There are two prevalent criticisms of financial derivatives – to do with their role in speculation and in the misrepresentation of financial accounts. We will identify them as the issues of speculation/leveraging and blending/disguise.

Speculation and leverage

There is a widespread belief that financial derivatives encourage speculation and hence increase the scale of speculation because they permit speculators to leverage (or 'gear up') their risk exposure.

What is meant by 'speculation' is an issue we must explore shortly. But suffice it to say here that, if speculation has something to do with investing funds in expectation of asset price movements, the leverage provided by derivatives exerts two important impacts. First, derivatives provide a cheap way of speculating. By being cheap, derivatives permit an increased risk exposure for a given expenditure. Second, a consequence of leverage is that futures and options enable the speculator to not only win or lose large amounts, but to lose more than the value of their initial investment.

If, for example, I believe that the value of the Euro will rise relative to the US dollar, I could buy Euros now and wait. If I spent $20 and purchased €10 (i.e. at an exchange rate of €2 per $1), and there was a 10 per cent appreciation in the Euro over 3 months, I will make $2 on my $20 investment. If it instead depreciated by 10 per cent, I would lose $2. These spot market (i.e. non-derivative) gains and losses are real, but rather small. But if I instead bought two $10 call options on €1000, I have increased my exposure to a 10 per cent appreciation of not €10, but €2000. The 10 per cent appreciation would give me a gain of $380 (€200 less the $20 spent on call options). Or if the Euro depreciated, I would lose my entire investment of $20. If instead of buying call options, I had sold put options and the Euro depreciated 10 per cent against my expectation, I would receive a $20 initial premium from the sale, but lose

$400, giving a net loss of $380 – that is, 19 times the value of my initial investment.

The illustration shows the range of concerns: the capacity of derivatives to leverage speculative positions and thereby accentuate both potential gains and losses, including losses greater than the initial investment. The effect, it is argued, is that derivatives attract high risk gamblers, although there can be no data on this claim, for reasons discussed below.

This capacity for leverage means that a speculator cannot only gamble much more, but if enough money is invested in derivatives, there may well be price effects in cash markets. That is, leverage creates the capacity for high volume trading that can move prices in ways that may be profitable for the initiator, but destabilising for the rest of the market. This is precisely the practice captured in the fears about hedge funds that are attributed with mounting speculative attacks against the British pound and Swedish kronor in 1992, as well as those that played a similar role in the Asian financial crisis of 1996–97.

So financial derivatives are not the cause of speculation, but they are often judged harshly for increasing the leverage in speculation, and therefore making prices even more volatile. Policy proposals to curtail speculation in general and derivatives in particular follow accordingly. But is this an adequate depiction of 'speculation', and so are policies predicated on this depiction likely to have the desired effects?

So what is 'speculation'? In our depiction of leverage, we presented the popular notion that 'speculation' is both a clearly delineable activity and exerts negative impacts that may warrant containment by public policy interventions. It will be seen that the more one looks at this notion in the context of derivatives, the less credible it seems.

A detailed consideration of this issue is presented in Appendix 8.1. We can, however, get an essential perspective on this issue by briefly comparing the different conceptual approaches to speculation in neoclassical and Keynesian economics.

For neoclassical economics, speculation does not itself occupy a central place, because all market participants are equally important in price formation. But inasmuch as speculation is seen to exist in the neoclassical discourse, speculators do two critical things: they add liquidity to market exchange and permit risk to be reallocated to those who have the capacity and desire to hold it. In both cases speculation should help prices to more closely reflect their 'fundamental values'. The clear implication for derivatives is that, by making it easier to undertake transactions and shift risk, derivatives markets should help to make price formation more efficient and prices more stable. In terms of international capital markets, derivatives should help ensure the neutrality of money on an international level.[1]

In Keynesian discourse, speculation is understood to play a much more important and often destabilising role. Keynes made a distinction between money (or finance) and the 'real' economy, and observed that money does not always exert a neutral effect on economic activity. Where finance serves to facilitate real activity, it performs a useful social role. But where finance assumes a life of its own, it may undermine productive activity, or at least prevent it from being fully employed. This is where speculation can be so damaging, because speculators may not drive prices closer to fundamental values, for money markets are characterised by the activity of strategic behaviour: attempting to make money simply predicting what other market participants will do. In Keynes' (1936: 156) words 'we devote our intelligences to anticipating what average opinion expects the average opinion to be'.

In this respect, by making speculative transactions easier, derivatives may at times undermine the real economy. This would constitute a powerful case for the control of derivatives markets, so that governments can continue to keep money at the service of the real economy.

So what can be concluded about the issue of speculation and derivatives? It must surely be somewhat ambiguous. If there is a distinct set of activities called 'speculation' then derivatives accentuate the impact of speculation. It is stretching credibility to argue, in the neoclassical tradition that speculation, amplified by derivatives, systematically cause markets to gravitate even more rapidly towards a stable equilibrium. Indeed, although derivatives are creatures of price instability, they do not seem to have made prices more stable. But it is also stretching credibility to argue, in the Keynesian tradition, that short-term financial transactions are motivated exclusively by risk taking, and hence that derivatives always accentuate risk taking beyond what is collectively desirable.

These two interpretations form the basis of most economic debates about speculation. As a polemic, it is clear that one is extolling the virtues of market forces; the other, depicting them as destabilising and in need of controls. But it is important also to notice two shared absences from this polemic which, we will see shortly, are of critical importance for issues of capital controls.

---

[1] This is the notion of purchasing power parity: that the same commodities cost the same amount in different currencies.

First, neither the Keynesians nor the neoclassicals can adequately differentiate between speculation (taking on risk) and hedging (laying off risk) because the two processes cannot be differentiated by behaviour in the market. For the neoclassical, market forces are independent of the motives of agents and, of the two, it is market forces that matter. For the Keynesians too, all traders are party to a market process which is, in sum, destabilising. The solution for the Keynesians is not to differentiate honourable (hedging) from dishonourable (speculative) positions, but to regulate for market stability such that speculation is unprofitable and hedging unnecessary.

Second, neither neoclassicals nor Keynesians can deal with the issue of space and speculation. For the neoclassicals, speculative markets have no systematic spatial characteristics, and so there is no engagement with the question of whether the capacities of regulators are challenged by the spatial expansion of market trading. For the Keynesians, as we saw in Chapter 6, there is the presumed ontological primacy of national economic units, and so the implicit assumption that markets operate within territorial boundaries. The reality that speculative activity may occur 'offshore', and outside of the jurisdiction of national regulators, creates concerns about nation-state capacities and national economic sovereignty. It is at the core of Keynesian demands for international regulatory agencies (e.g. Eatwell and Taylor 2000).

Blending and disguise

Unlike speculation and leverage, the issue of disguise has not hitherto been prominent in our analysis, although we have developed all the background analysis required for this proposition. It will be recalled that we have noted how derivatives permit both the 'binding' of the future price of an asset to its price in the present, or of the price in one place with those in another. They also permit the 'blending' of different sort of assets together, breaking down the differences between hitherto discrete asset forms. The issue of possible disguise arises because the capacity of blending also makes it possible for one asset form to be made to appear like another: debt can be made to appear like equity; short-term flows can be made to appear as long-term flows.[2] This capacity of derivatives to change

---

[2] This is at least part of the reason that empirical work by Claessens *et al.* (1995) shows that the labels 'short-term' and 'long-term' do not reveal information about the time-series properties of flows. Indeed, they find 'long-term' to be as volatile and unpredictable as 'short-term' flows.

the appearance of an asset is important if, for analytical and/or policy reasons, there is need to distinguish between different sorts of capital. Futures and options are part of this blending/disguise process because they can misrepresent profitability. It is possible, for example, to forward sell (or purchase) an asset so that future price rises (or falls) can have opposite effects on a firm's profitability to that which would be expected from on balance sheet positions.

However, swaps are at the centre of the blending/disguise process because with a swap the underlying asset need not change hands, only the future income flows arising from changes in relative prices. An interest rate swap, for example, may effectively convert a debt with a fixed rate interest payment into a debt with floating rate characteristics (or vice versa). Because swaps are off-balance-sheet transactions, what appears on an institution's balance sheet may be quite different from its actual financial exposures. The institution's accounts showing a fixed rate loan is not depicting its actual exposure to interest rate changes. So derivatives make it impossible to read from the balance sheet itself exactly what forms of capital an institution is holding and transacting.

This can be readily understood in relation to corporations, and it has been well documented in cases like Barings and Enron, where the evidence eventually showed that official company accounts were not revealing the 'true' story. But it is also an issue for national accounts – the balance of payments – and this has profound implications for policies such as capital controls, as we shall discuss later.

The ways in which derivatives can be deceptive in balance of payments accounts are extensive, and we will give here just a couple of illustrations. The two seminal works on this issue are, we believe, Garber (1998) and The United States National Academy of Science's Panel on International Capital Transactions (Kester 1994).[3] An illustration borrowed from each will suffice to demonstrate the point.

Garber (1998: 32), writing about the Mexican exchange rate crisis of 1994–95, gives the general following illustration of the deceptive use of derivatives:

> The acquisitions of a large block of equity is classified as foreign direct investment, but a buyer may be acquiring the block simply to hedge a short position in equity established through a derivative position.

[3] The Panel was funded initially by the US Bureau of Economic Analysis, and later also by the Federal Reserve Board and the State Department.

In the case of an equity swap[4] ... the foreign investment firm that sells the swap must acquire the shares to form a hedge. If the swap is large enough, the hedging operation may be booked as foreign direct investment because the offshore swap position is not included in the capital accounts, although the investment house in fact is making a short term floating rate loan in foreign currency.

The Panel on Foreign Trade Statistics, analysing the limitations of the balance of payments as a macroeconomic indicator, opens up a different dimension: where things get recorded as well as what gets recorded. For example an overseas investor in the US stock market could hedge the purchase by borrowing dollars from a US bank or through the sale of forward dollars. The dollars borrowed from the US bank enter the US balance of payments but the forward sale will not (Kester 1994: 126).

This sort of concern is really an application to national balance of payments of an argument we elaborated in Chapters 3 and 4: that derivatives permit the separation of actual ownership of an asset from other attributes (such as future price movements). The problem of balance of payments data is that they are records of asset ownership, not of exposure to the attributes of assets.

The implications of blending/disguise are profound when governments seek to regulate inter-national capital flows: there are no 'true' data of the actual nature of these flows, and any attempt to differentiate some forms of capital flow as 'good' (e.g. direct investment) and others as bad (e.g., short-term foreign currency loans) is bound to fail, as Garber's illustration shows. Via swaps, capital can simply enter a country in whatever form is deemed acceptable, and convert once inside. Moreover, the conversion itself may be conducted in an off-shore financial market.

When we combine the concerns regarding leverage/speculation and blending/disguise, two important implications for policy become apparent.

First, neither framework provides a mechanism to distinguish between different forms of appearance of capital. The concern for speculation/leverage does not have the capacity to distinguish between speculation and hedging. The concern for blending/disguise shows that there is no effective substance to a distinction between, say,

---

[4] An equity swap is the exchange of the total return on a share or share index (including both share dividends and capital gains) for some interest yield.

international direct investment and short-term foreign currency transactions. It follows that it would be virtually impossible to operate any sort of capital controls that seek to differentiate between different forms of capital.

Second, neither framework can address the question of capital mobility and space – except by assumption. The analysis of speculation/hedging has no particular spatial dimension. The popular concern that hedge fund speculation involves a rapid shift of money in or out of a country is a misunderstanding of space. Speculation on the currency, interest rates or stock prices in country X does not require movements of capital into or out of country X if country X's currency, or stocks originating from country X (or even various currency or stock derivatives that relate to currency and stock derived from country X, but perhaps not even having origins in country X) are traded on a significant scale outside of country X. The concepts of 'speculation' and 'cross-border flows' are quite different. The same point applies to disguise: while there is an 'initial' flow into or out of country X as recorded in its balance of payments, the transformation into another asset form may occur in swaps markets offshore from country X.

These two points, we will see, become critical in the assessment of policies to contain the activities of derivative trading.

Differentiating 'threats'

Speculation/leverage and hedging/disguise may manifest in many different forms and sites. It is not our proposal to address them all. It is convenient to divide the threats that supposedly come with speculation/leverage and hedging/disguise into two distinct categories: we will call them internal threats and external threats. We could have used the terms 'micro' and 'macro' threats, and the popular meaning of these terms expresses our categories approximately; but only approximately.

By *internal threats* we refer to the dangers of speculation/leverage and hedging/disguise that arise within institutions (especially corporations) or within individual contracts. These are the concerns that arise about corporations (their managers or in-house rogue traders) that can use derivatives to 'gamble', and contracts in financial markets where one party or the other may be exposed to more than a manageable amount of risk, and for this to be hidden from public view. In these situations, speculation/leverage and hedging/disguise often go together, and many notable derivatives-linked corporate crashes of the last 20 years could be described as involving speculative practices that were only discovered when it was too late because the company books were not transparent. This would characterise Nick Leeson's options trading at Barings, the insolvency at Orange County, or the fraudulent operations of Enron, to name but a few infamous cases.

By *external threats* we refer to the dangers of speculation/leverage and hedging/disguise that impact on unknowing parties. To be more specific, we have in mind the threats that are thought to impact on nation states via leveraged speculative 'raids' on currencies, and by deceptive forms of recording financial flows, such that speculative flows cannot be readily identified in balance of payments financial account data.

There are clear similarities in speculation/leverage and hedging/ disguise in both internal and external threats, but we have a particular reason for highlighting a difference. It is about different policy responses to each threat. With internal threats, the almost-universally-adhered-to policy response involves a focus on two agendas: increased requirements for transparency in the financial positions and operations of institutions (corporations and financial institutions) and more effectively and tightly framed mechanisms of state prudential supervision. This policy programme is advocated by a broad spectrum covering neoclassical economists (BIS 2002), Keynesians (e.g. Partnoy 2002; Dodd 2005) and radicals (e.g. Epstein and Crotty 2001). While there remains intensive debate about the clearest guidelines for transparency and the most appropriate form of prudential supervision, they agree on this fundamental policy direction.

These are indeed important debates. The appropriate measurement of corporate (and national) economic performance in the midst of financial derivatives will almost certainly require different prudential supervision, and different accounting measures. We do not, however, see them as central to the project of this book. Our study of derivatives as an expression of capitalist accumulation has not focused on the correct legal specification of property rights and improved information flows. Nor are we expert in the accounting and legal dimensions that inevitably lie at the basis of these debates.

External threats, on the other hand, while not incompatible with the prudential regulation and transparency (Epstein *et al.* 2003), lead to policies that involve not the refinement of market processes, but the over-ruling of market processes, and this is what makes them central to our analysis. Accordingly, this chapter focuses on 'external' threats that are commonly associated with derivatives: how leverage/speculation impacts on nations and nation states via 'hot money', and how the blending/disguise associated with derivatives challenges nation-state capacities, including the capacity to regulate against 'hot money'.

We focus on two prominent policy debates about the regulation of externally generated, speculative threats: the proposals for a Tobin tax, and the case for national capital controls to avert 'capital flight'. Both have been extensively discussed, and over a long period. Our primary focus here is their association with financial derivatives.

The Tobin tax

A Tobin tax, as is well known, is a tax on turnover in foreign exchange markets. It was first proposed in 1972 by Nobel Prize-winning economist James Tobin (1974).[5] While it is now popularly presented as a policy to counter 'hot', speculative money, at the time Tobin proposed it, 'hot' money was not (yet) a problem. Tobin was seeking to address the increasing problem of indistinguishability between forms of capital movement. Dodd (2004: 23) reminds us of Tobin: 'his primary motivation for the policy ... was not to reduce volatility or finance development, but rather to enhance the effectiveness of monetary and fiscal policy'. The tax's impact on speculation was at best a second-order issue, a sort of useful (unintended) consequence of restoring macro-economic policy effectiveness.

But it is as a counter to speculative capital that the Tobin tax has achieved popularity. It is believed that, by reducing 'noise' in market trading, exchange rates would gravitate towards some long-term, sustainable value. This rather simple proposal has received significant support from a range of sources – from eminent conventional economists (e.g. Stiglitz 1989; Summers and Summers 1989; Frankel 1996) to radicals (e.g. ul Haq *et al.* 1996), and from some advanced capitalist governments and international organisations (e.g. BBC 2001; Reisen 2002) to third-world-oriented NGOs (e.g. Oxfam 2002; ATTAC[6]).

As a proposal with a substantial and diverse political momentum, the specific details of the proposed tax vary widely. Essentially, it involves a small tax on foreign exchange transactions so as, to use Tobin's famous phrase, to 'throw sand in the wheels of international finance'. But there

---

[5] Although many references to Tobin's proposal source it to an article in 1978 (Tobin 1978), it was in fact proposed in his 1972 Janeway Lectures at Princeton University (Tobin 1974).

[6] ATTAC is the Association for the Taxation of Financial Transactions for the Aid of Citizens. See for example, http://www.attac.org/indexen/index.html

remain disagreements amongst its advocates, for example:

• Should the tax apply to all kinds of financial transaction, or only some?
• Should the tax rate be uniform across markets and instruments?
• Should it be implemented within nations, and by discrete nation states, or does it require international co-operation?
• Is it necessary that all countries participate in the tax, or is it sufficient that it is implemented just in leading financial centres?
• Is the objective of the tax to restrict financial transactions or to separate capital markets and raise revenue?[7]

It is the underlying proposal, not the specifics of implementation, which is of concern here. We can consider the tax proposal via the issues of leverage/speculation and blending/disguise.

The underlying premises of the Tobin tax as it is popularly understood are that

1. financial markets are volatile,
2. volatility is due to speculation,
3. speculation involves short-term, hot money, and
4. a turnover tax on foreign exchange markets would reduce such short-term movement, and add to exchange rate stability.

We can accept proposition 1 as a general depiction of financial markets. However, proposition 2 can be read as one, but only one, possible explanation for volatility. If volatility is attributable entirely to speculation, it follows that, in the absence of speculation, exchange rates would gravitate to stable values. Those stable values must be assumed to be not just an empirical trend, but to have a material foundation: implicitly, there is the notion that, in the absence of speculation, exchange rates will gravitate towards 'fundamental value'. In earlier chapters, we challenged the idea that there is any notion of a 'fundamental value' which determines 'speculation-free' exchange rates. In this respect, the Tobin tax remains within the neoclassical vision that money should be neutral, and that 'pure' market processes (with appropriate government guidance and taxation) will generate prices that reveal 'real' forces. This is a rather limited perspective on the causes of volatility.

---

[7] For a discussion of some of these issues, see for instance Eichengreen *et al.* (1995).

The problem specific to the Tobin tax proposal shows primarily with proposition 3. Two conspicuous problems arise which have the effect of undermining the conclusion, proposition 4.

First, as argued by Paul Davidson (1997), at its most effective the Tobin tax would only deter speculation over small price movements (or what is known as 'noise' trading), not on all speculation *per se*. This would mean it is likely to be ineffective precisely when it would be most warranted: when markets are highly volatile. Any exchange rate movement in excess of the rate of a Tobin tax will still facilitate 'speculative trading'. That would include all the major exchange rate crises of the past 20 years.[8]

Second, while speculation may involve short-term movement of money, so too does hedging. While the target of a Tobin tax is so-called short-term 'hot' monetary movement, it is a tax on all turnover. That is, it would not discriminate between types of transaction: between 'legitimate' and 'speculative' trading. It would thus act also as a tax on international trade and production. Moreover, if speculation is not the sole source of exchange rate volatility, it would remain necessary for financial institutions and corporations to take up short-term positions in financial markets to avert losses from unexpected exchange rate variation.[9] As Grahl and Lysandrou (2003) convincingly argue, the danger of a Tobin tax, which cannot differentiate 'speculation' from 'hedging', is that it creates a disincentive for financial institutions and corporations to hedge their foreign exchange exposures. The effect then may well be to increase the risk of financial crises, not reduce them, as advocates of the tax contend.

In short, in the context of speculation and leverage, the problem of a Tobin tax in conception (regardless of the problems of practical implementation) is that it must contend either that it can eradicate the need for hedging, or that there is no basis to a differentiation between speculation and hedging, and both are to be discouraged. Neither is a persuasive argument.

Where do derivatives fit into this evaluation? When originally proposed by Tobin in 1972, derivatives were virtually unknown in financial markets. Indeed, Tobin's original proposal addressed only spot markets.

---

[8] Some have suggested that a two-stage Tobin tax would resolve the problem so that when large-scale flows do occur a larger tax would kick in. But the problem here is that these flows could well have occurred before regulators could implement the tax.

[9] This has led to a number of proposals for transaction and institutional exemptions from the tax, and this raises the problem of avoidance behaviour to exploit such loopholes.

The development of derivatives (and issues of disguise and leverage that comes with them) raises an additional set of issues for a Tobin tax. One issue here is that various forms of currency derivatives mean that, in practical implementation, the regulatory coverage could not just focus on taxing the main global centres of international finance: the regulatory process would need to be ubiquitous. This need is now widely understood, though the consequences are not. As Spahn (1996) has noted,

> The problem cannot be resolved simply by extending the tax to transactions in derivatives because the size of such transactions cannot be related to the underlying long transactions in a straightforward manner. A Tobin tax on the transactions themselves would grossly understate the volume of funds that can be channeled through foreign exchange markets; however, taxing the notional value of a derivatives contract would probably severely damage the derivatives markets and might even destroy them completely. Given the important role played by the forward and futures markets in hedging risks related to exchange rate fluctuations, the eventual disappearance of these markets would threaten the stability of foreign exchange markets.

But perhaps some would welcome this consequence!

The blending/disguise capacities of derivatives raise wider issues for the Tobin tax. As we have argued in Chapter 6, derivatives break down the distinction between money and capital, such that it is not possible to just tax 'money' transactions. The blending capacity of derivatives means that foreign exchange transactions are not just cash-like conversions such as occur in spot markets. They may involve all sorts of assets in one currency being 'converted' into all sorts of assets in another currency. All transactions in all of these assets would need to be taxed.

In addition to the need to cover 'capital' as well as 'money' the tax would have to cover not just foreign exchange related transactions, but a raft of domestic transactions, too. Take the example of short-term speculative transactions trying to gain advantage of, for example, interest rate increases in country X. The connection to flows of hot money is not at all obvious. There is need to consider the following:

1. the derivative transaction that gives exposure to country X interest rates need not involve any international flows of funds into country X: it can be transacted in 'off-shore' markets, and
2. Derivatives make it possible to gain exposure to interest rates in country X without exposure to the currency of country X.

So taxing international foreign exchange transactions will miss this speculative venture, both because there may be no cross-national exchange and no foreign currency exchange. What is true of interest rates is true of all other financial transactions, too. The implication for a Tobin tax is that it must tax all forms of capital transaction, not just the foreign exchange market. It must be a turnover tax on every transaction, domestic as well as international, if it is to achieve its objective.

It seems that the Tobin tax cannot deal with the complexities of either the speculation/leverage or disguise/blending that are associated with derivative.[10] It is probably the case that its primary attribute as a policy is its simplicity, for therein lies its essentially rhetorical value, and on that basis alone its popularity will continue.

National agendas for social change: are capital controls a priority?

The fear that some international capital flows are dominated by speculative or destabilising motives has driven renewed support for policies to control international capital flows. In particular, the experiences of the recent Asian financial crisis as well as financial crises in Latin and South America have revived debates about national capital controls. Much of this analysis, and most of the policy debate, has addressed the use of short-term controls on the inflow of capital. Our concern, however, is the use of controls on capital outflows, designed to prevent so-called 'capital flight'.

In the 1930s, Keynes argued forcefully for the implementation of national capital controls to restrict the forms and volume of international capital movements so as to increase national policy sovereignty (Crotty 1983). He expressed the view that 'advisable domestic policies might often be easier to compass if the phenomenon known as "capital flight" could be ruled out' (Keynes 1933: 757). By capital flight, Keynes was understood to be referring to capital which exits a nation as a response to national policies (particularly interest rate policies) that its owners perceive will be inconsistent with globally competitive rates of profit and with their corporate discretion on investment.

---

[10] Dodd (2003) develops a similar critique of such policies on the basis of an engagement with the technical details of financial derivatives, what they do and how they work. From a broadly Keynesian view of the need for derivatives to be controlled, he has concluded that a Tobin tax is bad politics because it probably can't be achieved politically, bad technically because it would be costly to implement, and bad policy because it won't achieve what its proponents expect it to.

This is not the only definition of capital flight. Some wish to define it through a balance of payments framework as net unrecorded capital outflows (Epstein 2005). But our concern here is with the Keynesian or nationalist project of using capital controls to create insulation from the vicissitudes of global financial markets. While not exclusively concerned with issues of 'hot money' and 'speculation', policies to deal with capital flight represent an attempt by nation states to assert policy autonomy in the face of capital mobility.

Here, as with Tobin tax, issues of capital controls are only partially related to financial derivatives, but it is this relationship, rather than capital controls *per se*, that is central to our analysis. Accordingly, the focus is on the issues of both speculation/leverage and hedging/disguise that come with financial derivatives.

So the question is: should the first, immediate act of a government intent on subordinating capital to a social agenda be to impose capital controls so as to lock capital in territorially before it has a chance to 'fly'? Many would argue that it is, and for essentially the reasons that Keynes nominated: capital in fear of the transformations will exit as quickly as possible. The government must corral capital and preserve it for the pursuit of its alternative strategy.[11]

In evaluating this strategic proposition, the critical concern is the relationship between money and accumulation, and we have seen that derivatives, by merging the categories of money and capital, will have an effect in the way capital controls impact upon accumulation. Because of the blending/disguise characteristic of derivatives, just what capital will be corralled by capital controls will be uncertain. The essential problem is that the accumulation consequences of policies to prevent capital flight cannot be known in advance.

But what, exactly, *is* the capital that supposedly flies in the process of capital flight? The answer to the question takes us back to the multiple meanings of capital, addressed in Chapter 7. There we identified four different ways in which the term 'capital' is employed.

K1 Capital as a stock of means of production, as in 'capital equipment'
K2 Capital as a stock of wealth, as in 'the investment of capital'
K3 Capital as an 'individual capital' in reference to a single process of production and exchange

---

[11] For advocates of capital controls on the left along these lines, see Epstein and Schor 1992, Block 1993, Crotty and Epstein 1996, Wade and Veneroso 1998.

K4   Capital as 'social capital' – a social relation, in reference to the capitalist system of property ownership and surplus appropriation.

What form of capital flies in the process of capital flight? It is not K1, for by and large, these are physical assets that are internationally immobile. It is only K2 (a stock of monetary wealth) that is prone to flight (or depreciation), via decisions made within K3. National capital controls are directed to K3 to contain the movement of K2.

In any project for social change requiring some containment of capital, two immediate problems arise. First, a financial stock of capital is or can readily be held offshore while appearing on the books of the company subject to capital controls. So K2 may already be outside the territory in which controls are exerted. Indeed, with financial derivatives, ownership of K2 can readily be moved, for instance by the owner buying an option to sell the wealth to another corporation, or by swapping the returns on that wealth with the returns from say a US government bond.

Second, K2 has meaning as a stock of capital only in the context of K3 – an individual capital's accumulation process. It is 'capital' because it is to be advanced for accumulation, and so is a claim on future output by K1. Without that claim, it is just a fund of money. Although we tend to think of a capital control as the prevention of an international relocation of money, the objective is not to simply retain money, it is to secure the conversion of money capital into productive inputs. A national outflow of capital means that the purchase of K1 (the conversion of K2 into K1) will be relocated to another country. Capital flight means, in effect, the loss of effective demand for locally produced K1.

A capital control therefore must do more that retain a pile of quarantined money – it must ensure effective demand via a positive conversion into nationally located K1. As capital flight is K3's escape from this positive conversion, there is reason to believe that it will not be spontaneously forthcoming: capital controls must secure an alternative path to ensure on-going domestic accumulation (the conversion of K2 to K1). But is it apparent that the on-going domestic conversion of K2 into K1 is contingent upon the de-mobilisation of escaping K2?

The argument in favour of controls on capital flight seems to conflate two propositions:

1. Capital flight causes unemployment and a loss of local production: the flight of K1 internationally precludes its conversion to K1 domestically; and

2. A reformist state cannot maintain accumulation domestically unless it can retain the use of corralled K2.

At issue is the question of what is required to 'trigger' K3 – the co-ordinated conversion of K2 into K1, etc. In proposition 1, there is a historical statement that 'flown' K2 is no longer expressing effective demand for local K1 – such that, with capital flight, K3 fails to occur domestically and unemployment is a consequence. In proposition 2, there is a positive statement that without the flown K2, local K1 *cannot* be mobilised in accumulation (K3).

The difference pivots on whether we understand K2 as money capital or just as a fund of money. Proposition 1 identifies the flight of money *capital* – a loss of claim on future K1. But it leaves the country merely as money: a book entry. Proposition 2 identifies only the need to retain a fund of money, without addressing its on-going role as money capital. But capital flight causes a decline in future production within the nation only because the transferred claims are not replaced by other claims. It is this loss of replacement of impetus for K3, not the flight of money, that explains unemployment in the aftermath of capital flight.

The policy alternatives are therefore basically of two kinds. One is that the reformist state must replace the *claims* of flown K2 with its own claims – it must socialise not control over mobility of money, but over production generally, with alternative signals for the processes of production and distribution. This is a direct and immediate confrontation with K4, the social relations of production. This, of course, is not the Keynesian agenda.

The other policy direction is that the state may invoke capital controls to de-mobilise escaping money, but it must then ensure that this corralled money is realised domestically as money capital: as claims on K1, in a process of K3. The reformist state would therefore need to address incentives which would ensure the conditions of K3 (that corralled K2 would indeed be advanced for the purchase of K1). So as part of the policy of immediate imposition of capital controls, the reformist state would, at the same time, have to ensure that the globally de-mobilised K2 would earn a rate of return that is sufficient to retain it in accumulation. The alternative would be to see K2 lying idle, awaiting its first opportunity to circumvent the controls (presumably via derivative transactions).

Andrew Glynn (1995) has highlighted the consequences of this requirement. Capital controls in themselves will not secure full employment and greater egalitarianism. They would need to be backed up by a commitment by labour to an economic environment conducive to high and stable profitability (or, as he put it, to a non-inflationary wage environment). Specifically, Glynn recommended that the task of national economic policy requires some of the costs of stability to be 'explicitly counted and willingly shouldered by the mass of wage and salary earners' (1995: 55).

In effect, when capital controls are adopted as the initial policy by a reformist government to stop capital flight, what is changed are accounting book entries. Corporations are prevented from transferring money offshore; the financial account of the balance of payments will not show a capital outflow. But what is not changed by this emphatic policy intervention is the conditions under which money is advanced as capital for the process of accumulation. The demobilised money must still be enticed into production, by the conventional incentives of profitability.

As the first, decisive, step in a reform programme, this hardly constitutes a challenge to individual capitals (K3), let alone capitalist social relations (K4). Indeed, as a policy, it is not far from the case made by orthodox economists, that capital controls can at best create a breathing space for governments to implement 'structural reform'.[12]

A project for radical social change within any nation does not need capital controls but the development of a new monetary regime to mobilise K1. In essence, the confrontation is not with the mobility of capital *per se* (K2 and K3), but with K4, the social relations of capital themselves. This confrontation is not enhanced by policies to prevent the outflow of currency. Indeed, the opposite is the effect, for the focus on the containment of money flows requires that the state take on the guarantees that will bring forward the advance of money as capital for accumulation, with all the implications that follow for securing labour productivity and wages consistent with global rates of profit.

This is indeed what derivatives emphasise about capitalism: that processes of exchange and competition are now saturated with capital, not just at the border, via 'leakages', but in all phases of economic activity.

Conclusion

This chapter has explored the issue of speculation in derivatives markets in order to consider the implications for monetary and financial stability. We have considered proposals for capital controls and Tobin taxes, both in terms of their potential to stabilise financial markets, and restore national government policy autonomy.

[12] Eichengreen (1998: 7) for instance, supports the orthodox case for capital controls for developing countries. Specifically he concludes that 'any recourse to capital controls ... should not be taken as an excuse to slow down the fundamental process of institutional development and policy reform'.

Neither policy is claimed by its advocates to be easy to implement, but financial derivatives, which are often not specifically considered by these advocates, create a near impossibility. Financial derivatives are now at the centre of global finance, and we established in earlier chapters that they have important implications for money, competition and capital. In short, they are an important expression of capitalist relations, not a pathological growth that can be excised by carefully targetted government policy.

For controls over capital movements, derivatives have the capacity to add leverage to financial markets, and the capacity to disguise forms of capital. This makes any attempts to regulate capital flows based around distinctions between 'hot', speculative money and long-term productive investment even more difficult than before. It also adds significant complications for proposals to tax international transactions, because derivatives can be written outside of national jurisdictions, and effectively transform the cash flow effects of assets in different national jurisdictions.

Our argument, therefore, is not affirming of national strategies that centre on control of money. In Chapter 6, it was explained how derivatives have created the merging of money and capital. National controls that seek to contain money flows finish up not neutralising derivatives, but 're-separating' money and capital and thereby neutralising capital.

Is this, of itself, an argument against nationally located strategies for social change? Not at all. It is a caution about how to understand finance in the process of change.

Appendix 8.1: speculation, derivatives and money

This Appendix explores the way speculation is understood conceptually. Within Chapter 8, we considered briefly the concept of speculation in the context of derivatives. But speculation has a wider ambit than derivatives, and any discussion of derivatives and speculation must lie within this wider analytical context. The particular object of this Appendix is the role of speculation in the determination of monetary values and the role of derivatives therein.

Speculation has proven to be a difficult concept to define. At its core, it is about strategies utilising uncertainty or segmentation in the market so as to buy in one 'part' of the market and sell at another price in another 'part' of the market. These markets may be segmented by time, space or regulation. But speculation is also about risk and the distribution and redistribution of risk among market participants. Beyond difficulties with a formal definition, there is a series of juxtapositions that can be used to highlight the difficulties of giving substance to the role of speculation. In the following analysis, we compare 'speculation' with the concepts of 'productive activity', 'gambling' and 'hedging'.

Speculative compared with productive activity

For neoclassical economics, a distinct activity of speculation relative to productive activity remains elusive, for the focus is on market interactions and price determination. Hence there is no distinct activity of 'production' that creates 'new value'. Indeed, as all market interactions are thought to help drive markets towards equilibrium,[13] each market participant is as important as the other in price determination. After all, liquid markets are thought to be the hallmark of efficient price discovery. Moreover, and specifically in relation to finance, with money conceived of as neutral with respect to economic activity, what Milton Friedman (1953) termed stabilising speculation in financial markets is indeed the means to secure the neutrality of money by ensuring that prices reflect underlying values.

Neoclassical economics is not, however, devoid of a discourse on speculation, although there is not a single conception of speculation. In one conception (the other is considered in the context of speculation and hedging), speculation can be understood as an activity associated with buying and selling in order to profit from changes in market prices. How this differs from normal commercial activity, such as that of a merchant is not easy to clearly delineate. Typically, a distinct activity of speculation is conceived in terms of either informational differences between market participants, or differences in beliefs about likely future circumstances. Speculators who use information or beliefs rationally will make money and their activities will tend to bring prices closer to their equilibrium levels that reflect fundamental value. Those who do not will lose money and go out of business. Both of these activities are seen to have stabilising propensities.

Money neutrality is here secured directly out of the process of buying and selling in product and financial markets, including the activities of speculators. The notion that stabilising speculation would enable freely floating currencies to be more stable than currencies subject to governmental controls was part of the rationale advanced for the introduction of floating exchange rate in the 1960s. We have seen in Chapter 5 that free-floating exchange rates have not resulted in stable currency values (and this instability of exchange rates has provided one of the proximate causes of the rise of derivatives as a way of contriving currency stability for users).

Indeed, many neoclassical economists and market participants have expressed concern at the sorts of destabilising speculation that may be associated with financial derivatives. The well-known CEO of investment firm Berkshire Hathaway, Warren Buffet has suggested that the ability to make or lose large amounts of money from even quite small price movements has a serious destabilising potential, not just for the firms involved, but because of the contagion across the economy that is likely to follow if some firms become insolvent. He referred to the contagion-like consequences of large losses from derivatives as a 'daisy chain' effect, and it will be recalled that this was precisely the fear that prompted the Alan Greenspan, the Federal Reserve Chairman, to intervene and arrange a bailout of LTCM. It is also for this reason that Buffet referred to financial derivatives as financial weapons of mass destruction.

However, it is outside of neoclassical economics, amongst post-Keynesians, radicals and (some) Marxists, where debates about the stabilising properties of

---

[13] Speculative bubbles will be considered briefly shortly.

speculation arise much more intensely. This in part arises because it is here that a conceptual distinction is made between 'money' and the 'real' economy (and hence between speculation and productive activity), and where money is not understood not to be neutral.[14]

The argument is remarkably similar amongst them. It is that the process of producing and selling goods and services are the legitimate (productive) economic activities. But there are also speculative activities which, while often benign, can come to overwhelm and undermine productive activity.[15] Finance, with all the historical associations with usury, can often be thought of as an analogue for speculation. Where finance serves to facilitate production and trade it performs a useful role. But often finance can instead assume a life of its own, and act to create bubbles and undermine productive activity.

Keynes was quite clear about the problem. He said that facilitating full employment and a stable economy (which he considered to be key goals of economic policy) required the subversion of finance and investment to these national productive needs. Through state management, money would be directed to the service of the real economy. For example:

> [I]n my view the whole management of the domestic economy depends upon being free to have the appropriate rate of interest without reference to the rates prevailing elsewhere in the world. Capital controls are a corollary to this.[16]

Keynes questioned the scale and motives of Britain's foreign investment, and suggested that his proposed economic programme may even require bringing the rate of interest down to very low levels (which he thought may even require the 'euthanasia of the rentier') (Vernenego and Rochon 2000: 6). He recognised that this would probably require controls over capital movements to weed out those that were not driven by fundamentals. Keynes' attitude to speculation follows from this approach.

But this is not as clear a position as at first appears. The decision to invest in production also carries with it the decision about timing – to invest now or wait – and thus even seemingly clear productive activities 'might involve some degree of speculation about market timing' (Dodd 2003: 9). In many respects a Keynesian juxtaposition of speculation and production faces the same analytical and policy dilemmas as the neoclassical tradition.

---

[14] Keynes for instance stressed that one difference between his approach and that of laissez-faire economics, was that he wanted to explicitly recognise that money was not neutral (or that the social costs of making it so were unrealistic). See for instance his notes on the monetary theory of production (1933, 408–12).

[15] Keynes constructed this notion in the *General Theory*, when he observed that, in the United States, there seemed to have developed 'the dominance of speculation over enterprise' (cited in Dodd 2002a: 2).

[16] Keynes, letter to Roy Harrod, 1942, cited in Crotty 1983: 62–3.

'Necessary' speculation compared with 'gambling'

The impossibility of putting a tight conceptual boundary around 'speculation' leads to a fallback judgement, especially with a focus on finance. There may be recognition that buying cheap and selling dear is an integral part of accumulation, and even that futures markets can add to price stability, especially in agricultural markets. But there is also identified a sphere of trading that is opportunist, and plays no useful role. It is akin to gambling on (short-term) price movements.

With volatile market prices, there is uncertainty about input prices (including the cost of credit), output prices, and the value of money (inflation and exchange rates). This is an environment that will certainly attract gambling. But 'producers', too, are caught in an environment of speculation on the future, whether they like it or not. Hence, they may well enter further 'speculative' trades but with the effect of closing off their exposure to existing risks, and managing new ones. They will, for instance, enter futures contracts to secure stable commodity prices, trade futures or options to avoid windfall foreign exchange losses, etc. In short, they hedge. So the difference between gambling and hedging really comes down to the motivation for a trade – is it to create an open (unhedged) position, or to close (hedge) a position?

A problem arises for the neoclassicals, however, with the empirical observation that markets do not systematically gravitate towards fundamental values and may depart from fundamentals for extended periods.[17] Where speculation is not attributed the virtue of being an agent of equilibration and efficiency, perhaps it has the characteristics of gambling.

The development of 'behavioural finance' has been the neoclassical response to such evidence. Here we consider the most popular case, the existence of so-called 'speculative bubbles' where prices move continually away from fundamentals, but with the recognition by market participants that this movement is not sustainable. During such a bubble, it is said some speculators may act rationally when they stay invested or continue buying in a rising market, even though they know that prices are already out of alignment with fundamental values. These speculators may calculate that the probability of ongoing buying by others will push prices up further before any price correction occurs. Under this scenario, speculators can systematically profit from on-going price misalignments.

How this concept of speculation fits into a neoclassical framework is difficult to identify. Clearly, it is not to be legitimised in terms of its equilibrating function so it is not 'necessary' speculation, but there is a clear reluctance to attribute the label of 'gambling'. Here, no doubt, there is recourse to the case for the intrinsic legitimacy of all market interactions, without imposing moral judgements!

For Keynes and the post-Keynesians, this whole activity of trading over uncertain price movements is generally seen as a zero-sum game, where different types of traders simply pit their wits against each other. It is this zero-sum dimension that attracts the label of 'gambling'.

An important element here, that differentiates this analysis from the neoclassicals, is that market participants do not simply attempt to speculate on how close prices may be to fundamental values. They may also speculate on what other

---

[17] The volatility of prices has provided fertile grounds for notions of destabilising speculation and alternative concepts of risk transfer (see for instance Baumol 1957, Aliber 1964, Johnson 1976, and Hart 1977).

investors are likely to do. Keynes (1936: 156) presented the famous analogy with a beauty contest:

> [P]rofessional investment may be likened to those newspaper competitions in which the competitors have to pick out the six prettiest faces from a hundred photographs, the prize being awarded to the competitor whose choice most nearly corresponds to the average preferences of the competitors as a whole; so that each competitor has to pick, not those faces which he himself finds prettiest, but those which he thinks likeliest to catch the fancy of the other competitors, all of whom are looking at the problem from the same point of view. It is not a case of choosing those which, to the best of one's judgment, are really the prettiest, nor even those which average opinion genuinely thinks the prettiest. We have reached the third degree where we devote our intelligences to anticipating what average opinion expects the average opinion to be. And there are some, I believe, who practise the fourth, fifth and higher degrees.

So unlike the benign views of neoclassical economics, Keynes concluded that stock market prices do not always move according to 'fundamentals', but are often affected by popular perceptions about risk and future potential. In this case, money is to be made simply by guessing popular perception (demand) correctly. With each new 'degree', the gambling dimension rises.

For the post-Keynesians, this essential theme remains. Markets by themselves cannot be guaranteed to secure price stability and, by extension, the neutrality of money. This is because market participants do not always act in terms of fundamentals, and so prices do not always reflect fundamental values.[18]

Speculation compared with hedging

In comparing speculation with 'productive activity', we identified one neoclassical conception of speculation as a process of arbitrage. Another neoclassical conception is defined in terms of risk and uncertainty. In this framework there can be understood to be two basic types of market participants: hedgers and speculators. In an uncertain market, hedgers are those who want to reduce their existing risks, while speculators are those that are prepared to take on additional risks. While there will be both sellers and buyers who wish to reduce or hedge their unwanted risks, there will often be imbalances in either the demand for or supply of hedging opportunities. Any imbalances must be filled by market participants who do not have any offsetting positions: they must take on risk. So in order for some market participants to reduce their risks about future purchases or sales, other market participants must be available to take on these risks. Hedgers are thus driven by their desire to protect their fundamental positions (in production), while speculators are those that do not have a position to protect.

What makes this speculative activity different from gambling is its role in the equilibration of markets, which is analytically privileged over the motivations of the speculator. Once again, speculation is understood to be functional to money

---

[18] There is indeed mixed evidence that changes in price movements (volatility) affect the behaviour of some market participants (Schleifer and Summers 1990; Goetzmann and Massa 1999).

neutrality, this time indirectly, by way of risk transfer rather than directly via price stability. This stylised distinction between hedgers and speculators provides an interesting way of looking at risk transfer. Unfortunately, in actual markets, the behavioural differences between the two types of market participants are much harder to delineate. Studies have not only found a range of reasons for (or types of) both hedging and speculation, but, at any point in time, market participants may be engaged in both speculative-type and hedging-type activities (Kwast 1986; Peck 1992).

In this neoclassical approach, financial derivatives are thought to offer new and lower cost means of transferring risk and securing price stability. However, empirically, it is not clear that prices are inherently more stable, and conceptually, the whole distinction between hedging and speculation, always highly stylised, is rendered problematic. Such issues are increasingly being discussed in corporate financial policy in terms of risk management rather than hedging policy (Shapiro and Titman 1986; Froot *et al.* 1993; Hunter and Smith 2002). In this discourse, both hedging and speculation can be considered complementary elements in risk management (Kwast 1986).

While neoclassical economists would see the hedging potential as a case for derivative markets, many (though certainly not all) post-Keynesians are reluctant to adopt this interpretation. Moreover, while hedging may permit limited micro-level price stability (via hedging transactions between, for example, futures contract participants), it cannot secure macro-price stability, and nor can it eliminate macro-type risks associated with exogenous shocks (such as a large oil price increase, or the national effects of a global recession). Derivative markets do not seem to have stabilised individual commodity prices, or relative prices as a whole, and there is considerable evidence that there is much more trading than that needed simply for hedging purposes.

Moreover, the use of derivatives may in fact have created a set of new risks of their own. Eatwell (1996: 20), for instance, argues that,

> The growth of derivatives markets may have increased systemic risk, both because the very complexity of some derivative instruments and hedging strategies creates severe informational problems for both management and regulators and because derivatives trading may increase exposure to liquidity crises.[19]

There is a need, it is argued, to regulate against volatility on a global and national scale, not rely on imperfect market substitutes. Intervention can in this way supersede the whole need to rely on the sphere of 'gambling' to secure prices.

---

[19] A similar argument is made by Kregel (1998) about the role of derivatives in the Asian financial crisis.

9
Derivatives and the Development of Capitalist Relations

In earlier chapters, we identified the growth of financial derivatives, and especially their generalised use by large corporations for risk management, as an emerging and decisive change in capitalist development. We contended that the growth of financial derivatives in the 1980s is akin to the watershed created by the growth of joint stock companies in the middle-to-late nineteenth century. Derivatives are transforming our understanding of capital and of money and, indirectly thereby, of competition. There are also wider potential implications that warrant consideration. Just as it could be said that the joint stock company gave rise to new capacities for corporations, with now well-recognised social implications, so we here look to possible broader social and economic implications of financial derivatives growth.

First, however, two important caveats. As derivatives are only now emerging on a wide scale, there are dangers of projections on the basis of such a short history. Further, it is important not to exaggerate developments in derivatives (or finance generally) as a driver of social change. The issues of this chapter should be interpreted in this light.

Our path to this objective is via an evaluation of a rather widespread interpretation that situates finance and derivatives within a discourse of 'deregulation' and 'neoliberalism'. We raised this issue in the context of Chapter 5, and there are some further dimensions that warrant consideration here. Our contention is that we have seen not a process of 'deregulation', but a change of regulation, in which derivatives are central, both in terms of finance and social order generally.

'Deregulation' and 'reregulation'

The popular history of the last 25 years of finance centres on one key word: 'deregulation'. It has served as a huge diversion in depicting the recent history of capitalist development.

Broadly, the argument is put, some time after the end of Bretton Woods (formally 1971) many governments terminated national capital controls and fixed exchange rates. They supposedly 'deregulated' their financial sectors. Moreover, this initiative in finance sector policy then had repercussions in other policy areas as well. The argument goes that financial flexibility demanded other forms of market flexibility – an end to industry protectionism, the breaking of the power of unions in the labour market, privatisation of state-owned commercial (and potentially commercial) assets, balanced government budgets etc. Even within the sector of finance itself, one deregulation has led to another. The lifting of capital controls generated the demand for 'free market' solutions within finance and insurance.

Some extol the virtues of this outcome, seeing deregulation as the assertion of market rationality over arbitrary or politically compromised government-administered arrangements. Others describe the same process in terms of the anarchy of the market and anti-social allocation that follows from deregulation.

Within this intense debate, there is a shared point of agreement: the 1970s was a watershed in economic order. There was, from the late 1970s (although at different times in different countries), a process of deregulation involving the retreat of the state from economic management and a renewed focus on market calculation and the individual. The advocates characterised deregulation in terms of the individual's right to accumulate without interference from the state, and the obligation on the individual to take responsibility for their own well-being. The critics characterised it as 'neoliberalism' (Overbeek and van der Pilj 1993).

In international finance, the 1970s was a watershed not so much of regulation, but of economic nationalism, and we should not conflate the two. In terms of regulation, there was certainly the end of a regime of formal adherence to fixed exchange rates and controls on capital mobility but, as we discussed in Chapter 5, we should not exaggerate regulation of the period before the watershed, nor diminish the extent of regulation after it. In the so-called 'regulated' period, capital flowed with increasing freedom. In the period after 1971 there was no sustained 'deregulation' in the sense of a decline for the role of financial regulation. While it is impossible to quantify regulation, there is now a widespread recognition that regulation is now no less necessary, and undoubtedly more demanding, than it was in the 1950s and 60s, when central bank decrees ruled financial institutions in a relatively closed national financial system. The post-1970s tasks of prudential regulation and inflation management now demand more regulators and detailed regulations than ever before.

The challenge to economic nationalism associated with the end of the Bretton Woods Agreement was the removal of one of the central pillars that had permitted nationalists to think of nations as discrete economic units, directly responsive to the policies of nation states. The early 1970s showed that the global economy could be seen neither as stable nor predictable, and that economic processes once thought of as 'domestic' were now responding intensively to global competitive forces. Nationalist presumptions in national policy were being undermined.

The watershed of the 1970s shows as a challenge to nationalism also in the way national policy responded to the change. Nation states did not move to some model of 'de-regulation', as the popular history suggests. Rather, over more than a decade, and in different processes in different countries, one set of regulations was replaced, usually in a rather *ad hoc* reform process, by another. Regulation of international finance stumbled towards its late twentieth-century order, and the central source of confusion was how to facilitate financial stability in an era when earlier nation-centred policies were no longer working. Goodman and Pauly (1993) make the point that what became known as 'deregulation' was often a recognition by national governments *de jure* of what had *de facto* been happening for a number of years – that, in a different international financial environment, existing regulations were no longer working. The problem was not one of a capacity to regulate, but the need to shift the objectives of regulation away from the national containment of capital and towards the facilitation of its orderly international mobility.

Financial derivatives seem to stand outside this alternative explanation. They appear to be insulated from any form of government regulation – apparently as true models of 'deregulation'. We saw in Chapter 5 that financial derivatives markets started to emerge with the growth of Eurofinance markets. In particular, both grew outside the systems of nation-state regulation, and so as to avoid particular national regulations. Rapid derivatives growth from the 1980s has also been largely outside of formal national regulatory systems, and many derivative products are designed specifically so as to avert various national capital controls. Derivatives, and especially OTC derivatives, are, it would

206 Capitalism with Derivatives

appear, largely unregulated by nation (or supra-national) state authorities. They seem to be the quintessential expression of deregulation.

Moreover, it is apparent that derivatives have indeed been used in ways that are flagrantly illegal, and where it would appear that regulators have turned a blind eye to illegal practices. Particularly in the context of the collapse of Enron, Frank Partnoy (2002b) has been outspoken about these illegal practices and the regulatory culture that gave them tacit approval:

> [We] moved through a period [the 1980s and 1990s] where most of the people in power, at companies and at regulatory bodies, had been trained by efficient market theorists. And so, not surprisingly, the arguments that won the day in Washington were primarily deregulatory in focus. So, there was a wave of deregulation in the financial markets that included allowing the movement of securities into private placements or offshore funds; removing the registration requirements to allow shelf registrations etc. But in addition to this wave of financial deregulation, the approach to the prosecution of financial market criminal behavior changed as well. So we had a deregulatory focus in terms of the prudential approach, but we also had a dramatic reduction in the number of criminal cases brought. In my opinion, with this latter shift regulators were sending the signal that basically we rely on the morals of the market place.

Partnoy (2002a) argues that regulators went soft on illegal practices and misuse of derivatives, especially where OTC derivatives (as distinct from exchange-traded derivatives where reporting requirements are more stringent) are used to disguise 'real' positions on company books. In the context of Enron, he has contended that the problem lies with regulatory failure:

> The collapse of Enron makes it plain that the key gatekeeper institutions that support our system of market capitalism have failed. The institutions sharing the blame include auditors, law firms, banks, securities analysts, independent directors, and credit rating agencies ...

No doubt, the question of how best to regulate so as to secure legal practices in derivative markets and in the recording of derivatives in company accounts is, and will remain, a critical issue in commercial law. But, contrary to the Keynesians preoccupied with 'speculation', Partnoy's is not an argument that derivatives are inherently undesirable and require regulation to reduce their use. He is not classifying derivatives as 'hot money' but as risk management tools that are being abused by a lack of transparency.

What is required, he contends, is a 'reregulation' of financial markets, to address the use of derivatives for corporate deception, and empower the gatekeepers. The arguments here are compelling: the regulatory procedures associated with derivatives have been found wanting.

But they are also a limited perspective on the regulatory issues to do with derivatives. Derivatives themselves stand outside the 1950s and 60s conventions of 'regulation'. The suggestion that 'reregulation' is the antidote to 'deregulation' leaves entirely open to question how any new form of regulation would be appropriate to globally integrated finance rather than simply the aspiration of a return to the financial regime of the 1950s.

Derivatives' role in regulation

Posed in the framework of empowering the gatekeepers, we stay entrapped in (domestic) market efficiency, an innately nationalist, conception of regulation. If, instead, we see state regulation as facilitating the global integration of financial markets, derivatives show up in different (additional) light. Derivatives in this context are not the extreme case of deregulation, but on the contrary, part of a newly emerging regulatory process.

With financial institutions now globally integrated, the territorial limitations of nation-state regulatory capacity mean that the old forms of regulation (supervising the domestic operations of financial institutions and controlling cross-territorial flows of capital, including derivatives) is now highly limited. States require other forms of regulation, and the regulation of accumulation requires something more than states can deliver. In both of these dimensions derivatives are central to regulation precisely because they transcend nation-state regulations.

We can pose three regulatory dimensions of financial derivatives which we will consider in turn:

- Regulation derivatives provide to nation states,
- Regulation derivatives provide beyond nation states, and
- Regulation of derivative markets.

What forms of regulation do derivatives provide to nation states? With finance (including national currencies) circulating spatially beyond the territorial jurisdiction of nation states, derivatives permit national monetary authorities to exercise extra-territorial influence in financial markets so as to pursue domestic policy agendas. For example, when national central banks seek to intervene in foreign exchange markets (because they believe that the national currency has become unsustainably over- or under-valued) they generally do so by trading in international currency swaps markets. The reasons for this are straightforward: derivatives permit a central bank to leverage its interventions (and so cheapen the costs of any market intervention) and currency derivative markets are now the drivers of currency markets generally.

Another form of regulation is where state prudential supervision of financial institutions demand systematic risk management. Prudential regulators require that institutions with exposures to exchange rates, interest rates, equities, etc. are all hedged in derivative markets.[1]

In effect, in a world of globally integrated finance, where nation-state regulatory capacities are territorially bounded, though finance is not, derivatives are at the centre of the nation state's role in the regulation of finance. It is their independence from particular national regulators, and even a coalition of national regulators, that enables them to be used for the purpose of regulation: if they were not so independent, they would themselves be the objects, not the subjects of regulation.

What do financial derivatives contribute to regulation beyond the capacities of the nation state? In Chapter 5 we showed that derivatives now anchor the international financial system in a way comparable to the role of gold in the nineteenth century. In the absence of derivatives, volatility in interest rates, exchange rates, share values and commodity values would feed directly into volatility in prices, profit rates and thereby into investment. The global financial system is regulated, in the sense of being kept orderly, by processes and conventions in which derivatives play a central role.

What regulates derivative markets? The Gold Standard was not directly regulated by states – at least not in the way the term regulation is currently used – but it remained a stable and orderly system in which nation-state monetary regimes served to secure a global monetary system over which none of them, nor any supra-national agency, exerted direct supervision. Similarly, there is a process of regulation of financial derivatives in which nation states make a contribution, but no nation states, individually or collectively, exert direct regulation. The following

[1] This requirement is integral to the Basle II Accord of the BIS.

are the key modes of regulation of derivatives:

- For exchange-traded derivatives, the exchanges regulate practices, and these exchanges are regulated by the prudential supervision of the nation states within which the exchanges are located.
- For OTC derivatives, the International Swaps and Derivatives Association, whose members transact over 80 per cent of derivatives trades, require the use of standard contracts, which are enforced by ISDA.
- Around 70 per cent of derivatives transactions involve banks as counterparties – either in their own right, or as agents for another corporation, and these banks are themselves subject to state-based prudential regulation.
- The credibility of counterparties is determined by credit ratings agencies, and these agencies are charged with providing on-going supervision of their creditworthiness.

No one, except the most ardent advocate of *laissez faire*, could look upon this system of financial regulation with deep confidence (although the same could be said also of all previous eras of regulation!). It is clearly vulnerable to crisis whenever a large financial or corporate institution reveals extensive indebtedness and inability to meet its financial obligations. In this sense, derivatives have made it likely that any financial crisis will have a more pervasive and speedy impact than was previously the case.

It is in this context that nation states do, indeed, remain at the centre of the process of regulation, for it is only nation states that currently have the capacity to arrange bailouts of financial and corporate failures. Which crises will bring forth state-led bailouts – and which will not – has no laws. This adds a random and highly political dimension to the process of regulation. It also begs the question of how such bailouts are funded by states.

There are no decisive answers here and, we argue, it would be deceptive to contend that there are. There is a popular vision that financial crises could be better averted by a process called 'reregulation'. This, it seems, would involve a return to the sorts of practices of the 1950s and 60s – or even that these sorts of practices would be 'updated' and undertaken by a global financial authority (Eatwell and Taylor 2000). It lacks credibility. Its strongest argument is that it is offering *some* policy alternative, as a statement of resistance.

As we discussed in Chapter 8, in the context of capital controls, this policy alternative not only exaggerates the capacities of state regulation, but it conflates control over money with control over capital. It fails to acknowledge the way in which the changing nature of global finance is itself an expression of the way in which the organisation of institutions within capitalism, and the system of calculation within those institutions, has itself changed. And this change cannot simply be regulated away. The contradictions of international finance are not found so much in a propensity towards anarchy (as those who emphasise speculation and deregulation suggest), but in the accentuation of competition and the opposed interests of labour and capital on a global scale.

Indeed, it is through these contradictions that we can see a potential for the 'logic' of derivatives to take on a broader social significance.

Derivatives as the model of the future

In its simplest form, the capacity of corporations to hedge against commercial risk via derivatives stands as a model for broader social policy. As well as their application to financial and commodity risk, derivatives suggest the capacity of individuals to 'take positions' on a range of other risks they are exposed to in their daily lives, and hence the possible development of new sorts of risk markets.

We refer here to the growth of insurance against personal and other life risks. Insurance policies – for death, health, buildings, etc., have an established history in capitalist societies, and the history of derivatives is itself bound up with forms of insurance. The insurance companies that historically provided such policies were generally modelled on mutual funds. Participants in the fund simply recognized that they share a common risk and pay a premium to ensure that whoever actually came to be affected, would be compensated from the fund. In house insurance, for example, the premiums of all are calculated to be sufficient to compensate the unlucky homeowners whose houses burn down. But as the insurance industry has itself become more competitive, the mutual society model has been surpassed by a more calculating way of managing the pool of insurance funds.

There developed more advanced ways of managing risk, via hedging exposures across markets. We can now think of insurance not as the activity of a mutual society, but as the activity of a hedge fund.

In this context, derivatives are integral to insurance: insurance can be framed as an option. With house insurance, for example, you choose the value for which you want the house to be insured (the amount of protection) and you are covered against the loss of that specified value for a year. You are purchasing a form of put option. And the insurance company which has sold the put option can use the premiums to hedge its position.

By moving from mutual societies and insurance to risk management through derivatives, the possibilities for private insurance have expanded. This is already seen in most parts of the advanced capitalist world in health care: that a public health system is being replaced by private insurance where individuals purchase a put option: for an annual fee, you choose the extent and type of health care you wish to invoke over the year, should you need it.

The parallels between finance and health care are close. In both cases, in the post-war period risks were borne by the state (via fixed exchange rates and regulated domestic money markets on the one hand; by public health systems on the other). From the 1980s, we have seen financial risk management (associated with interest rate and exchange rate variability in particular, but also commodity price variability) dispersed to individuals via derivative markets and health risk management dispersed to individuals via private health insurance.

Indeed, within neoclassical economics, there is already the vision of a risk-management utopia in which all facets of life have insurance markets, and each individual can 'choose' a personal life-risk profile. Robert Shiller, Professor of Economics at Yale, has presented such a vision in a book titled *The New Financial Order*, subtitled *Risk in the 21st Century* (2003). His vision warrants quoting at length:

> Picture vast international markets that trade major macroeconomic aggregates such as the total outputs of countries such as the United States, Japan, Paraguay, and Singapore, or indexes of single-family home prices both in cities – from New York to Paris to Sydney – and in regions, such as shoreline properties on the Riviera or agricultural property in the corn belt or the rubber plantations of Indonesia. Portfolio investors will be able to take positions in a wide array of such markets with little cost. International markets for human capital will emerge as well for occupations from medical and scientific professions to the careers of actors and performers to common labor. These markets will facilitate the creation of livelihood insurance policies on every major career and job category, and home equity insurance policies on the value of everyone's home. Massive electronic databases made accessible by user-friendly designs will enable people everywhere to engage these markets to manage their real risks.
>
> As these markets transform our appreciation of risks, our concepts and patterns of thought will change accordingly. People will set prices

in light of the prices in these markets; countries will make international agreements that parallel some of the risk management afforded in these markets and will similarly revise their welfare and social security systems. Our economies will run more efficiently because these markets provide the means to control our risks. The presence of these new markets will make it easier for firms to offer livelihood insurance, home equity insurance, and income-linked loans to individuals. Our fundamental risks will thus be insured against, hedged, diversified, making for a safer world. By lightening the burden of risk, a new democratic finance will encourage all of us to be more venturesome, more inspired in our activities. (2003: 6)

In essence, Shiller wants to apply risk management techniques from finance to all facets of life so that, to use his phrase, people can 'pursue their dreams with greater confidence than they can under existing modes of risk management' (Shiller 2003: ix). We may readily recognise this as the ideas of a radical neoclassical, swept away by the infinite virtues and possibilities of market mechanisms. Even on its own terms, the volume of information and the expectations of agent rationality (specifically defined) make this a utopian fiction. Shiller himself no doubt sees these ideas as a vision rather than as a practical policy program.

But it is not difficult to see state policies that are borne of this vision emerging. The shift from the welfare state to private insurance (in particular related to health care and old age) and the shift to privately funded tertiary education where fees are based on future income are amongst the wide-spread trends towards Shiller's vision.

Moreover, this is, indeed, a development that we might anticipate with capitalist development. The technology permits the relevant data to be collected on an on-going basis and computed into contracts. It is, almost certainly, a potentially profitable further dimension of the financial services industry. It would be naive not to expect developments in this direction. And with this growth in insurance will no doubt come the secondary markets, where these contracts are on-sold as the insurers themselves seek to hedge their exposure. Traders will be buying options on the right to purchase your health insurance contract at some date and price. The parties to that contract will be taking different positions on your health six months hence!

An immediately apparent critique points to the image of an Orwellian dystopia, based on the need of the market for 'perfect' (i.e. infinite) information. Personal life circumstances have become commodified; your well-being is being traded. But beyond this civil liberties concern is the fact that wherever the market moves, the imposition of competition follows.

Conclusion

True believers in market forces such as Shiller must be feeling confident about their vision of the future: it would seem to be compatible with a current trend towards individualism, and it engages the individual's fear of insecurity. This trend, it must be said, is not just part of a neoclassical economic vision; it is also consistent with emerging trends in European social democracy – the so-called 'third way'. The 'third way' itself is gravitating towards embracing market dynamism, creativity and innovation, and these are all the hallmarks of volatility. Shiller's vision asserts the market's version of social democracy: it is social democracy for those who can afford it!

For those of us who are not so enchanted, we need a refutation. At one level, this refutation could be about critiques of *laissez faire*, individualism, neoliberalism, etc. But there is also need for a critical evaluation of the finance that is involved. Perhaps here, too, there is an array of ready-made responses about 'casino capitalism' and talk of inevitable financial crises that come from the anarchy of markets.

But none of these responses actually engages finance – its operation, the connections between finance and accumulation, and the issue of dealing with a form of finance that will be, for the foreseeable future, not under significant control by nation states.

This concern has driven our analysis of financial derivatives – not to discover a new formula for crisis, not to determine how finance can be delivered back to nation states, cowering and eager to please – but to determine how capitalism is evolving. Only then can its changing contradictions be identified.

On first sight, financial derivatives are esoteric, technical tools of risk management that have only recently emerged to prominence. They are that, but they are clearly also much more than that. They are transforming economic calculation, and are intensifying the process of competition wherever they expand. They make capitalism more dynamic and more fragile; more complex and more integrated.

Perhaps their most important impact, however, is that they give a grounding, or a materiality, to finance. They reveal finance as a driver of accumulation not just in terms of providing the funds that are used in investment or exchange, but in computing the value of assets, and thereby determining the benchmarks of asset performance. This is what inserts derivatives into the explanation of class relations and of social change.

Are we opposed to derivatives?[2] Many people concerned for social change are, but we think it is the wrong question. As will be apparent to any reader who has got this far, we see that derivatives are an integral expression of capitalism. Any proposal that derivatives can be 'picked off' and strangled by empowered regulatory agencies is, we believe, failing to understand just how they are integral. Either that, or they are part of an essentially opportunist politics that peddles the idea that advocacy of emphatic state policies equates to decisive strategy. To confront derivatives is to confront the class nature of capitalism itself. For better or worse, that is the challenge of those who would resist.

---

[2] In a speech 'On the Question of Free Trade', delivered to the Democratic Association of Brussels January 9, 1848, Marx concluded with these words:

> In general, the protective system of our day is conservative, while the free trade system is destructive. It breaks up old nationalities and pushes the antagonism of the proletariat and the bourgeoisie to the extreme point. In a word, the free trade system hastens the social revolution. It is in this revolutionary sense alone, gentlemen, that I vote in favour of free trade.

No doubt the same case can be made in relation to derivatives.

References

Ackland, N, 2000, The Role of Swaps in the Development of the International Financial System, PhD Thesis, Faculty of Economics, University of Sydney, mimeo.

Aglietta, M, and Breton, R, 2001, Financial Systems, Corporate Control and Capital Accumulation, *Economy & Society*, Vol. 30, 4, 433–66.

Aglietta, M, 2002, Whence and Wither Money? in OECD (ed.) *The Future of Money*, OECD, Paris.

Akthar, M, 1983, Financial Innovations and Their Implications for Monetary Policy: An International Perspective, BIS Economic Papers No. 9, Basel, December.

Alchian, A, and Demsetz, H, 1972, Production, Information Costs and Economic Organisations, *American Economic Review*, Vol. 62, 5, 777–95.

Aliber, R, 1964, Speculation and Price Stability Once Again, *Journal of Political Economy*, Vol. 72, 607–9.

Arditti, F, 1996, *Derivatives: A Comprehensive Resource for Options, Futures, Interest Rate Swaps and Mortgage Securities*, Harvard Business School Press, Boston.

Arshanpalli, B, and Doukas, J, 1997, The Linkages of S&P 500 Stock Index and S&P Index Futures Prices during October 1987, *Journal of Economics and Business*, Vol. 49, 243–66.

Bank for International Settlements (BIS), 1984, Financial Innovation and Monetary Policy, Monetary and Economics Department, BIS, Basle.

Bank for International Settlements, 1995, The BIS Statistics On International Banking and Financial Market Activity, BIS Monetary and Economic Department, Basle, August, BOPCOM98/1/20.

Bank for International Settlements (BIS), 2003, Annual Report. BIS, Basel.

Bank for International Settlements (BIS), 2004, International Convergence of Capital Measurement and Capital Standards: A Revised Framework, Basle Committee on Banking Supervision, Basle, June.

Bank for International Settlements (BIS), 2005, Triennial Central Bank Survey of Foreign Exchange and Derivatives Market Activity 2004 – Final Result, BIS, Basel, 17 March.

Baskin, J, 1988, The Development of Corporate Financial Markets in Britain and the United States, 1600–1914: Overcoming Asymmetric Information, *Business History*, Vol. 62, 2, 199–237.

Baskin, J, and Miranti, Jr., P, 1997, *A History of Corporate Finance*, Cambridge University Press, Cambridge.

Battilossi, S, 2000, Financial Innovation and the Golden Ages of International Banking: 1890–1931 and 1958–81, *Financial History Review*, Vol. 7, 141–75.

Bauman, Z, 2000, *Liquid Modernity*, Cambridge: Polity Press.

Baumol, W, 1957, Speculation, Profitability and Stability, *The Review of Economics and Statistics*, Vol. 39, 3, Aug., 263–71.

BBC News, 2001, France Backs Tobin Tax Wednesday, 29 August 2001 http://news.bbc.co.uk/1/hi/business/1514647.stm

215

Beck, U, 1992, *Risk Society: Towards a New Modernity* (Translated by Mark Ritter) Sage Publications, London.

Beck, U, 1999, *What is Globalization?* (Translated by Patrick Camilleri) Polity Press, Cambridge.

Beck, U, 2000, *Brave New World of Work* (Translated by Patrick Camilleri), Polity Press, Cambridge.

Beechey, M, Gruen, D, and Vickery, J, 2000, The Efficient Markets Hypothesis: A Survey, Reserve Bank of Australia Discussion Paper, RBA, 2000–01, Sydney.

Bell, S, 2001, The Role of the State in the Hierarchy of Money, *Cambridge Journal of Economics*, Vol. 25, 2, 149–63.

Berle, A, 1959, *Power Without Property: A New Development in American Political Economy*, Harvest Books, New York.

Bernstein, P, 1996, *Against the Gods: The Remarkable Story of Risk*. John Wiley & Sons, New York.

Black, F, and Scholes, M, 1973, The Pricing of Options and Corporate Liabilities, *Journal of Political Economics*, Vol. 81, 637–54.

Blair, M, 2003, Shareholder Value, Corporate Governance and Corporate Performance, in P, Cornelius and B, Kogut (eds) *Corporate Governance and Capital Flows in a Global Economy*, Oxford University Press, Oxford.

Blake, B, 1949, *Elements of Marxian Economic Theory and Its Criticism*, Gordon Co., New York.

Blanchard, O, and Watson, M, 1982, Bubbles, Rational Expectations, and Financial Markets, in P, Wachtel (ed.) *Crisis in the Economic and Financial Structure*, Lexington Books, New York.

Block, F, 1993, Remaking Our Economy: New Strategies for Structural Reform, *Dissent Magazine*, Spring, 166–71.

Bonfim, A, 1999, Profits, and Balance Sheet Developments at U.S. Commercial Banks, *Federal Reserve Bank Bulletin*, June.

Boyer, R, 2000a, 'Is a Finance-led growth regime a viable alternative to Fordism? A preliminary analysis', *Economy & Society*, Vol. 29, 1, 111–45.

Braudel, F, 1984, *Civilisation and Capitalism*: 15th–18th century – Vol. III, The perspective of the world, translated by S, Reynolds, Collins, London.

Breuer, P, 2002, Measuring Off-balance-sheet leverage, *Journal Of Banking and Finance*, Vol. 26, 2–3, March, 223–42.

Brewer, E, Jackson, W, and Moser, J, 2001, The Value of Using Interest Rate Derivatives to Manage Risk at U.S. Banking Organisations, *Economic Perspectives*, Federal Reserve Bank of Chicago, Third Quarter.

Broz, J, 1999, Origins of the Federal Reserve System: International Incentives and the Domestic Free-rider Problem, *International Organisation*, Vol. 53, 1, Winter, 39–70.

Bryan, D, 1995, *The Chase Across the Globe: International Capital and the Contradictions for Nation States*, Westview Press, Colorado.

Bryan, D, and Rafferty, M, 1999, *The Global Economy in Australia*, Allen & Unwin, Sydney.

Burn, G, 1999, The State, the City and the Euromarkets, *Review of International Political Economy*, Vol. 6, 2, 225–61.

Cagan, P, and Schwartz, A, 1975, Has the Growth of Money Substitutes Hindered Monetary Policy? *Journal of Money, Credit and Banking*, Vol. 7, 2, May, 137–59.

Callon, M (ed.), 1998, *The Laws of the Markets*, Blackwell Publishing, Oxford.

Calvo, G, and Reinhart, C, 2002, Fear Of Floating, *Quarterly Journal of Economics*, Vol. 117, 2, 379–408.

Carlos, A, and Nicholas, S, 1996, Theory and History: Seventeenth-Century Joint-Stock Chartered Trading Companies, *The Journal of Economic History*, Vol. 56, 4, Dec., 916–24.

Carlton, D, 1984, Futures Markets: Their Purpose, Their History, Their Growth, Their Successes and Failures, *Journal of Futures Markets*, Vol. 4, 209–47.

Castells, M, 1996, *The Information Age: Economy, Society and Culture* Vol.I: The Rise of the Network Society, Blackwell Publishers, Cambridge MA. and Oxford.

Chandler, A, 1978, *The Visible Hand: The Managerial Revolution in American Business*, Harvard University Press, Boston.

Chicago Mercantile Exchange (CME), 2005, Products, downloaded from http://www.cme.com/prd/wec/usweather3612.html.

Claessens, S, Dooley, M, and Warner, A, 1995, Portfolio Capital Flows: Hot or Cold, *The World Bank Economic Review*, Vol. 9, 1, January.

Clark, G, 2000, *Pension Fund Capitalism*, Oxford University Press, Oxford.

Clifton, J, 1977, Competition and the Evolution of the Capitalist Mode of Production, *Cambridge Journal of Economics*, Vol. 1, 137–51.

Coase, R, 1960, The Problem of Social Cost, *Journal of Law and Economics*, Vol. 3, 1, October, 145–9.

Cohen, B, 1998, *The Geography of Money*, Cornell University Press, Ithaca.

Cooper, R, 1982, The Gold Standard: Historical Facts and Future Prospects, Brookings Papers on Economic Activity, No. 1, 1–45.

Corbridge, S, Martin, R, and Thrift, N (eds), 1994, *Money, Power and Space*, Blackwell, Oxford.

Cowen, M, 1976, *Capital Peasant Households*, University of Nairobi, mimeo July 1976.

Cowen, M, 1977, Some Problems of Capital and Class in Kenya, Institute of Development Studies, University of Nairobi, Occasional Paper No. 26.

Cowen, M, 1982, The British State and Agrarian Accumulation in Africa, in M, Fransman (ed.) *Industry and Accumulation in Africa*, Heinemann, London.

Cowen, M, and Shenton, B, 1996, *Doctrines of Development*, Routledge, London.

Cox, 1976, Futures Prices and Market Information, *Review of Economics and Statistics*, Vol. 65, May, 289–97.

Crotty, J, 1983, On Keynes and Capital Flight, *Journal of Economic Literature*, Vol. 21, 59–65.

Crotty, J, and Epstein, G, 1996, *In Defence of Capital Controls*, The Socialist Register. http://www.yorku.ca/socreg/crotty-epstein96.txt

Davidson, P, 1972, *Money and the Real World*, John Wiley and Sons, New York.

Davidson, Paul, 1997, Are Grains of Sand in the Wheels of International Finance Sufficient to do the Job when Boulders are Often Required?, *The Economic Journal*, Vol. 107, May, 671–86.

Day, C., 2004, Bits and Pieces and Moral Authority: The Paradox of Success in the 'unregulated' 19th century New York Capital Markets, Syracuse University College of Law, mimeo (downloaded from SSRN.com).

De Cecco, M, 1974, *Money and Empire: The International Gold Standard*, Blackwell, London.

Dodd, N, 1994, *The Sociology of Money: Economic Reason and Contemporary Society*, Polity Press, Cambridge.

Dodd, R, 1996, Memorandum on OTC Clearing to the Off-Exchange Task Force of the Commodity Futures Trading Commission. Washington, DC 12 December.

Dodd, R, 2002a, Derivatives, the Shape of International Capital Flows and the Virtues of Prudential Regulation, UNU/WIDER, Discussion Paper 2002/93.

Dodd, R, 2002b, The Role of Derivatives in the East Asian Financial Crisis, in J, Eatwell and L, Taylor (eds) *International Capital Markets: Systems in Transition*, Oxford University Press, Oxford.

Dodd, R, 2003, Lessons for Tobin Tax Advocates: The Politics of Policy and the Economics of Market Microstructure, Financial Policy Forum, Derivatives Study Center, Washington, January.

Dodd, R, 2004, The Virtues of Prudential Regulation in Financial Markets, Derivatives Study Center, Financial Policy Forum, mimeo, Washington DC.

Dodd, R, 2005, Derivatives Markets: Sources of Vulnerability in U.S. Financial Markets, in Gerald Epstein (ed.) *Financialization and the World Economy*, Edward Elgar, London.

Donaldson, R, and Kamstra, M, 1996, Stare Down the Barrel and Centre the Crosshairs: Targeting the ex ante Equity Premium, Federal Reserve Bank of Atlanta, Working Paper 4, February.

Dore, R, 2000, *Stock Market Capitalism: Welfare Capitalism: Japan and Germany Versus the Anglo-Saxons*, Oxford University Press, Oxford.

Dufey, G, and Giddy, I, 1978, *The International Money Market*, Englewood Cliffs, New Jersey.

Dumenil, G, and Levy, D, 2004, *Capital Resurgent: Roots of the Neoliberal Revolution*, Harvard University Press, Cambridge.

Easterbrook, F, 1986, Monopoly, Manipulation and The Regulation of Financial Markets, *Journal of Business*, Vol. 59, s103.

Eatwell, J, 1996, International Capital Liberalisation: The Impact on World Development, Center for Economic Policy Analysis, New School for Social Research Working Paper No. 1, October. Accessed January 2004 at http://www.newschool.edu/cepa/publications/working papers/archive/cepa0101.pdf.

Eatwell, J, and Taylor, L, 1998, International Capital Markets and the Future of Economic Policy, CEPA Working Paper Series III, New School for Social Research, No. 9, September.

Eatwell, J, and Taylor, L, 2000, *Global Finance at Risk: The Case for International Regulation*. New York: New Press.

Eatwell, J, and Taylor, L, (eds) 2002, *International Capital Markets: Systems in Transition*, Oxford University Press, Oxford.

Edey, M, and Hyvbig, K, 1995, An Assessment of Financial Reform In OECD Countries, OECD Economic Studies, No. 25, 11.

Edwards, S, 1999, The Mirage of Capital Controls, UCLA Graduate School of Management, mimeo, May.

Eichengreen, B, 1998, Globalizing Capital: A History of the International Money System, Princeton University Press, Princeton, NJ.

Eichengreen, B, and Sussman, N, 2000, The International Monetary System in the (Very) Long Run, IMF Working Papers 00/43, International Monetary Fund, Washington.

Eichengreen, B, J, Tobin and C, Wyplosz, 1995, The Case for Sand in the Wheels of International Finance, *The Economic Journal*, Vol. 105, 162–72.

Eklund, R, and Tollinson, R, 1980, Mercantilist Origins of the Corporation, *The Bell Journal of Economics*, Vol. 11, 2, Autumn, 715–20.

Elliot, L, and Atkinson, D, 1998, *The Age of Insecurity*, Verso, London.

Emery, H, 1899, Futures in the Grain Market, *The Economic Journal*, Vol. 9, 3, March, 45–67.

Epstein, G, and Crotty, J, 2001, *In Defence of Capital Controls*, Socialist Register, Vol. 32, edited by L. Pantich.

Epstein, G, and Schor, J, 1992, The Structural Determinants and Economic Effects of Capital Controls in the OECD, in T, Banuri and J, Schor (eds) *Financial Openness and National Autonomy*, Oxford University Press, Oxford.

Epstein, G, Grabel, I and Jomo, K, 2003, Capital Management Techniques in Developing Countries: An Assessment of Experiences from the 1990s and Lessons for the Future, paper prepared for G24.

Epstein, G, (ed.) 2005, Financialization and the World Economy, Edward Elgar, London.

Fama, E, 1965, The Behaviour of Stock Markets, *Journal of Business*, 38.

Fine, B, and Lapavitsas, C, 2000, Markets and Money in Social Theory: What Role for Economics?, *Economy & Society*, Vol. 29, 3, 357–82.

Fisher, I, 1904, Precedents for Defining Capital, *The Quarterly Journal of Economics*, Vol. 18, 3, May, 386–408.

Fleetwood, S, 2000, 'A Marxist Theory of Commodity Money Revisited' in J, Smithin (ed.) *What is Money*, Routledge, London.

Flood, R, and Garber, P, 1980, An Economic Theory of Monetary Reform, *Journal of Political Economy*, Vol. 88, 1, 24–58.

Foley, D, 1987, Money in Economic Activity, in J, Eatwell, M, Millgate and Peter Newman (eds), *The New Palgrave: Money*, Macmillan, London, 248–62.

Foley, D, 1998, Asset Speculation in Marx's Theory of Money, in R, Bellofiore (ed.) *Marxian Economics: A Reappraisal*: Essays on Volume III of Capital, Vol. 1. St Martins Press, New York.

Forrester, R, 1931, Commodity Exchanges in England, *Annals of the American Academy of Political and Social Science*, Vol. 155, 1, 196–207.

Frankel, J, 1996, How Well do Foreign Exchange Markets Function: Might a Tobin Tax Help?, NBER Working Paper No. W5, Cambridge.

Frankfurter, G, and Wood, B G, Jr., 1997, The Evolution of Corporate Dividend Policy, *Journal of Financial Education*, Vol. 23, 16–33.

Franks, J, and Meyer, C, 2002, The Origination and Evolution of Ownership and Control, London Business School, mimeo, December, downloaded from SSRN.com.

Friedman, M, 1951, A Commodity Reserve Currency, *Journal of Political Economy*, Vol. 59, June, 203–32. Reprinted in M, Friedman, 1953, *Essays in Positive Economics*, University of Chicago Press, Chicago.

Friedman, M, 1953, *Essays in Positive Economics*, University of Chicago Press, Chicago.

Friedman, T, 2000, *The Lexus and the Olive Tree – Understanding Globalization*, Anchor Books, New York.

Froot, K, Scharfstein, D, and Stein, J, 1993, Risk Management: Coordinating Corporate Investment and Financing Policies, *Journal of Finance*, December, 1629–58.

Froud, J, Johal, S, and Williams, K, 2002, Financialisation and the Coupon Pool, *Capital & Class*, No. 78 Autumn, 119–52.

Froud, J, Haslam, C, Sukhdev, J, and Williams, K, 2000, Restructuring for Shareholder Value and its Implications for Labour, *Cambridge Journal of Economics* Vol. 24, 771–97.

Galbraith, J, 1967, The New Industrial State, New American Library, New York.

Garbade, K, 2001, Pricing Corporate Securities as Contingent Claims, MIT Press, Cambridge.

Garbade, K, and Silber, W, 1983, Price Movements and Price Discovery in Futures and Cash Markets, Review of Economics and Statistics, Vol. 65, May.

Garber, P, 1998, Derivatives in International Capital Flow, NBER Working Paper No. 6623, NBER, Cambridge MA, June, http://www.nber.org/papers/w6623

Garber, P, 2001, *Famous First Bubbles: The Fundamentals of Early Manias*, MIT Press, Cambridge.

Garber, P, and Taylor, M, 1995, Sand in the Wheels of Foreign Exchange Markets: A Skeptical Note, *Economic Journal*, Vol. 105, January, 173–80.

Gastineau, G, and Kritzman, M, 1992, *A Dictionary of Financial Risk Management*, Frank J. Fabozzi Associates, New York.

Geisst, C, 2002, *Wheels of Fortune: The History of Speculation From Scandal to Respectability*, Wiley, New York.

Gibson, R, and Zimmerman, H, 1994, The Benefits and Risks of Derivative Instruments, University of Lausanne, mimeo, downloaded from www.finance.wat.ch/genevap/papers.html.

Giddy, I, and Dufey, G, 1995, Uses and Abuses of Currency Options, *Journal of Applied Corporate Finance*, Vol. 8, 3, 83–93.

Glaeser, E and Schleifer, A, 2001, The Rise of the Regulatory State, NBER, Working Paper 8650, Dec.

Glynn, A, 1995, Social Democracy and Full Employment, New Left Review, Vol. 211, 33–35.

Goedhart, M, Koller, T and Wesseels, 2005, Do Fundamentals – or Emotions – Drive the Stock Market?, *McKinsey Quarterly*, Special edition, Value and Performance.

Goetzmann, W, and Massa, M, 1999, Index Funds and Stock Market Growth, NBER Working Paper No. 7033, Cambridge.

Goldberg, M, 1985, The Effect of Futures Markets on Money Demand, US Federal Reserve Board, Washington, April.

Gonzalez-Hermosillo, B, 1994, The Microstructure of Financial Derivative Markets: Exchange Traded Versus Over-the-Counter Markets, Bank of Canada Working Paper, March.

Goodhart, C, 1995, Financial Globalisation, Derivatives, Volatility and the Challenge for the Policies of Central Banks, Special Paper No. 74, LSE Financial Markets Group, October.

Goodman, J, and Pauly, L, 1993, The Obsolescence of Capital Controls? *World Politics*, 46, 50–82.

Gordon, 1999, *The Great Game: The Emergence of Wall Street as a World Power*, HarperCollins, New York.

Gordon, M, 1962, The Investment, Financing and Valuation of the Corporation, Irwin, Homewood.

Gosh, A, Gulde, A, and Wolf, H, 2002, Exchange Rate Regimes: Choices and Consequences, MIT Press, Cambridge.

Gosh, S, Gilbert, C, and Hughes-Hallet, A, 1987, *Stabilizing Speculative Commodity Markets*, Clarendon Press, Oxford.

Grabel, I, 2002, Neoliberal Finance and Crisis in the Developing World – Argentina, Mexico, Turkey, and other countries, *Monthly Review*, Vol. 53, 11, April, 34–46.

Graham, B, 1944, *World Commodities and World Currencies*, McGraw-Hill, New York.

Graham, F, 1941, Transition to a Commodity Reserve Currency, *American Economic Review*, Vol. 31, 3, 520–5.

Graham, F, 1944, Keynes versus Hayek on a Commodity Reserve Currency, *Economic Journal*, Vol. 54, December, 422–9.

Grahl, J, and Lysandrou, P, 2003, Sand in the Wheels or Spanner in the Works? The Tobin Tax and Global Finance, *Cambridge Journal of Economics*, Vol. 27, 4, 597–621.

Grahl, J, and Teague, P, 2000, The Regulation School, the Employment Relation and Financialization, *Economy and Society*, Vol. 29, 1 February, 160–78.

Gray, J, 1998, *False Dawn: The Delusions of Global Capitalism*, The New Press, New York.

Gray, J, 2000, Meta-risks, *Journal of Portfolio Management*, Vol. 26, 3, Spring.

Gray, R, and Peterson, J, 1974, *The Economic Development of the United States*, Irwin Inc, Homewood, Ill.

Greenspan, A, 2000, Testimony on Over-the-Counter Derivatives, BIS Review No. 12, 1–3.

Grossman, S, 1989, *The Informational Role of Prices*, The MIT Press, Cambridge.

Grubel, H, 1966, The Case Against an International Commodity Reserve Currency, Oxford Economic Papers, Vol. 17.

Hall, B, and Murphy, K, 2000, Optimal Exercise Prices for Risk Averse Executives, *American Economic Review*, May, 209–14.

Handlin, O and Handlin, M, 1945, Origins of the American Business Corporation, *The Journal of Economic History*, Vol. 5, 1, May, 1–23.

Hannah, L, 1984, *The Rise of the Corporate Economy*, 2nd edition, Methuen, London.

Harcourt, G, 1969, Some Cambridge Controversies in the Theory of Capital, *Journal of Economic Literature*, Vol. 7, 2, June, 369–405.

Harris, R, 1997, Political Economy, Interest Groups, Legal Institutions, and the Repeal of the Bubble Act in 1825, Economic History Review, Vol. 50, 4, 675–96.

Hart, A, Kaldor, N, and Tinbergen, J, 1963, The Case for an International Commodity Reserve Currency. UNCTAD, Geneva, Reprinted in N, Kaldor, 1964, Essays on Economic Policy II: Vol. IV of Collected Economic Essays of Nicholas Kaldor. 1980 edition, Holmes and Meier, New York.

Hart, O, 1977, On the Profitability of Speculation, *The Quarterly Journal of Economics*, MIT Press, Vol. 91, 4, 579–97.

Haugen, R, 1995, The New Finance: The Case Against Efficient Markets, Prentice Hall, New York.

Hayek, F, 1943, A Commodity Reserve Currency, *Economic Journal*, Vol. 53, 210, 176–84. Reprinted in F, A, Hayek, 1948, *Individualism and Economic Order*. University of Chicago Press, Chicago.

Hayek, F, 1978, *Denationalisation of Money – The Argument Refined, An Analysis of the Theory and Practice of Concurrent Currencies*, 2nd edition, Institute of Economic Affairs, London.

Heath, R, 1998, The Statistical Measurement of Financial Derivatives, IMF Working Paper 98/24, IMF Washington.

Hefeker, C, 2000, Sense and Nonsense of Fixed Exchange Rates: On Theories and Crises, *Cato Journal*, Vol. 20, 2, Fall, 159–78.

Held, D, McGrew, G, Goldblatt, D, and Perraton, J, 1998, *Global Transformations: Politics, Economics, and Culture*, Polity Press, Cambridge.

Helleiner, E, 1994, *States and the Re-emergence of Global Finance: From Bretton Woods to the 1990s,* Cornell University Press, Ithaca, New York.

Helleiner, E, 1995, Handling 'Hot Money': US Policy Toward Latin American Capital Flight in Historical Perspective, *Alternatives,* Vol. 20, 83–84.

Helleiner, E, 2003, *The Making of National Money: Territorial Currencies in Historical Perspective,* Cornell University Press, Ithaca.

Henderson, S, and Price, J, 1988, *Currency and Interest Rate Swaps,* 2nd edition, Butterworths, London.

Henwood, D, 1999, Marxing up the Millennium, paper presented at Marx at the Millennium Conference, University of Florida, March 19, downloaded from http://www.leftbusinessobserver.com/MillMarx.doc

Herring, R, 1994, International Financial Integration: The Continuing Process, Wharton Financial Institutions Centre, WP 94–23.

Herring, R, and Chatusripatak, N, 2000, The Case of the Missing Market: The Bond Market and Why it Matters for Financial Development, Asian Development Bank Institute (ADBI), Working Paper No. 11, Tokyo, July.

Hicks, J, 1967, *Critical Essays in Monetary Theory,* Oxford at the Clarendon Press, London.

Hilferding, R, 1910/1981, *Finance Capital: A Study of the Latest Phase of Capitalist Development,* London: Routledge & Kegan Paul.

Hirst, P, and Thompson, G, 1999, *Globalization in Question: The International Economy and the Possibilities of Governance,* Polity Press, Cambridge.

Hodrick, R, 1990, Volatility in the Foreign Exchange and Stock Markets: Is it Excessive?, AEA Papers and Proceedings, Vol. 80, 2.

Hunt, B, 1935, The Joint-Stock Company in England, 1830–1844, *Journal of Political Economy,* Vol. 43, 3, Jun., 331–64.

Hunter, W, and Smith, S, 2002, Risk Management in the Global Economy: A Review Essay, *Journal of Banking and Finance,* Vol. 26, 205–21.

Ingham, G, 2000, Babylonian Madness: On the Historical and Sociological Origins of Money, in J, Smithin (ed.), *What is Money?* Routledge, London.

Ingham, G, 2001, Fundamentals of a Theory of Money: Untangling Fine, Lapavitsas, and Zeizer, *Economy & Society,* Vol. 30, 3, August, 304–23.

Ingham, G, 2002, New Money Spaces, in OECD, *The Future of Money,* Paris.

Ingham, G, 2004, *The Nature of Money,* Polity Press, Cambridge.

International Monetary Fund (IMF), 1993, System of National Accounts, IMF, Washington, March.

International Monetary Fund (IMF), 1998, Financial Derivatives, Eleventh Meeting of the Committee on Balance of Payments Statistics, Prepared by the Statistics Department, IMF, Washington, DC, October 21–23.

International Monetary Fund (IMF), 1998, *International Capital Markets – Developments, Prospects and Key Policy Issues.* IMF, Washington, September.

International Swaps and Derivatives Association (ISDA), 2002, Master Agreement http://www.isda.org

International Swaps and Derivatives Association (ISDA), 2003a, Over 90% of the World's 500 Largest Companies Use Derivatives to Help Manage Their Risks, According to New ISDA Survey, Media Release April 9, downloaded March 2004, from, http://www.isda.org/

International Swaps and Derivatives Association (ISDA), 2003b, Derivatives – Product Descriptions downloaded at: http://isda.org/productdescriptions

Jensen, M, and Meckling, W, 1976, Theory of the Firm: Managerial Behavior, Agency Costs and Ownership Structure, *Journal of Financial Economics*, Vol. 3, 305–60.

John, K, and John, T, 1993, Top Management Compensation and Capital Structure, *The Journal of Finance*, 1993, Vol. 48, 3.

Johnson, H, 1964, Major Issues in Monetary and Fiscal Policies, Federal Reserve Bulletin Vol. 50, Nov., 1400–1413, reprinted in W, Smith and R, Teigen (eds) *Readings in Money, National Income, and Stabilization Policy*, revised edition, Irwin, Homewood, 1970.

Johnson, H, 1976, Destabilizing Speculation: A General Equilibrium Approach, *Journal of Political Economy*, Vol. 84, 11, 101–8.

Johnson, P, 1998, *The Government of Money: Monetarism in Germany and the United States*, Cornell University Press, Ithaca, NY.

Jones, S, and Ville, S, 1996, Efficient Transactors or Rent-Seeking Monopolists? The Rationale for Early Chartered Trading Companies, *The Journal of Economic History*, Vol. 56, 4, Dec., 898–915.

Josephson, M, 1934, The Robber Barons, 1978, Harcourt Brace, New York.

Kamstra, M, 2001, Rational exuberance: the fundamentals of pricing firms, from blue chip to 'dotcom' Federal Reserve Bank of Atlanta Working Paper 21, November.

Kay, G, 1991, The Nature of the Epoch – Notes on Machover, *Critique*, Vol. 23.

Kay, G, 1999, Abstract Labour and Capital, *Historical Materialism*, 5, 1, Winter, 255–80.

Kay, G, and Mott, J, 1982, *Political Order and the Law of Labour*, MacMillan, London.

Kelly, R, 1995, Derivatives – A Growing Threat to the International Financial System, in J, Michie and J, Grieve Smith (eds) *Managing the Global Economy*, Oxford University Press, Oxford.

Keynes, J, 1930/1971, *A Treatise on Money*, Macmillan, London, reprinted in *The Collected Works of John Maynard Keynes*, Macmillan, London and Basingstoke.

Keynes, J, 1933, *A Monetary Theory of Production*, reprinted in *The Collected Works of John Maynard Keynes*, Vol. XIII, The General Theory and After, Part I, Preparations, pp. 408–11.

Keynes, J, 1936, The General Theory of Employment, Interest, and Money, in *The Collected Writings*, MacMillan, London, 1973.

Keynes, J, 1938, The Policy of Government Storage of Foodstuffs and Raw Materials, *Economic Journal*, September.

Keynes, J, 1943a, Proposals for an International Clearing Union, in *The Collected Writings*, Vol. 25, Activities 1940–45, Shaping the Post-War World: The Clearing Union, MacMillan, London, 1980.

Keynes, J, 1943b, The Objective of Price Stability, *Economic Journal*, Vol. 53, 210, pp. 185–7.

Keynes, J, 1933, National Self-Sufficiency, *The Yale Review*, Vol. 22, 4, 755–69.

Kindleberger, C, 1973, *The World Economy in Depression: 1929–1939*, University of Califormia Press, Berkeley.

Kindleberger, C, 1984, *A Financial History of Western Europe*, Allen & Unwin, London.

Kindleberger, C, 1989, Time and Money, in *International Money – A Collection of Essays*, George, Allen & Unwin, London.

Knapp, G, 1924, *The State Theory of Money*, MacMillan, London.

Knorr, C, and Bruegger, U, 2002, Global Microstructure in Virtual Societies of Financial Markets, *American Journal of Sociology*, Vol. 107, 905–50.

Kohn, M, 2001, Payments and the Development of Finance in Pre-industrial Europe, Working Paper 01–15, Department of Economics, Dartmouth College.

Krawiec, K, 1998, *Derivatives, Corporate Hedging and Shareholder Wealth: Modigliani Miller Forty Years Later*, University of Illinois Law Review, No. 1.

Kregel, J, 1998, Derivatives and Global Capital Flows: Applications to Asia, Working Paper 246, Jeremy Levy Economics Institute, New York, August.

Krugman, P, 1999, Labor Pains, *The New York Times Magazine*, 5/23/99 downloaded from: http://web.mit.edu/krugman/www/

Kwaller, I, Koch, O, and Koch, T, 1987, The Temporal Relationship Between S&P 500 Futures and the S&P 500 Index, *The Journal of Finance*, Vol. 42, 5, 309–29.

Kwast, M, 1986, An Overview of Financial Futures and Options in the U.S. Economy, in M, Kwast (ed.) *Financial Futures and Options in the U.S. Economy, a Study by the Staff of the Federal Reserve System*, Federal Reserve Bank, Board of Governors, Washington.

Lazonick, W, and O'Sullivan, M, 2000, Maximizing Shareholder Value: A New Ideology for Corporate Governance, *Economy and Society*, Vol. 29, 1, Feb., 13–36.

LeRoy, S, and Porter, R, 1981, The Present-Value Relation: Tests Based on Implied Variance Bounds, *Econometrica*, Vol. 49, 3, 555–74.

Leyshon, A and Thrift, N, 1997, *Money/Space: Geographies of Monetary Transformation*, Routledge, London.

LiPuma, E, and Lee, B, 2004, *Financial Derivatives and the Globalization of Risk*, Duke University Press, Durham.

Lowenstein, R, 2001, *When Genius Failed: The Rise and Fall of Long-Term Capital Management*, Fourth Estate, London.

Luskin, D, 1992, If Derivatives are So Great Why Don't More People Use Them?, in K, Brown (ed.) *Derivative Strategies for Managing Risk*, Association for Investment Management and Research.

Luttwak, E, 2000, *Turbo-Capitalism: Winners and Losers in the Global Economy*, HarperCollins Publishers, New York.

Machlup, F, 1964, Plans for Reform of the International Monetary System, Princeton University Special Papers on International Economics, No. 3, Princeton.

MacWilliam, S, 1992, Introduction, in S, MacWilliam and H, Thompson, Political Economy of Papua New Guinea, *Journal Of Contempoary Asia*, Manilla, 1–13.

Marris, R, 1964, *The Theory of Managerial Capitalism*, The Free Press, London.

Marsh, A, 1911, Cotton Exchanges and Their Economic Functions, *Annals of the American Academy of Political and Social Sciences*, Vol. 38, 2, Sep., 253–80.

Martin, R, (ed.), 1999, *Money and the Space Economy*, John Wiley & Sons, Chichester.

Marx, K, 1867, *Capital*, Vol. I. Harmondsworth: Penguin.

Marx, K, 1885, *Capital*, Vol. II. Harmondsworth: Penguin.

Marx, K, 1894, *Capital*, Vol. III. Harmondsworth: Penguin.

Marx, K, 1939, *Grundrisse*. Harmondsworth: Penguin, 1970.

Marx, K, 1849, Wage Labour and Capital, in Marx, K, and Engels, F, *Selected Works* Vol. 1. Moscow: Progress Publishers 1969.

Maurer, B, 2002, Repressed Futures: Financial Derivatives, Theological Unconscious, *Economy and Society*, Vol. 31, 1 Feb., 15–36.

Mayhew, S, 2000, The Impact of Derivatives on Cash Markets: What Have We Learned?, University of Georgia, Department of Banking and Finance, mimeo, downloaded from SSRN.com

McCormick, R, 1981, *From Realignment to Reform: Political Change in New York 1893–1910*, Cornell University Press, Ithaca.

McDonough, J, 1998, The Role of Central Banks in the Global Financial Market, Remarks by the President of the Federal Reserve Bank of New York to the Economics Club of New York, 14 December, downloaded from BIS website: www.bis.org

McKenzie, D, 2004, Is Economics Performative? Option Theory and the Construction of Derivatives Markets, Paper presented to the Harvard-MIT Economic Sociology seminar, 16 November.

McKenzie, D, and Millo, Y, 2003, Negotiating a Market, Performing Theory: The Historical Sociology of a Financial Derivatives Exchange, *American Journal of Sociology*, 109, 107–45.

McKinnon, R, 1981, The Exchange Rate and Macroeconomic Policy: Changing Postwar Policy Prescriptions, *Journal of Economic Literature*, Vol. 19, 2, Jun., 531–57.

McKinnon, R, 1993, The Rules of the Game: International Money in Historical Perspective, *Journal of Economic Literature*, Vol. 31, Mar., 1–44.

Meade, J, 1948, National Income, National Expenditure and the Balance of Payments, *The Economic Journal*, Pt I, Vol. 58, 232, Dec., 483–505.

Meade, J, 1949, National Income, National Expenditure and the Balance of Payments, *The Economic Journal*, Pt II, Vol. 59, 233, Mar., 17–39.

Meese, R, and Rogoff, K, 1983, Empirical Exchange Rate Models of the Seventies: Do they Fit Out of Sample?, *Journal of International Economics*, Vol. 14, 1–2, 3–24.

Mendelsohn, M, 1980, *Money on the Move: The Modern International Capital Market*, McGraw-Hill, New York.

Menger, K, 1892, On the Origin of Money, *Economic Journal*, Vol. 2, 239–55.

Minns, R, 2001, *The Cold War in Welfare: Stock Markets Versus Pensions*, London: Verso, London.

Minsky, H, 1982, *Can 'It' Happen Again? Essays on Instability and Finance*, M.E. Sharpe, New York.

Minsky, H, 1986, *Stabilizing an Unstable Economy*, Yale University Press, New Haven.

Minsky, H, 1989, Comments and Discussion, in *Brookings Paper on Economic Activity*, No. 2, the Brookings Institution, Washington.

Mirowski, P, 1990, Learning the Meaning of a Dollar: Conservation Principles and the Social Theory of Value in Economic Theory, *Social Research*, Vol. 57, 3.

Mirowski, P, 1991, Postmodernism and the Social Theory of Value, *Journal of Post Keynesian Economics*, Vol. 13, 4, Summer.

Mirowski, P, 1999, *More Heat than Light: Economics as Social Physics, Physics as Nature's Economics*, Cambridge University Press, Cambridge.

Moore, B, 1988, *Horizontalists and Verticalists: The Macroeconomics of Credit Money*, Cambridge University Press, Cambridge.

Mundell, R, 1962, The Appropriate Use of Monetary and Fiscal Policy for Internal and External Balance, IMF Staff Papers, No. 9, 1, Mar., 70–7.

Murrill, R, and Caputo, M, 2004, Making Executive Pay Work, Ivey Management Services. May/June Reprint No.9B04TC08, downloaded from http://www.ivey-businessjournal.com/view_article.asp?intArticle_ID = 484.

Näslund, B, Presentation speech at The Bank of Sweden Prize in Economic Sciences in Memory of Alfred Nobel, Dec., 1997.

Negri, A, 1968, Keynes and the Capitalist Theory of the State, reprinted in Negri 1994, Labor of Dionysus: A Critique of the State-Form [translated and written in collaboration with Michael Hardt] University of Minnesota Press, Minneapolis.

Nordin, D, 1974, *Rich Harvest: A History of the Grange*, University of Mississippi, Jackson.

Nurkse, R, 1944, *International Currency Experience*, League of Nations, Geneva.

O'Brien, R, 1992, Global Financial Integration: The End of Geography. Council on Foreign Relations Press (for the Royal Institute of International Affairs), New York.

Obstfeld, M, 1985, Floating Exchange Rates: Experiences and Prospects, Brookings Papers on Economic Activity, Vol. 2, 369–450.

Obstfeld, M, and Rogoff, K, 1995, The Mirage of Fixed Exchange Rates, *Journal of Economic Perspectives*, Vol, 9, 4, Fall, 73–96.

Obstfeld, M, Shambaugh, J, and Taylor A, 2004a, The Trilemma in History: Trade-offs Among Exchange Rates, Monetary Policies and Capital Mobility, C.E.P.R. Discussion Papers No. 4352, downloaded from http://www.cepr.org/pubs/dps/DP4352.asp

Obstfeld, M, Shambaugh, J, and Taylor A, 2004b, Monetary Sovereignty, Exchange Rates, and Capital Controls: The Trilemma in the Interwar Period, NBER Working Papers 10393, National Bureau of Economic Research, Cambridge.

Ohmae, K, 1990, *The Borderless World*, HarperCollins, New York.

Ollermann, C, and Farris, P, 1985, Futures or Cash: Which Market Leads Live Beef Prices?, *Journal of Futures Markets*, Vol. 5, 4, Winter, 529–38.

Overbeek, H, and van der Pilj, K, 1993, Restructuring Capital and Restructuring Hegemony: Neo-Liberalism and the Unmaking of the Post-War Order, in H, Overbeek (ed.) *Restructuring Hegemony in the Global Political Economy: The Rise of Transnational Neo-Liberalism in the 1980s*, Routledge, London.

Oxelheim, L, and Rafferty, M, 2003, Dynamic Efficiency of Secondary Bond Markets, Lund University, Department of Economics, Working Paper 2003/3.

OXFAM America, 2002, Global Finance Hurts the Poor – Analysis of the Impact of North-South Private Capital Flows on Growth, Inequality and Poverty, Oxfam America, Boston, May.

Panitch, L, and Gindin, S, 2004, *Global Capitalism and American Empire*, The Merlin Press, London.

Parguez A, and Seccareccia, M, 2000, The Credit Theory of Money: The Money Circuit Approach, in John Smithin (ed.) *What is Money*, London: Routledge, 101–23.

Parsons, J, 1988, Bubble Bubble, How Much Trouble? Financial Markets, Capitalist Development and Capitalist Crisis, *Science and Society*, Vol. 52, 3, 260–90.

Parsons, J, 1999, Futures and Derivatives Markets, Charles River Associates International, downloaded April 2004, from www.crai.com

Parsons, J, and Mello, A, 1995, Maturity Structure of a Hedge Matters: Lessons from the Metallgesellschaft Debacle, *Journal of Applied Corporate Finance*, Vol. 8, Spring, 106–20.

Partnoy, F, 1997, *F.I.A.S.C.O.: Blood in the Water on Wall Street*, W.W. Norton, New York.

Partnoy, F, 1999, Adding Derivatives to the Corporate Law Mix, University of San Diego, School of Law and Economics Research paper, No. 3.

Partnoy, F, 2000, Why Markets Crash and What Law Can Do about it, University of San Diego Law School, mimeo.

Partnoy, F, 2002a, ISDA, NASD, CFMA, and SYNY: the Four Horsemen of Derivatives Regulation?, University of San Diego Law School, WP 39, Spring.

Partnoy, F, 2002b, Testimony to US Senate, Committee on Governmental Affairs, January, mimeo.

Partnoy, F, 2003a, A Revisionist History of Enron and the Sudden Death of 'May', *Vilenova Law Review*, Vol. 48, 4, 1245–80.

Pashigian, B, 1986, The Political Economy of Futures Market Regulation, *Journal of Business*, Vol. 59, 2, pt 2, s55–84.

Pawley, M, 1993, *Financial Innovation and Monetary Policy*, Routledge, London.

Peck, A, 1992, The Economic Role of Financial Futures, in A, Peck (ed.) *Futures Markets: Their Economic Role*, American Enterprise Institute for Public Policy Research, Washington.

Perlod, A, 1995, The Payment System and Derivative Instruments in R, Merton and Z, Bodie (eds) *The Global Financial System – A Functional Perspective*, Harvard Business School Press, Boston, Mass.

Pirrong, S, 1995, The Self-Regulation of Commodity Exchanges: The Case of Market Manipulation, *Journal of Law and Economics*, Vol. 38, 1, April, 141–206.

Pontiff, J, 1997, Excess Volatility and Closed-End Funds, *American Economic Review*, 87, 1, 155–69.

Pryke, M, and Allen, J, 2000, Monetized Time-Space: Derivatives – Money's 'New Imaginary, *Economy and Society*, Vol. 29, 2, May, 264–84.

Radice, H, 1988, Keynes and the Policy of Practical Protectionism, in J, Hillard (ed.) *J.M. Keynes in Retrospect*, London: Edward Elgar, 153–71.

Rees, G, 1972, *Britain's Commodity Markets*, Paul Elec Books, London.

Reisen, H, 2002, Tobin tax: could it work? OECD Observer March http://www. oecdobserver.org/news/fullstory.php/aid/664/Tobin_tax:_could_it_work__.html

Robinson, J, 1956, *The Accumulation of Capital*, Macmillan, London.

Rochon, L,-P, and Rossi, S, 2003, Money and Endogenous Money, in L, -P, Rochon, and S, Rossi (eds) *Modern Theories of Money*, Edward Elgar, Cheltenham.

Rule, J, 1993, The Labouring Classes, in J, Rule and R, Malcolmson (eds) *In Protest and Survival The Historical Experience*, Merlin.

Sawyer, M, 2003, Money: Means of Payment or Store of Wealth, in L, Rochon and S, Rossi (eds) *Modern Theories of Money: The Nature and Role of Money in Capitalist Economies*, Edward Elgar, Cheltenham.

Schleifer, A, and Summers, L, 1990, The Noise Trader Approach to Finance, *Journal of Economic Perspectives*, Vol. 4, 2.

Scholes, M, 1998, Derivatives in a Dynamic Environment, *American Economic Review*, Vol. 88, 3, June, 350–70.

Schumpeter, J, 1954, *A History of Economic Analysis*, George Allen and Unwin, London.

Schwartz, A, (ed.), 1992, *Commodity Monies*, Edward Elgar, London.

Semmler, W, 1984, *Competition, Monopoly, and Differential Profit Rates: On The Relevance of the Classical and Marxian Theories of Production Prices for Modern Industrial and Corporate Pricing*. Columbia University Press, New York.

Sennett, R, 1998, *Corrosion of Character: The Personal Consequences of Work in the New Capitalism*, W. W. Norton and Co, New York.

Shiller, R, 1987, The Volatility of Stock Market Prices, Cowles Foundation Paper No. 670, Reprint Series, Vol. 235, Jan, 33–7.

Shiller, R, 1991, *Market Volatility*, Cambridge: Cambridge University Press.

Shiller, R, 1981, Do Stock Markets Move too Much to be Justified by Subsequent Movements in Dividends?, *American Economic Review*, Vol. 71, 3, 421–36.

Shiller, R, 2003, The New Financial Order: Risk in the 21st Century, Princeton University Press, Princeton, NJ.

Shleifer, A, and Vishny, R, 1997, The Limits of Arbitrage, *Journal of Finance*, Vol. 52, 1, 35–55.

Simmel, G, 1907, *The Philosophy of Money*, Routledge, London (1990).

Simons, H, 1991, Organisations and Markets, *Journal of Economic Perspectives*, Vol. 5, Spring, 25–44.

Smith, A, 1776, *An Inquiry Into the Nature and Causes of the Wealth of Nations*, Vol, I, from A, Skinner and R, Campbell (eds) The Glasgow edition of the works and correspondence of Adam Smith, Oxford, 1976.

Sobel, A, 1988, The Politics of Increasing Internationalization in Securities Markets, Foundation for Advanced Information Research, Tokyo.

Solomon, R, 1977, *The International Monetary System, 1945–76*, Harper and Row, New York.

Spahn, P, 1996, The Tobin Tax and Exchange Rate Stability World Bank Finance and Development, Guest Article, downloaded from, http://www.worldbank.org/fandd/english/0696/articles/0130696.htm

Stark, D, and Beunza, D, 2004, 'Trading rooms as ecologies of value', in Karin Knorr Cetina and Alexa Preda (eds) *The Sociology of Financial Markets*, Oxford University Press, Oxford.

Stiglitz, J, 1989, Using Tax Policy To Curb Speculative Short-Term Trading, *Journal of Financial Services Research*, Vol. 3, 101–15.

Stiglitz, J, 2001, *Whither Socialism*, Yale University Press, New Haven.

Stockhammer, E, 2004, Financialisation and the Slowdown of Accumulation, *Cambridge Journal of Economics*, Vol. 28, 5, 719–41.

Stoll, H, and Whaley, R, 1990, Stock Market Structure and Volatility, *The Review of Financial Studies*, Vol. 3, 37–71.

Strange, S, 1986, *Casino Capitalism*, Basil Blackwell, New York.

Strange, S, 1996, The Retreat of the State: The Diffusion of Power in the World Economy, Cambridge University Press, Cambridge.

Strange, S, 1998, What Theory? The Theory in Mad Money, Centre for the Study of Globalisation and Regionalisation, University of Warwick, Working Paper 18/98, December.

Summers, L, 1986, Does the Stock Market Rationally Reflect Fundamental Values?, *Journal of Finance*, Vol. 41, 3, 591–601.

Summers, L, and Summers, V, 1989, When Financial Markets Work too Well: A Cautious Case for a Securities Transactions Tax, *Journal of Financial Services Research*, Vol. 3, 261–286.

Swan, E, 2000, *Building the Global Market: A 400 Year History of Derivatives*, Kluwer Law International, London.

Swaps Monitor, 2002, Data on the Global OTC Derivatives Market, downloaded from www.SwapsMonitor.com

Taulli, T, 2003, Can Financial Instruments Become a Force for Evil? A review of Frank Partnoy's Infectious Greed, downloaded from Findlaw's Book Reviews http//:www.writ.corporate.findlaw.com/books/reviews/20030711_taulli.html

Taylor, J, 1995, Changes in American Economic Policy in the 1980s: Watershed or Pendulum Swing?, *Journal of Economic Literature*, Vol. XXXIII, June.

Telser, L, 1986, Futures and Actual Markets: How are they Related?, *Journal of Business*, Vol. 59, 2, pt 2, s5–19.

Thompson, E, 1963, *The Making of the English Working Class*, V. Gollancz, London.

Tobin, J, 1974, The New Economics One Decade Older, The Eliot Janeway Lectures on Historical Economics in Honour of Joseph Schumpeter, 1972, Princeton University Press, Princeton.

Tobin, J, 1978, A Proposal for International Monetary Reform, *Eastern Economic Journal*, Vol. 4, nos 3–4, 1153–9, Reprinted in James Tobin, *Essays in Economics: Theory and Policy*, The MIT Press, Cambridge MA.

Toms, J, 2002, The Rise of Modern Accounting and the Fall of the Public Company: The Lancashire Cotton Mills 1870–1914, *Accounting, Organizations and Society*, Vol. 27, 61–84.

Toporowski, J, 2000, *The End of Finance: The Theory of Capital Market Inflation, Financial Derivatives, and Pension Fund Capitalism*, Routledge, London and New York.

Ul Haq, M, Kaul, I, and Grunberg, I (eds), 1996, *The Tobin Tax: Coping with Financial Volatility*, Oxford University Press, Oxford.

Vernenego, M, 2000, *Exchange Rate Regimes and Capital Controls*, Challenge, November.

Volcker, P, 2000, Commanding Heights, interview with Paul Volcker on PBS radio transcript 26 September, downloaded from http://www.pbs.org/wgbh/commandingheights/shared/minitextlo/int_paulvolcker.html

Volcker, P, and Goyhten, T, 1992, *Changing Frontiers: The World's Money and the Threat to American Leadership*, Times Books, N.Y.

Vrolijk, C, 1997, Derivatives Effect on Monetary Policy Transmission, IMF Monetary and Exchange Department, Working Paper, WP-97-121, Washington, September.

Watkins, G, 1907, The Growth of Large Fortunes, *American Economic Review*, Vol. 8, 4, Nov.

Weber, M, 1895, The Stock Exchange, in W. Runciman (ed.) Max Weber: *Selections in Translation*, Cambridge University Press, Cambridge (1978), 374–77.

Weeks, J, 1981, *Capital and Exploitation*, Princeton: Princeton University Press.

Weeks, J, 1999, Surfing the Global Waters of Global Turbulence: A Comment, *Historical Materialism*, 5, Winter, 211–30.

Weiss, L, 1998, *The Myth of the Powerless State*, Cornell University Press, New York.

Whitman, M, 1974, The Current and Future Role of the Dollar: How Much Symmetry, Brookings Papers on Economic Activity, Vol. 1974, 3, 539–91.

Williams, K, 2000, From Shareholder Value to Present-Day Capitalism, *Economy & Society*, Vol. 29, 1, 1–12.

Williamson, O, 1964, *The Economics of Discretionary Behaviour, Managerial Objectives in a Theory of the Firm*, Prentice Hall, Englewood Cliffs, NJ.

Williamson, J, 1983, Keynes and the International Economic Order, in *Political Economy and International Money: Selected Essays of John Williamson*, NYU Press, New York.

Wolfers, J, and Zitzewitz, E, 2003, The Furore Over 'Terrorism Futures', *Washington Post*, 31 July, A19.

Working, H, 1961, New Concepts Concerning Futures Markets and Prices, *American Economic Review*, 51, 2, 160–3.

Wray, R, 2000, Modern Money, in J, Smithin (ed.) *What is Money?*, Routledge, London.

Wray, R, 1999, *Understanding Modern Money*, Edward Elgar, Cheltenham.

Zaloom, C, 2003, Ambiguous Numbers: Trading and Technologies in Global Financial Markets, *American Ethnologist*, Vol. 30, 2, 258–72.

Name Index

Subject Index

CPSIA information can be obtained at www.ICGtesting.com
Printed in the USA
LVOW11*1738010516

486188LV00002B/7/P